bestie

'This is simply the best book about football in recent years.'
***The Herald* (Glasgow)**

'. . . it is hard to imagine a better book on the subject.'
The Independent

'Lovejoy's treatment of the saga is even-handed and refreshingly bereft of misty-eyed genuflection'
***Evening Telegraph* (Kettering)**

'. . . a magnetic, gut-wrenchingly honest authorized biography . . .'
Express on Sunday

'A superb read for old fans and Bestie newcomers alike . . . exhaustingly researched, impassioned and mercifully football-cliché free . . .'
FHM

'Joe Lovejoy's outstanding biography is such a compelling read . . . that Bestie subverts the stereotype, reflects credit on author and subject . . .'
Four Four Two

Joe Lovejoy has been a sportswriter for 30 years. He is the Football Correspondent of the *Sunday Times*, having worked previously for the *Independent* and the *Mail on Sunday*. This is his first book.

JOE LOVEJOY

bestie

a portrait of a legend

PAN BOOKS

First published 1998 by Sidgwick & Jackson

First published in paperback 1999 by Pan Books

This edition published 2007 by Pan Books
an imprint of Pan Macmillan Ltd
Pan Macmillan, 20 New Wharf Road, London N1 9RR
Basingstoke and Oxford
Associated companies throughout the world
www.panmacmillan.com

ISBN 978-0-230-76853-6

1 3 5 7 9 8 6 4 2

A CIP catalogue record for this book is available from
the British Library.

Typeset by SetSystems Ltd, Saffron Walden, Essex

Printed and bound by CPI Group (UK) Ltd, Croydon, CR0 4YY

To my wife, Lesley

'The Wind Beneath My Wings'

acknowledgements

First, I must thank my literary agent, David Godwin, for coming up with such an irresistible subject. I had been asked to write several football biographies before, but always declined for lack of motivation. To chronicle the life of George Best, a genius before the description became devalued, was an offer simply too good to refuse.

Despite countless warnings about his bohemian interpretation of the word 'appointment', George could not have been more cooperative. Possibly because we usually met at his local, he went on what he calls 'the missing list' only twice in eighteen months. He was unfailingly courteous, always good company, and I thank him for that. Whenever arrangements had to be made, and on the rare occasions when wires became crossed, his good friend and agent, Phil Hughes, was an obliging and effective conduit.

George's memory is not the most reliable, and every fact needed corroboration. For that, and for much time, freely given, I owe a huge debt of gratitude to his old team-mates and friends, such as Pat Crerand, Denis Law, David Sadler, Brian Kidd, Sir Bobby Charlton, Johnny Giles, Terry Neil, Wilf McGuinness, Mike Summerbee, Rodney Marsh, Terry Venables, Malcolm 'Waggy' Wagner, Brian Fugler and last, but by no means least, Felix, from the 'Gorilla Grill'.

George's father, Dickie, was the most welcoming of hosts, his pride in his son second only to his hospitality. Dickie was a mine of information, as was Belfast's leading football reporter, Malcolm Brodie, a friend of the Best family for nearly forty years.

My earliest memories of George date from the 1968 European

Cup final. For events before that climactic watershed, and to fill in the many gaps elsewhere, I relied on the finest sportswriters of that, or indeed any, era. First among equals must be Geoffrey Green, doyen football correspondent of *The Times* from 1938 to 1976, but even more valuable than Green's peerless prose was the 20:20 insight provided by Hugh McIlvanney, my colleague at the *Sunday Times*, who has been among George's most loyal friends for thirty years – and was a confidant of Sir Matt Busby for even longer. Thanks for digging out the relevant cuttings are due here to the ever helpful staff at the *News International* reference library.

Various books written about George over the years were of great value when researching this one. Among them were: *George Best: An Intimate Biography* by Michael Parkinson, *Where Do I Go From Here?*, an autobiography with Graeme Wright and *The Good, The Bad and The Bubbly*, with Ross Benson. Essential reference works included *The Illustrated History of Manchester United* by Tom Tyrell and David Meek, and *Back Page United* and *The Old Trafford Encyclopaedia*, both by Stephen Kelly.

David Meek, who reported Manchester United's day-to-day affairs for the *Manchester Evening News* from Munich to Alex Ferguson's 'Double Double' was the ultimate arbiter when separating fact from fiction.

David Godwin was always supportive when the going got tough, Susan Hill at Macmillan was a sympathetic editor, and of the many others who offered encouragement, none deserves more thanks than Ian Ridley, author and respected football correspondent of the *Independent on Sunday*, who supplied advice above and beyond the duties of friendship.

Finally, heartfelt gratitude, too, to Peter Edwardson, for his technical assistance, and to all at The Parkhouse.

'You beauties!'

'Genius does what it must, talent does what it can.'

Owen Meredith, Earl of Lytton. *Poet.*

bestie

chapter one

They are queuing inside and out, forming a ragged crocodile on the forecourt and for a hundred yards around the aisles, boys of all ages, from six to sixty, craning and tiptoeing for a glimpse of 'Yer Man'.

No one goes away disappointed. They all get something – an autograph here, a photograph there. The girl from local radio gets her interview, and is charmed into the bargain. It was ever thus.

The owners of the Belfast cash and carry have paid £2,000 – £1,000 an hour – for their star attraction, and are fawning in overdrive, falling over themselves to thank him for his time. For the money he smiles constantly, despite feeling like death, presses more flesh than a politician on the stump, exchanges banal chit-chat with tongue-tied fans and plays stooge to a Wheeltappers and Shunters comic, dressed in drag.

This is how George Best, the most gifted and charismatic footballer Britain has produced, earns his corn these days. On a treadmill of personal appearances where his 'team-mates' are as likely to be Faith Brown and Mick Miller as Denis Law or Rodney Marsh. He has always professed to hate it, always insisted that he wanted to be judged as a person, rather than a cardboard cut-out celebrity, but twenty-four years after he last played for Manchester United, he is still milking the name for all it is worth. Or rather as much as his libertine lifestyle allows.

In fairness, it is some name. There are those who say Pele was a better player (witnesses to be called later will argue that he was not). That there should even be a debate about it goes some way towards explaining Best's magical, enduring appeal, and the cult status he enjoys among admirers too young ever to have seen him in his pomp.

At his best George most certainly is not on this balmy afternoon in Belfast. The last time I had seen a smile that fixed it was accompanied by a strong whiff of formaldehyde.

The day had not begun well. When the feet that launched a thousand chips dragged him into Heathrow for the 8.30 shuttle he was sporting the sort of eye that normally demands a referee's intervention, a disfigurement which had forced him to pull out of his regular Saturday spot with Sky TV. Fortunately, Sky has become accustomed to such things and, as usual, had a replacement, Clive Allen, standing by. George's wife, Alex, some twenty-six years his junior at twenty-five, accompanies him everywhere, as his personal assistant. For once, she was not her usual chirpy self, and mention of the 'shiner' saw her decamp to another part of the departure lounge. Best, the errant husband, was in familiar territory. The doghouse.

'A bird rang the flat when I wasn't in,' he said, with the incorrigible air of a schoolboy caught in the act behind the bikesheds. 'When Alex answered, the girl asked for George. Alex went ballistic, but I don't even know who it was. I'd been on the same phone number for ten years [he changed it, sharpish], so it could have been anybody.'

Not a good start. Mrs B, once a stewardess with Virgin Airways, was in such a state that she forgot to check them in. The flight had closed, and mere mortals would have missed the plane, but the Bests were ushered to the most coveted seats. The front row.

George had done what he always does in times of marital or any other difficulty, and hit the bottle, big time. Having had no sleep (he is within the odd catnap of being an insomniac) he would have looked on the seedy side of jaded, even without the black eye, but at least he was dressed for the job, eschewing the usual shellsuit for something by Armani. Alex, too, looked the part as a celebrity's moll, a minuscule pelmet of a dress showing off her svelte figure and ever-present tan to maximum advantage.

The one-hour flight was whiled away with the *Daily Mirror* quizword, a ritual the Bests never miss, even when relations are strained gossamer thin. Alex's entries tend to be from the Stanley Unwin school of English, and the consequent laughter is good marital medicine. The BA breakfast was viewed with distaste, and left untouched. Like most alcoholics, George eats like a bird, and Alex has the appetite of an anorexic. Stewardesses miss nothing, and as we disembarked at Belfast International I overheard one turn to another and, fingering an eye, trill knowingly: 'Obviously he hasn't changed.'

At Heathrow there had been a minimum of fuss, just the one middle-aged businessman asking for an autograph, 'for my son'. Back 'home', heads turn with every step, and progress resembles a royal procession. Three teenagers, who could never have seen Best play, are gobsmacked, the most forward of them exclaiming: 'Jesus, it's George Best. Amazing!' He proffers a bare forearm for an autograph ('Have you got a pen, Geordie?' – everyone in Belfast calls Best 'Geordie'), which is duly inscribed.

Quickly into a chauffeur-driven Mercedes, complete with driver who makes Vinnie Jones look like Julian Clary. He is, we are told later, the strong, silent type, but in the presence of his hero the macho ice melts and he gabbles like an auctioneer. 'You know, Geordie, we are distantly related.' George has heard this one more often than 'Last orders'. 'Really?' he responds, switching to autopilot and gazing blankly out of a window that frames the concrete-grey topography and where-there's-life-there's-hope bustle of the town he used to call home.

At last an interruption, to prevent the mouth with wheels from completing his full family tree. Disorganized as ever, George has come out with exactly one pound in his pocket. The pick-up at the gig is not in 'readies', so a detour is required to find a cashpoint. Alex clambers out of the limo to withdraw a modest fifty pounds – 'I didn't think I should push my luck until we pay something in' – then it is on to the venue, which turns out to be a warehouse-cum-hypermarket in an unprepossessing suburb that could have been anywhere, from London's East End to Manchester's Moss Side.

A crowd, mostly frazzled mums with small boys in Manchester United shirts, has gathered outside, and the object of its affections switches on the smile again and the reflex 'Hi, how are yous?'

Inside, it is bedlam. Managers and their gofers are all over George (one or two indicate, out of earshot, that they would prefer to be all over Alex), but no one has the gumption to tell him precisely what he is expected to do. Left to fend for himself, he is besieged and, without assistance, organizes his public into something like a queue. Alex, understandably bored, looks on from a distance, and mutters conspiratorially, 'Isn't there somewhere we can go for a coffee, or something?' There isn't, and tedium turns to embarrassment when she is identified and asked to sign a few autographs herself. Rumbled, we take refuge in the manager's office, leaving George to the masses, armed only with a Biro.

After forty-five minutes of working the crowd, back to back with the gag in drag, he joins us for a quick break. His dad, Dickie, appears and, oblivious to the onset of writer's cramp, asks George to sign a few old posters left over from his testimonial match. Then a smartly dressed man with a minor speech impediment joins the group. 'My brother-in-law, Norman,' says George, by way of introduction. 'We call him Stormin' Norman.' Family gossip exhausted, Norman excuses himself to go back to work and someone says, 'Lovely man, pity about the stutter.' George does sympathize with his sister's husband, but it is nothing to do with the way he talks. 'You'd have a stutter, too, if you had his job. He's in bomb disposal.'

Outside again, where someone wins a transit van. 'He's a big lad,' says the comic. 'That'll be handy for his meat and two veg.' A hint, perhaps? While a growing entourage enjoys lunch upstairs, the man of the hour and his painted sidekick are spirited away to meet honoured clients in the 'business suite'.

In their absence, Dickie regales us with stories of Harry Gregg (the irascible Manchester United and Northern Ireland goal-keeper who now runs a hotel in Coleraine), Bobby Campbell's kindness as manager when George played for Fulham, and trips to Scotland with his mates, 'for the horse racing'. Close your eyes and it could have been Best the Younger speaking when he tells the tale of how he passed out unnoticed and spent the night under the table in a Scottish pub. 'When I woke up the next morning, I thought I'd died and gone to heaven.'

Eventually, George and the comic, who is unrecognizable in mufti, are freed from their chores to join in the banter. Still, however, there is work to be done. Someone appears with a box of footballs for George to sign, a task he is so used to performing that he can do it while carrying on a normal conversation, undistracted.

When his food is served, he looks queasy, and leaves it untouched. Everyone notices, and the comedian, clearly accus-tomed to dealing with awkward silences, breaks this one by reverting to his alter ego, hitching up imaginary breasts and mincing: 'I've got everything a woman could want.'

'Yeah,' says George, wearily. 'Balls signed by George Best.'

Later, he confides that he had been 'as sick as a dog' in the toilet mid-visit, and suffered throughout with a blinding head-ache. There is no need to ask why. He has good and bad days.

Now, he just wants to get away. 'Have you got the cheque?' he asks Alex. She hadn't. Having to ask for the money always embarrasses her, but she had summoned the courage to do so three times, to no avail. George is not pleased, and makes no attempt to disguise it. The agent who made the booking was not one of his favourite people. There is no question of leaving until further enquiries, and phone calls, bring satisfactory guarantees. Only then is the Merc summoned for the return trip to Belfast International.

In the airport bar, a chance meeting with Derek Dougan, an old Northern Ireland team-mate George had not seen for years, provides the excuse (as if any were needed) for a hair of the dog which is in danger of becoming the full coat by the time the flight is called. Again BA's cuisine is spurned, this time in favour of another glass or two, and a fairly typical day in the life of a living legend winds down with a couple of hours in his Chelsea local and a visit to his favourite West End casino, where he orders dinner but walks out without eating it, pleading tiredness.

Back in Belfast, Lois Lane has turned a snatched, five-minute interview into George Best: *This is Your Life.*

chapter two

The rest of the world was preoccupied with the Nuremberg war crimes trials, the constitutional crisis in India and the Chinese civil war, but on 22 May 1946 the centre of the universe for Dickie and Ann Best was Belfast's Royal Maternity Hospital, where their first born, George, was making his first public appearance. Matt Busby, incidentally, had just become manager of Manchester United.

The Bests, a devoted young couple, wanted a big family (they were to have five more children) and were delighted to have made a start. Ann was a good-looking woman of pure Irish stock, and Dickie, whose antecedents came from Scotland, was deemed to have made a good catch when they married, in June 1945.

George was born into a solid, working class background. Presbyterian, for those interested in such details. His father, then twenty-seven, worked long hours, on alternate day and night shifts, at an iron turner's lathe in Belfast's Harland and Wolff shipyard. 'Mam', who died in 1978 at the age of fifty-four, was a brunette bundle of energy who worked on the production line in Gallagher's tobacco factory and played hockey, to just short of international standard, for relaxation.

Married for only eleven months, the Bests were living with Ann's parents, still looking for a home of their own, when George arrived kicking and screaming the first rebel yell. For a long time, even after his parents had found their own place, 'home' for George meant Granny Withers's house on Donard Street. 'Family life always seemed to centre around my grandparents,' he says. 'Even after we moved to Burren Way, my primary school was near Donard Street, and I was in and out of there every day.' Part of the attraction was that the Withers' first grandchild was the apple of their eye. George had been named after his maternal grandfather, who doted on the boy. By January 1949, when Dickie and Ann became the first, proud tenants on Burren Way, the council's new estate off the Cregagh Road, there was a granddaughter for old George to spoil, too. Carol, the eldest of four sisters, had been born in October 1947.

Dickie Best played amateur football until he was thirty-six, but it was the patriarchal George, rather than his father, who first introduced Ireland's finest to the game. 'The earliest photograph of me I've seen is at fourteen months, kicking a ball around at my grandparents' house. From when I was a year old, I always had a ball. From then, I was never without one. I even took it to bed with me.' Dickie smiles at the memory. 'As soon as he could walk, all he wanted to do was kick a ball. Those photos at fourteen months were taken with a small box camera – I didn't think they'd come out. Now you mention it, George has had them off me, and I never got them back. All he ever wanted to do was get a ball in his hand and kick it along the street. Then, when we moved up here [Dickie has lived in the same terraced council house for forty-nine years] there was a field where some flats are now, and he was in his element.'

Those peerless skills were developed in a way which seems clichéd and *passé* to the virtual reality generation. Street football is low on street cred, to the regret of the nation's youth coaches, who are left bemoaning the lack of basic ball control among even the best of their charges. 'When we moved to the Cregagh estate,' George says, 'there were some garages at the bottom of the street and, if there were no other kids around to play with, I used to go down there on my own and kick a tennis ball against the garage doors for hour after hour. It used to drive the neighbours nuts.'

On Saturday afternoons, after working in the shipyard until 12.20, Dickie would play football, 'a pretty good amateur', according to George. 'One of his pals told me he was a full-back who kicked the shit out of everybody. A bit of a hard man, apparently.' George wouldn't know, he never saw him play. Instead, he would go with his mother to her hockey matches. 'I remember thinking she was good,' he says. 'I think everyone regarded her as a bit of a star.' Dickie did, for one. 'She was good all right. They say she would have played for Northern Ireland, had not the war years intervened when she was at her best.'

While Ann played, George would dribble a tennis ball between spectators, practice which was to stand him in good stead when it was his turn on the other side of the touchline. He was proud of his mother's sporting prowess, but there was never the slightest chance of his following in her footsteps. Hockey never interested him. 'From day one, all I ever wanted was to play football, and that's all I did.'

His earliest memories include 'chasing beside my grandad, George, to a dustbowl known as the Hen Run to play my first football match', but it was his other grandfather, Dickie's dad, who took him to his first big game. James 'Scottie' Best was so called because he was taken to Glasgow at the age of two, and raised there, working in the Clydeside shipyards before returning to Belfast. 'He lived right by Glentoran's ground, The Oval, and he used to take me there sometimes. If there was anyone who really fuelled my interest, it was him. He used to lift me over, as we called it in those days. He'd help me over the turnstiles and pass me down over all the heads. They used to get a good crowd there.' Glentoran, although only semi-professional, rivalled Linfield, also of Belfast, for supremacy in the Irish League. Champions in 1951 and 1953, the club regularly drew attendances of

3,000-plus. George was occasionally among them, but generally he was one for playing rather than watching the game:

> We kicked a ball around at every opportunity, from dawn till dusk. We did it because we loved it, but also because in those days there was nothing else for kids to do. There was very little football on television, and there were no computer games, or anything like that, so when it was playtime, all you had was a kickabout in the street. That's what we did, all the time.
>
> When I went to primary school [Nettlefield Primary], which was near my grandmother's, it was the same thing. I took a tennis ball, kicked it all the way to school, did my lessons and dashed home at lunchtime for a piece of toast and a cup of tea at grandma's. Then it was quickly back to the playground for a kickabout. I was always the first kid back because my gran's was just around the corner. I was there and back in about five minutes flat. The first couple back would play one against one, then two against two, and by the time everyone got back from lunch it was probably thirty-a-side. It was all good grounding. You learned not to give the ball away when you got it, because if you did, you might not get another kick. As it was, if you got six touches you were a good player.
>
> After school we'd play again, usually until bedtime. My parents had to come looking for me every night. As soon as it got dark, all the other kids were being called in by their mums and dads, all over the estate, but they had to drag me off the streets. Even when it was pitch black I'd still be there, smashing a ball against those garage doors.

Shoes were 'a nightmare' for his parents, each pair lasting no more than a couple of months. The expense of bringing up two children was such that Ann Best went back to work, part-time in the evenings. Dickie remembers it all fondly, as if it were yesterday. 'We had a great life in those days. It was a hard life at times, but we loved it.' Wherever the Bests went, they went together. Socially, that usually meant dancing, at any one of a number of working men's clubs in Belfast. Dickie liked a drink, but never to excess; Ann was teetotal until she was past forty. They had no worries yet about George. 'We never had trouble finding him,' Dickie says. 'If you wanted him, you looked in the field at the end of the road, or by the garages, and he'd be there with a ball. Then, when they laid the football pitches on the estate, he'd be up there all day.'

Whether he had company or not, George would be happy enough, as long as he had a ball. He had the ability to make it talk, after all. 'If I was on my own in the street, and couldn't knock a tennis ball back and forth with a pal, I would try and hit the kerbstone so that the ball would come straight back to me. That was one of the things I would practise. With the garage doors, I would try to hit the knob on the door. Accuracy was the key.'

Shy, bordering on being introverted, he was prone to loneliness. By the time he was six he had two sisters, Barbara joining Carol on the distaff side in October 1952, but he could hardly share his growing passion for football with a baby girl. Nevertheless, his childhood was both 'normal' and 'happy', he says. 'Someone wrote a piece in one of the newspapers recently – some psychiatrist – talking about my upbringing as being abnormal and difficult. He couldn't have been further from the truth. Ours was a happy home, and the way the children were brought up was top class.'

Though occasionally lonely, he was never a loner. He had his gang, and together they got into the usual childhood scrapes. One involved a rat of feline proportions which, when cornered, bit clean through a mate's Wellington boot. Another nearly precluded George's other career, as football's Don Juan. One of the gang's rituals involved jumping a stream which had a concrete slab on either bank, and a sewer pipe running between. One side was higher than the other, and the jump was always made downwards, which was much easier. Too easy for George, who had to be the first to try it the other way. After a run-up Fred Trueman would have deemed excessive, it was immediately apparent that the attempt was doomed to fail. George fell short, and landed on the pipe, wedding gear to the fore. The pain was excruciating as he staggered home, misty-eyed and preoccupied, for once, with balls which were not for kicking. Repeatedly urged to try again, it was one dare he would always decline.

Daredevil yes, tearaway no. There was no lack of discipline in the Best household:

> It was mum who provided it. Dad was a bit of a softy. If I stepped out of line, it was mum who used to smack me across the back of the legs. I'd get sent up to bed, then creep back down half an hour later and they'd let me stay up for another twenty minutes. Mum was definitely the disciplinarian. When they had to come looking for me, she was always the one who came and dragged me in eventually. She was the one who had to hand out the punishment, but she used to hate doing it. She'd chase me up the stairs and I'd crawl under the bed. When she did get to smack me, it hurt her more than it hurt me, I was that skinny and bony.

Dickie is amiable and chatty, but certainly not timid, and he baulks at the description 'softy'. If he was reluctant to punish the boy, it was because his early behaviour rarely warranted it. 'We didn't have to bother too much with discipline. George wasn't hard to work with. He didn't give us any worries. He didn't run about with a bad lot, or look for bother. If you wanted George, you looked in that field, and he'd be there with a ball. I don't think I ever raised my hand to George at all. I can't remember having to. His mum might slap his legs – if she could catch him. He'd run upstairs and roll himself in a ball in the bedclothes, and she'd hurt herself more than she'd hurt him.'

It was a religious family, but in an entirely non-political way. All six children were brought up as Free Presbyterians, and attended Sunday school, as well as church every Sunday. But there was, and never has been, any of the bigotry associated with Ulster sectarianism. George says:

> We always went to church on Sunday, morning or evening. My mum's dad, George, was the one that made us do it. He was the guv'nor, the religious one. He wasn't a soapbox type, but he believed in Christianity, and the children had to go to Sunday school and be good. One of my sisters, Carol, is still very religious. You can't watch television or play football at her house on a Sunday, and my grandad was the same. Mind you, we used to cheat a bit with the telly. When he went upstairs for his afternoon siesta, all the kids would crowd round the set. We had to take it in turns to keep watch at the bottom of the stairway. When we heard him get up, the telly was straight off.

The religious divide has been woven, seemingly inextricably, into the fabric of everyday life in Northern Ireland since partition nearly eighty years ago, but while the socio-economic problems were always there, the violence, at least, was less intrusive when young George was growing up:

> The Troubles, as we know them now, hadn't started then. Our troubles amounted to name calling, no more than that. The street my dad has lived on for forty-nine years is totally mixed. The next-door neighbours I knew are still there, and they are Catholic. The woman there, Melda, was my mum's best friend. A couple of doors away there is another Catholic

> family, living happily next to a Protestant one. Everyone gets on so well that my dad can still leave his front door open, like he used to do when he was a kid.
>
> The only trouble we had was a bit of name-calling. You were either Fenians or proddy dogs. That's what the kids used to call each other. That distinction was always there, but the way it has escalated is too sad for words. The place has gone nuts.

Dickie says George has been away too long if he believes anyone can still leave the front door open in modern Belfast. On the contrary, he keeps a piece of wood not unlike a baseball bat behind the bolted door, and another upstairs, by the bed. There was an intruder at the house not too long ago, an occurrence unlikely to happen again. The Bests have friends in deterrent places.

Despite the constant distraction of football, which always came first, George did well at his lessons. Well enough to pass the eleven-plus and gain a scholarship to the local grammar school, Grosvenor High. 'He always did his homework, he had no bad habits until he went to England,' says Dickie, with feeling.

The celebrations were muted. The grandfather after whom George had been named, and whom he loved as dearly as his parents, died while he was sitting the exams. The fact was kept from him, for obvious reasons at such an important time, but he discovered it, cruelly, on the day he sat the final paper. 'I called into the shop, to buy a couple of pencils and a rubber, and I thought it was funny when the woman serving said: "When is your grandfather getting married?" I actually laughed on the way out. It wasn't until much later that it dawned on me. She had been asking when he was getting buried.' Utterly distraught when his worst fears were proved true, young George walked until he could go no further, then sat under a lamppost and cried like a baby. The house that was his second home was never the same. He was to call it 'the passing of my childhood'.

The sadness lingers to this day, but life had to go on. 'When I passed the eleven-plus to go to grammar school, mum and dad were so pleased,' George says, still proud at the memory. 'Most of my pals hadn't passed, but I was going to Grosvenor High, which was *the* place, and they were a bit chuffed, to say the least, to think that their lad had made it.' Chuffed or not, Dickie never demanded academic success of any of his children. Let them find their own way, free of pressure, was his parental philosophy. It was an attitude he extended to George's football:

> I never had any ambitions for him as a footballer. When his big chance came along, obviously I was pleased about it, but I never tried to push football on George. I didn't go to watch him play and tell him he should be doing this or that differently. I left him to get on with it, and just enjoy himself. I firmly believe that's the proper thing to do with children. You can encourage them, but don't put them under any pressure. Too many parents try to fulfil their own ambitions through their kids.
>
> When it came to the eleven-plus, I told all my children: 'If you get it or you don't, it doesn't matter as far as our feelings towards you are concerned. We will always love you, regardless. Try your best. That's all you can do.' Four out of the six passed, and Julia [one of twins born in July 1963] would have done had she not been taken seriously ill during the exams.

If grammar school was a blessing, it soon proved to be a mixed one for young Master Best. It was never going to work out. For one thing the school played rugby, not football. For another, getting to and fro necessitated a fraught return journey which took George, and his Protestant blazer, through a Catholic enclave. Most important of all, he missed his old mates:

> I was always getting into trouble, always being kept behind in detention to do my lines, and when I came out of school, on my own, I had to walk through this Catholic area with my Protestant uniform on, and it was like running the gauntlet most afternoons. But that wasn't the reason I left. It was a combination of the fact that I couldn't play football there, and that most of my pals were at the secondary school. There is no point being at a grammar school if you are unhappy and not working well. That was the bottom line really. I didn't want to be there, so I wasn't learning anything.

For a year he played rugby, at fly-half, 'and quite enjoyed it'. So much so that he used to climb over the wall to watch Ireland's Five Nations matches in the days when they played within a long touch kick of Burren Way, at the Ravenhill ground, which is still used for B internationals today. It may seem strange, scarcely believable, that the greatest talent British football has produced played rugby at such a crucial stage in his development, but such things are not unknown. John Toshack, a distinguished striker with Liverpool and Wales, played only rugby throughout his schooldays in Cardiff. Coincidentally, also at fly-half.

Mostly at Grosvenor, George played truant:

> The work wasn't really a problem. I was up to that. My two best subjects were English, which I loved, and arithmetic. There were a couple I didn't like. History and geography I found boring. But I felt out of place. The other kids were all strangers to me, and I couldn't wait to come home to meet all my pals from the estate. Basically, I just didn't want to be at the grammar school. The routine became regular. We'd break for lunch, and if we had to be back at one o'clock, I'd go in the boys' toilets at two minutes to one and hide until

> everyone had gone into class. Then I'd climb out over the roof and head off for the afternoon.

He would hide his bag-cum-satchel behind the dustbin at his Auntie Margaret's house, then walk up the Upper Newtownards Road and into the city centre, wandering around the shops until it was time to go home for the pre-prandial kickabout.

Truanting eventually cost the reluctant grammarian his scholarship and, with great relief, he was transferred to Lisnasharragh Intermediate, a secondary modern school which was nearer to home, played his beloved football and reunited him with his friends. 'The first day there, I can remember my first lesson was art. I went in, and all the girls were drawing and all the boys were huddled in a corner, picking a football team to play for the school that weekend. I went across to see what they were doing, and they asked me if I wanted to play. That was the start of it. I was in the school team.'

Inwardly, Dickie must have been disappointed at his son's downgrading. Outwardly, it was a case of *c'est la vie*:

> I think the journey to and from the grammar school bothered George more than he lets on. He had to get a bus through a Catholic area, and you know what kids are like. He'd go through with his badge clearly visible, and they'd throw stones and call him names. Now George didn't look for trouble, but if trouble came along he didn't run from it. If someone had a go at him, he'd have a go back. I remember him telling us one day that he'd got chased and he gave the kids some abuse back and timed it so that he jumped on the bus just before they could catch up with him. He was much happier at Lisnasharragh, which is just over the road. He was top of the class, or near it, in most things, and of course they had a football team, which is all he was ever really interested in.

By the age of eleven or twelve, the game had become an obsession. Family holidays – mostly trips down the coast to Bangor – were unwelcome diversions from the latest make believe Cup Final. All the boy ever wanted, come Christmas or his birthday, was a football or a pair of boots. There was one exception. When he was eleven, he wanted a bike which, times being hard, was bought on hire purchase. Dickie shakes his head, recalling what happened. 'He'd only had it three or four days that Christmas when a friend of mine called Bud McFarlane asked him to deliver a message. It was icy out, and George took the bike against my advice. He was going down this steep hill, and of course he came off. The bike was badly buckled, and we had a bit of a row about that, but Bud paid for the repairs.' Any debt was made good with handsome interest. Bud McFarlane it was who 'discovered' George Best nearly four years later, recommending him to Bob Bishop, Manchester United's Northern Ireland scout.

At the age of eleven, the fixated youngster was having to be dragged off the local pitch, behind the sewage works, almost every night. 'Sometimes, on a cold winter's day,' Dickie reminisced, 'he'd come home and his laces would be frozen solid. We'd have to cut them off. I used to keep him outside and hose him down to get all the mud off him before I'd let him in the house. Only then could he have a hot bath.'

George Best was never one for heroes, but by now he was supporting Wolverhampton Wanderers, chronicling the halcyon days of the Stan Cullis era, alongside events closer to home, in a treasured scrapbook. 'Because I used to go and watch Glentoran with my grandad, I stuck the reports out of the *Belfast Telegraph* on the Glentoran games in the front of the book, and then used to turn it upside down and use the back of the book for Wolves reports. In those days, they were playing the Russians and all the top teams from Europe, and to me they had to be *the* team because they were playing the glamour games, against the foreigners. I didn't really have an individual hero as such, but I suppose Peter Broadbent, the England inside-forward, was close.'

George's choice of an English club to support was not as strange as it might seem today. Wolves were the Manchester United of their day, winning the League championship in 1957–8 and again the following season before missing out on a hat-trick of titles when Burnley pipped them by a single point in 1959–60. That year, they had to be content with the FA Cup. As well as their domestic success, the pride of the Midlands also blazed a trail for English clubs in Europe with a series of prestigious, high-profile matches which brought Honved, Moscow Dinamo, Moscow Spartak and Real Madrid to Molineux. These were ostensibly friendly fixtures, but were played in an undeniably competitive spirit. Broadbent, still revered in the Black Country, was the archetypal playmaker, who called the shots and scored goals, too. He would have won many more than his seven England caps had he not been in competition for a place with the great Johnny Haynes.

By the time he was thirteen, young George was beginning to acquire a following of his own. When he played for the school, passers-by would stop to watch the six-stone weakling who looked as if a single sprint would exhaust him, yet tackled with the best of them and dribbled with the ball magnetized to his mesmeric right foot. Friends and acquaintances were telling Dickie: 'Your wee fella is going to be a good player, make sure all the clubs know about him.' They were wasting their breath. This was never one of football's pushy dads:

> I just said: 'Let's leave him alone. If he has any talent, someone will see it.' After George had gone to Manchester United, I met a mate of mine from work, out for a walk with his kids. He said: 'Your boy has gone to Manchester, I hear. How did you get him over there?' I said: 'I didn't get him over there. All I did was give him permission to go if he wanted to.' He

said: 'My boy is going to be a good player, and I'd like to push him.' I told him: 'Your best way to push him is to leave him alone. Let him go out and play his football and enjoy himself. If he's got talent, someone will see it.'

I hardly ever watched George play as a youngster, and people often asked me why. Not watching him was my way of letting him develop his own way. I never believed in putting pressure on my children. I wasn't the type to make them be what I wanted them to be, wanting to bask in reflected glory, if you like. But I was always quietly proud of George and his football.

That Best was better was never in any doubt. The boy had always sensed it. 'It sounds corny, and a bit arrogant,' he says, 'but I believe great sportsmen are born with a gift, and I was always better than all the other kids, as far back as I can remember. Obviously you don't realize how much better, but I always had something a little bit extra, or a little bit better. Others were keen, but maybe not as fanatical as I was.'

At thirteen, going on fourteen, George started playing for the local youth club, Cregagh Boys. He was still 'unbelievably thin', his body a 'disaster area', but his legs were strong, and if the girls ridiculed his physique, so what? He was on first-name terms with the ball, which was all that mattered. The Cregagh Boys Club team was run by the late Bud McFarlane, of bicycle fame, who was also reserve team coach at Glentoran. 'Bud was the one,' George says, 'who started telling me I could play, and that I could make it big time. The best advice I had was from him. One day he said: "You're a bit weak on your left foot," so all that week I practised with a tennis ball and my left foot. Come the Saturday, I played with a plimsoll on my right foot and a boot on my left. I never touched the ball with my right and we won 21–0. I scored twelve – all with my left foot.'

Scoring a dozen goals at a time, with his 'wrong' foot, he was creating quite a stir. But not, strangely, with the Northern Ireland Schools selectors. George Best was never considered good enough to win a schoolboy cap, a slight Dickie has never forgotten:

> People here still can't believe it. Lisnasharragh didn't play in a competitive league as such, they only played friendly games against other schools or boys clubs, and perhaps that counted against George. What did happen was that Bud McFarlane arranged a match between Cregagh Boys Club and the probable Schools international side. I slipped out of work to watch, which I didn't do very often, but the game was only five minutes away from where I was working, so I went along to have a look. George was just about the smallest player on the pitch, but he stood out head and shoulders above the rest of them. Cregagh won 2–1. After that, they put him in the possibles squad. In one of the trial games they were 2–0 down and brought him on and he scored two goals, but still he didn't get a cap. I think it was because of the school he played for.

Fortunately, George's mentor, Bud McFarlane, had influence, and Bud had a friend. Bob Bishop was a salt of the earth character with whom Bill Shankly, Jock Stein and Alex Ferguson would have had common cause. Teak tough, having worked as a riveter in the shipyards, he was really at home only among working men or football folk, and in the latter case only at the unspoiled, grass roots level. Bishop helped to run the celebrated Boyland Youth Club, whose success as a nursery for England's First Division had just seen him appointed, in 1961, as Manchester United's chief scout in Northern Ireland. It is impressive testimony to his excellence as a talent spotter that he was United's eyes and ears in Ulster for the next thirty-seven years, until his retirement, at the age of eighty-six, in 1987. Jimmy Nicholson,

Sammy McIlroy, David McCreery, Jimmy Nichol and Norman Whiteside – internationals all – were among his discoveries.

At Bud McFarlane's behest, Bishop had taken George to one of his weekend training camps for Boyland boys, held just outside Belfast, at Helen's Bay. Bishop liked what he saw, but was not sure. A scout from Leeds United had already been to watch George in a match, but left midway through the first half, telling McFarlane: 'That boy will never make a player. He's too skinny.' The poor man was never allowed to forget it but, in fairness, such stories are legion. Kenny Dalglish, a Rangers fan as a boy, was watched and rejected by the club he dreamed of joining, and Coventry City told Kevin Keegan he was 'too small'. Bishop was more circumspect. He watched George time and again, then asked McFarlane to play him against a better class of opposition. A special match was arranged, Cregagh Under-15s against Boyland, who fielded an older team, including seventeen- and eighteen-year-olds. It was a day George is unlikely to forget. 'They wanted to see if I could handle it against bigger boys because they were still worried about my size and weight. I only weighed about six stones. I was still skinny when I got in the first team at United, but when I was a kid it was pitiful.'

Again, Dickie just had to be there. 'Normally, I didn't go, and by the time George was fifteen I don't think I had seen him play more than six times, but obviously this was important. George was just fifteen, and he was up against a big lad of nearly eighteen, but he played really well and scored twice.' That clinched it. Bob Bishop was convinced. He sent Matt Busby his famous telegram: 'I think I've found you a genius.'

Old Bob was to die, in June 1990, with one great regret. 'George really was the best,' he said. 'When he first went to United, he was like Little Lord Fauntleroy – butter wouldn't melt in his mouth – and it's a shame how he turned out. George should have been a millionaire. I often thought if his parents had come over from Ireland and sorted him out, things might have been different. McIlroy, Nichol and Whiteside's parents all went across. There are things you don't do when your parents are about.'

The reasons Dickie and Ann Best stayed in Belfast will become apparent later. Back in Easter 1961, the questions that remained were rhetorical. Dickie had to be formally approached for his consent for George to go to Old Trafford. 'Only if he wants to go,' came the inevitable reply. They hardly had to ask. There would be a trial for two weeks during the school holidays, they said, and another Irish boy, Eric McMordie, would be going with him. He never heard the second part. Already he was up on cloud nine, telling grandad George that he was off to Manchester United.

chapter three

Potential genius or not, Manchester United treated the fifteen-year-old George Best in such an offhand way that they nearly lost him before he had kicked a ball for them.

In marked contrast to the painstaking nursery scheme that is Alex Ferguson's pride and joy, and which is serving the club so well today, United's youth development system in the early sixties was easy come, easy go. There was much more raw talent out there in the pre-computer age, and if one good boy fell by the wayside, so what? There were plenty more fish in the Irish Sea. So it was that George Best and Eric McMordie were left to find their own way from Belfast to Old Trafford, without a chaperon or anyone to meet them on arrival in England.

The story begins on a hot July day in 1961. The scene was replicated in the film *In the Name of the Father*, where the young Gerry Conlon, played by Daniel Day-Lewis, and his mate board the ferry for a new life weighed down with trepidation and a few quid of dad's hard-earned. George's mum, Ann, had also dug deep to equip him with his first pair of long trousers. Barely five feet tall, shorts had sufficed until now, but they were hardly the right travelling gear for the budding professional footballer. Great Adventure or not, it was an experience George recalls without affection:

> Eric and I didn't know each other, which didn't help. It was not as if I had one of my mates for company. It was all a bit

frightening really. We were a couple of soft kids who had never been out of Belfast before, and to be invited to Manchester United, one of the greatest clubs in the world, was intimidating, to say the least. It made it so much worse that we had to get on the boat and travel overnight on our own, with no mums and dads. In those days, kids were much less confident, less worldly, than they are today, and that was asking a bit much.

At fifteen you would have thought the club might have had someone travel with us, but even when we docked at Liverpool there was no one there to meet us. We were so nervous and inexperienced, we didn't know what we were doing, but we made it to Lime Street station and got a train to Manchester. Again, nobody met us. We were told the club would send a taxi, but if they did we missed it. When we got one of our own and asked for Old Trafford we ended up at the cricket ground, where Lancashire were playing at the time. It hadn't occurred to us that there were two Old Traffords, and that it was the cricket season.

When we finally arrived at the right place, we were immediately on the move again. Dear old Joe Armstrong, who was the chief scout, and a lovely man, took us to the training ground. This was before they had the modern complex where they train now, called The Cliff. They were using somewhere in Stretford at the time.

Because we arrived in the morning, after travelling all night, they thought it would be a good start to introduce us to the Irish players at the club. We met a guy called Sammy McMillan, who played a few first-team games, and two Northern Ireland internationals, Jimmy Nicholson and Harry Gregg. Harry was a legend – everyone's hero back home. To me, he looked like Superman. To two kids like us, he was a giant. I remember looking at him – and Jimmy Nicholson was a well built lad, too – and thinking: What chance have two little waifs like us got of making it in a game full of men like these?

Tired, after twenty-four hours on the move, and utterly overawed, the two 'waifs' were finally transported to their digs, a terraced house in the Manchester suburb of Chorlton which, although he would have ridiculed the notion at the time, was to be George's home, on and off, for more than a decade. Mrs Mary Fullaway was a widow with a three-up, three-down council house who boarded a couple of Manchester United players at a time in one spare room to help make ends meet. George was not the first, but he was to be the last. Recalling that first meeting, she said: 'I wanted to sit him down and fill him full of meat and potatoes. He was so thin, so tiny. He looked more like an apprentice jockey than a footballer. I didn't give him a hope of making it.'

That first night, George would not have argued. 'It had been such a frightening day. Having to fend for myself in such overwhelming circumstances was too much. Everything seemed to be a terrible problem, even our accents. Nobody understood what the hell we were talking about, which was so embarrassing for a youngster. Poor old Mrs Fullaway just couldn't understand a word we were saying. We decided to lock ourselves in our bedroom, and I remember turning to Eric and saying: "D'you fancy going home?" That first night we decided we wanted to go home, we weren't going to make it.' A fitful night's sleep in strange beds merely served to heighten their sense of alienation, and their resolve. In the morning they told Joe Armstrong: 'Thanks, but no thanks.'

We had to get two buses from Mrs Fullaway's, one to Trafford Bar and another from there to Old Trafford, and the embarrassment started all over again. You had to tell the conductor a dozen times what ticket you wanted, because he couldn't understand your accent. When we got to the ground and told them 'We want to go,' they didn't really argue. They just said, 'Okay, if that's what you want to do.' We didn't tell anyone at home, in case they tried to stop us, and that night we went back to Liverpool and did the reverse trip. United wouldn't give us the tickets, we had to buy them out of the little money we had.

Anyway, I just turned up the next morning at my mum and dad's house, knocked on the door and they freaked out. They assumed I must have done something wrong and got sent home. I said: 'No, we were just homesick, we wanted to come back.'

Dickie Best was not, and is not, the type of man given to 'freaking out', but he did require a more detailed explanation than the one word 'homesickness'. It had been his son's heart's desire to play for Manchester United. What had gone wrong to change all that in the space of twenty-four hours? The more he looked into it, the less impressed he was with United's cavalier treatment of the next generation of 'Busby Babes':

George and Eric McMordie had never been out of Belfast in their lives before, apart from trips to the seaside at Bangor, twelve miles away. Now, at fifteen years of age, they were expected to find their own way across to Old Trafford. No wonder they were a bit scared by it all – George probably more so than Eric, who was a nice lad, but worldly-wise for his age.

When they came back after just the one day United wanted to know why, and I had a message to get in touch with Joe Armstrong, the chief scout. We didn't have a phone in the house at the time, so I made the call from a box and reversed the charges. Joe said he was disappointed that the boys didn't give the club a chance. I said I could hardly believe that none of their young trialists had been homesick before. Anyhow, he said: 'We'd like your boy to come back and give it another go. Would he come?' I said: 'Only of his own free will. I've never put any pressure on him, and I'm not going to start now.'

Dickie Best knew his son. The softly, softly approach was the way to bring him round. He said nothing at first on his return from the phone box, playing on young George's curiosity. Eventually, the question burst out of the boy. 'Dad, what did Mr Armstrong want?'

Dickie, detachment personified, said: 'He's just disappointed that you didn't give it a better chance, that's all.' Deliberately, there was no mention of the invitation to try again. Time for a little parental psychology first.

George had been 'skulking'. There was no call for that. 'You have been over there, you've come back, and you're hiding in the house,' dad chided, gently. 'Why? No one thinks any the less of you for coming home. You've done nothing wrong, you were just homesick. We don't think there's anything wrong in that.'

There was tea, and sympathy, in the cosy kitchen at Burren Way, as father and son sat at the table, poring over the sports pages of the *Belfast Telegraph*. Judging the time to be right, Dickie went for it. 'George, would you like to go back to Manchester?'

'Yes, I would.'

'Well, they're talking about you going over at Christmas, for the holidays.'

'No dad, I want to go back now. I'm ready now.'

'You understand that if you do go back, you're going of your own accord, under no pressure from us?'

'What do I have to do?'

Dickie suggested a letter, stressing the boy's strong wish to play for Manchester United, would probably have the desired effect. George asked him to write it for him.

> I left it for a couple of hours, but George was full of the idea now, and said: 'Dad, are you not going to write my letter?' So I wrote the letter. He said: 'Can I see it?' so I gave it to him and asked him if he was happy with it. He was, so I sealed it, addressed it and said: 'Here you are, you put a stamp on it and post it when you want to post it.'
>
> The following day, we were going to Bangor on the train, my wife and I and the younger children, and George said: 'Can I go with you?' I said: 'Of course you can.' Anyway, we were halfway up the street when George said: 'I've forgotten the letter,' so he ran back for it, and we posted it in the post office in Bangor.

More important correspondence may have arrived in the Old Trafford mailroom, but none springs readily to mind. Had the letter not been written, or had it received no response, George Best might still have spent his life in newspapers – but as a printer.

Like any dutiful parent, Dickie wanted his boy to have something to fall back on in case a career in professional football failed to work out, and had been nudging him towards the print trade. George was not averse to the alternative. 'I was only interested in football, but I had taken the exams to become a printer before I was first invited to Old Trafford. I had passed them, too, so I had a job waiting for me, just in case.' At Dickie's behest, the apprenticeship was kept open for six months after George had joined United, but long before the offer expired it was evident that it would not be taken up.

The missive from Bangor had done the trick. There had been an inquiry at Old Trafford into why the 'genius' Busby had been promised had not materialized, and it was with some relief that Joe Armstrong reeled in 'the one that got away'. The prodigy was deemed sufficiently important for dad's letter to warrant a telegram in response – and no boats this time. There was a pre-paid air ticket awaiting collection at Belfast's Aldergrove airport. George Best was taking off.

Not that air travel was without its pitfalls. When the ingenuous fifteen-year-old arrived at Manchester Ringway there was again no one to meet him and, having no idea where to go, he followed the crowd and found himself in the biggest car park he had seen in his life. This time, though, nothing fazed him. He was ready. He was going to get there, and get on, come what may. 'I was determined to stick it out, and fortunately, quite quickly I met a couple of kids who were just like me, and we sort of clicked and got on well right from the start.' Those early brothers in arms included John Fitzpatrick, the combative Aberdonian who followed Best into the first team and played his part in the 1968 European Cup run, Jimmy Ryan, now back on the coaching staff at Old Trafford, and Peter McBride, a young wing-half who never quite made the grade and drifted into obscurity, first at Southport, then briefly at Bradford Park Avenue, after making just one first-team appearance for United. George smiles at the memory of the gauche new boys, trying to hide their self-consciousness. 'We all arrived at the same time and we were all homesick, and a bit scared, because it was our first time away from our families. We became good pals, and have remained so over the years.'

Back at Mrs Fullaway's, this time the landlady without the lingo was a sympathetic surrogate mum who spared no effort to overcome the pangs that afflict strangers in a strange land. Losing a couple of her charges after just the one night was an affront to the Fullaway hospitality. George would be happy this time, or else.

Best senior was still worried. What was happening over there? How was the boy getting on? Not having a phone with which to maintain regular communication hardly helped. Nor did United's attitude when it came to the rearing of apprentices:

> From various conversations I had with Joe Armstrong, the chief scout, I know they preferred parents to stay away from their boys while they settled in. Anyway, George went away in July, and by October, or it might even have been November, I'd had no contact with the club. So I rang Joe Armstrong again. We still had no phone, so I reversed the charges from a friend's house this time. I said: 'Mr Armstrong, how is the boy getting on? The only way we know he is actually in Manchester is from his weekly letter home.' The alarm bells rang in old Joe's head. Young Master Best was already regarded as 'something special' at Old Trafford. It would be silly to run the risk of losing him a second time. 'Okay Mr Best,' he said. 'We'll bring you over to see him.'

Dickie was satisfied. Briefly. 'After about a week, I got one ticket for the boat. First class. Meantime, although it was hard finding the money, I had booked two flights to Manchester. So when the boat ticket arrived, I rang Joe again and said: "Mr Armstrong, can you tell me what's going on here? You've sent me one ticket for the boat. Don't you think my wife would like to see our boy – maybe even more than I do?" He said: "Well, perhaps we can come to some arrangement." I said: "Don't bother, I'm sending your ticket back because I've booked two flights."'

The point had been well made, and anyway the Bests, with their prodigy, were a special case. Manchester United sent forty pounds, which in those pre-inflationary days paid for two return flights. It was money well spent. Parental fears were soon allayed by seeing George completely at ease, and happy, in his home from home:

> Once we met Mrs Fullaway we didn't have any worries about where he was living. She had two boys of her own, but had always kept boarders – policemen as well as footballers.

Another Belfast lad, a goalkeeper called Ronnie Briggs, was there for a while, and George was very happy.

After that first visit, we went back a couple of times at our own expense, but the club wasn't keen on the idea. Joe Armstrong's attitude was: 'It would be better if you stayed away from the lad. Let him settle.' For a year or so George was still a bit homesick. Now I can't get him home!

In football terms, settling in was never a problem, the technique honed on the streets of the Cregagh compensating in handsome measure for the young Best's lack of inches and avoirdupois. His puny build may have sown the seeds of doubt in his own mind ('I still didn't think I was going to make it'), but Busby and his coaching staff knew they had a rare talent to nurture. George's own fears were fuelled by the feeling that his development was being hampered, unfairly, by a protectionist rule which discriminated against boys from Northern Ireland and Scotland, whose respective Football Associations objected to English clubs cherry-picking their best young players, and would not allow them to sign on a professional basis until their seventeenth birthday. George, and his friend John Fitzpatrick, were required to play as amateurs, which meant earning their living, or at least having a job, outside the game. In reality, these 'jobs' were little more than sinecures with local employers, who were only too willing to oblige, in return for reciprocal favours when the big matches came along. Young Best, however, resented anything that impinged on time that could be spent playing football, and it always rankled that he had to be at work while his English contemporaries were out on the training field:

Of course we didn't think it was right. Just because we were Irish, or Scottish, we couldn't sign as apprentice professionals. We were amateurs, which meant we had to have a job and train on Tuesday and Thursday nights with the other amateurs, not with the full-time professionals. The club would find you a job and you had no choice, you had to do it.

I was a clerk, a gofer with the Manchester Ship Canal Company, making tea for everyone when I wanted to be playing football. I told the club I wanted to train every day with the other boys. I wasn't here to make tea for people, I wanted to play football. I told them I wasn't happy, but all they did was to move me to a different branch of the same company. Same work, different location. I wasn't having that, so then they found me a job in a builders' yard. I had to be there at eight o'clock in the morning on my first day. I stayed until lunchtime, then I went back to Old Trafford and said: 'I didn't come to Manchester to hump planks of wood.' I quit after half a day – and still went back and asked for the morning's wages.

United gave in and made allowances for George Best's extraordinary talent, which was to be the way of it for the next ten years. The bolshie fifteen-year-old had his way. Grinning at the memory, like the recalcitrant kid he was, he says: 'The club came up with a solution which was totally illegal, but worked to everyone's advantage. They found a Manchester United supporter who had an electrical business near The Cliff training ground, and Fitzy [John Fitzpatrick] and I used to clock on at nine in the morning, walk over to The Cliff, do our training, then go back to clock off. We got what we wanted – to train full-time with the rest of the boys.'

As a bogus electrician and 'amateur' footballer, George earned £4 1s 9d (£4.09) a week, three pounds of which he sent home to his parents. 'I lived on £1 1s 9d [£1.09] a week, and thought I was rich. The club paid for just about everything – digs, meals, bus fares etc. – and when I went out I could make one drink last all night. I always had money left at the end of the week.' Back in Burren Way, the financial help was welcome. 'As a family,' George says, 'we were never desperately poor, but there was never a lot of money. Everyone had to chip in, and that three pounds was a lot for mum to get.' Dickie is too proud to elaborate, but he was bringing up five younger children and, he says, 'it came in handy, right enough'.

George Best must have been exceptional for a club as big as Manchester United to bend the employment rules, and risk the wrath of the FA, to keep him happy, but opinion is divided as to what extent he stood out in fairly distinguished company. Johnny Giles, six years Best's senior, was a first-team regular at United at the time, before going on to attain greatness with Leeds United. He remembers watching the youth team, but has no recollection of George Best much before his first-team debut, at seventeen. Giles, now an acerbic columnist with the *Express* newspaper, told me:

> For his first year or so, George was just another groundstaff lad. He was always a nice, quiet, fairly shy lad. Matt Busby didn't have much to do with the young players. It was left to his assistant, Jimmy Murphy, to run the youth team, and I'm not sure, but I think it may be a myth that Matt saw George and said: 'Don't coach him, he's a genius.'
>
> As I remember it, George wasn't outstanding in the youth team, and there was a time when the other lads weren't keen on him playing. I certainly don't remember watching the youth team and seeing him as an outstanding player, and the word never went round the first-team dressing room that this was a player you had to see. George was just one of a crowd. He wasn't a boy genius.
>
> I played two games in the reserves before I left for Leeds, and George, who was seventeen, played in both. I played on the right wing and he played on the left. One was at Old Trafford and the other – my last game – was at Chesterfield. I didn't think then: 'This lad is going to be a great player.'

The case for the defence is put by the most celebrated of all the 'Red Devils'. The name Bobby Charlton is synonymous with Manchester United the world over. Sir Bobby, as he became in the 1994 Birthday Honours List, insists nobody should have been in any doubt that the club had a prodigy in its midst. The word had gone round, he says:

> The coaching staff usually tell you – it filters through if a really good kid comes in. Hundreds of young hopefuls pass through a big club and they leave, mostly without making any sort of a mark, almost on a daily basis. But now and again the coaching staff will say: 'There's a good lad just come. All things being equal, he's got a chance.' That's the way they talk. 'All things being equal, he's got a chance' is their way of saying they've got a really good player.
>
> That's what happened with George. Manchester United had got a lot of the best young players, mainly because we were the club they all wanted to join, so there was no shortage of good youngsters around the place, but when a really great young player comes along, the coaches can't tell you enough about it. Most people in the game will immediately recognize natural talent and sheer ability. The question marks are against the kids who have to learn something on the way to being a good player. But some just have it so naturally that it shines out, like a beacon. That's how it was with George.
>
> I remember Wilf McGuinness, who was on the coaching staff, winding me up by saying: 'Bloody hell, if you think you're a good player you should see this lad who has come in from Belfast.' Joking, I told him: 'But he can't be as good as me. I'm brilliant.' Wilf said: 'No, no, it's right.' Humouring him, I said: 'All right, I believe you.' I didn't, of course, but the next thing I knew George was in the first team.
>
> I think I know what Johnny Giles means. Like him, I can

only remember George in the first team. He all but missed the reserves, going straight from the youth team to the firsts. He was on top of us before we knew what had happened.

If Charlton was taken by surprise by the speed of the tyro's elevation, another of United's all-time greats most certainly was not. Scotland's Pat Crerand believes he was the first of the senior players to recognize that George was indeed a genius. The midfield organizer of Busby's European Cup-winning team had just signed from Celtic when, killing time, he went to watch a youth match. 'We had this fella playing inside-left, and I just couldn't believe it. I couldn't believe his ability. I went and spoke to Jack Crompton, the trainer, and said: "Jack, what about that bloody inside-left. Isn't he unbelievable? I have never seen anything like it in my life." Jack just looked up and said, matter of fact: "Oh, we know all about him." You could have put your house on that boy becoming one of the great players.'

Best himself accepts that he was not the star of the youth team – not at first, anyway. 'David Sadler [who was to play for England] was regarded as the one who was going to be the big star. When United signed him, all the big clubs had been after him. Eamonn Dunphy and Barry Fry were also regarded very highly. I was well down the list.' Sadler, now a successful businessman in corporate hospitality, runs the United ex-players association. He roomed with Best at Mrs Fullaway's for six years, and they remain good friends. George, he says, is the best player he has ever seen, but it was probably true to say that at one time even more was expected of David Sadler. At sixteen he had been working in a bank and playing amateur football for Maidstone United when United beat off half the old First Division to sign the most sought-after young player in the country:

Playing for Maidstone, I was doing well enough to get picked for the full England amateur side, and as a sixteen-year-old centre-forward who was scoring a few goals there was a bit of fuss made about me. There were a few clubs I could have joined, but I plumped for United and signed amateur forms with them late in 1962. I stayed down in Kent until I was seventeen, in February 1963, so after joining United I had another six months in the old National Provincial bank. It was then, when I was able to sign as a professional, that I first came across George and the other lads. I remember hearing one or two of them making sarky comments about the superstar southerner, and how the club had laid out a nice new tracksuit for me, while the others had crap stuff.

Sadler was to become as good a friend as Best has ever had, but the early memories are blurred. As with Johnny Giles, there was no immediate impression of being in the presence of potential greatness. 'It wasn't like I went training and all of a sudden there was this genius there. I came up at seventeen and got straight into the youth team a year before George. Barry Fry was in that side ahead of him. To be honest, there was nothing special about that team. It was the next lot, George's class if you like, which produced several players of note.' Sadler also agrees with Giles on the overplaying of the idea of Matt Busby ordaining that young Best should not be coached, to preserve his individuality:

I don't think that was peculiar to George. That was very much the United way at the time. They would pull you aside occasionally and say you were doing this or that wrong, but they never really did coach us individually. John Aston senior was the youth coach then. I don't know if he had any qualifications for coaching, but I would be surprised if he did.

John Aston took the youth team and Jimmy Murphy the reserves. They didn't really teach us much. They always talked in very simple terms, about keeping possession and so on. They didn't really coach you as we know it now. It wasn't just George they left alone. Their attitude was: You wouldn't be here, son, if we didn't think you had the ability to do it. We're just giving you the chance to show that ability. In all the time I was there, they never really talked about technique. Attitude – applying yourself – was more important than skills. Those they took for granted.

Deemed too young, and too frail, to play for the youth team in his first year, it was on his own initiative, then, that Best worked assiduously to improve the breadth of his skills. He was always first out on to the training pitch, always the most reluctant to leave it. The love of football, and the desire to be better than the rest, was all the motivation he ever needed, but he does recall one inspirational moment of great significance:

> When I was fifteen, United were playing Real Madrid, and I remember seeing [Francisco] Gento do something I had never seen before. It was during the pre-match warm-up, and the goalkeeper was drop-kicking the ball to him. Gento had a great left foot and he pretended to shoot, but he put such backspin on the ball that after it had gone about ten yards it would spin back to him. I watched, spellbound. I had never seen anything like it.
>
> The next day, in training, I had to do it. I was right-footed, but Gento had done it with his left, so I had to do the same. That was probably the start, the thing that made me determined to be genuinely two-footed. I made up my mind that I was going to be able to do everything with my 'other' foot. From then on, I worked on it all the time. I tried to keep the ball up with my left foot. If I could do it ten times, then I wanted to do it a dozen. After training, when everyone else

had gone, I'd take out six or seven balls and keep working at it. I set myself tasks. I would take corners with my left foot and try to score direct. Then I would stand on the eighteen-yard line and try to hit the crossbar time after time. By the time I was nineteen or twenty, most people couldn't tell which one was my stronger foot.

Heading the ball was a challenge, too. Something else that could be improved by diligent repetition. 'Our gym was at Old Trafford then – I think it's one of the players' lounges now. Jack Crompton, who was our trainer, used to hang a ball from the ceiling and swing it for heading practice. Once you were finding the height easy, you raised the ball. I was shorter than a lot of other players, but people forget I scored a good few goals with my head.'

Tackling, another of Best's strengths, came naturally:

That was a matter of pride. Sir Matt always said that I was probably the best tackler at the club, and that was a hell of a compliment. I actually enjoyed the physical side of it. I had people trying to kick me, and if they took the ball away from me, it was an insult. I wanted it back.

I remember once we played at Birmingham, and Noel Cantwell was captain at the time. It was a really muddy day, and towards the end of the game Noel made a run down the left, someone knocked the ball off to their right-winger and Noel was caught out of position, with no hope of getting back. 'George,' he said, 'd'you think you can get there?' I thought: I'll get back all right. I was a skinny eighteen-year-old kid, in six inches of mud, but I chased this winger for fifty or sixty yards and tackled him to get the ball out for a throw-in. I felt so chuffed. I felt like Superman when I got up after the tackle. I got him.

When it came to pace, George was always well blessed:

> I was naturally quick. In the training sprints, over ten or fifteen yards, the only one that could ever beat me was Bobby [Charlton]. When we worked on sprints, I used to have little challenges with my mates, who were the same age as me. I could run backwards and beat them when they were running forwards. We also had routines where you had to carry someone on your back from the eighteen-yard line to the halfway line, then switch over, and of course everyone would look for a lighter partner. Not me. I used to look for the heaviest. I didn't mind slinging Bill Foulkes [the first team's strapping centre-half] on my back, just to make it harder.
>
> Pre-season training was always hard work, but I actually enjoyed it. I enjoyed the competition. Whether it was cross-country or out on the pitch, I wanted to be the best. Over a short distance, Bobby Charlton was always red hot. Over the longer runs, the four or five miles cross-country, John Fitzpatrick was the only one who could ever beat me. I can still remember, when we used to turn right out of The Cliff, about half a dozen of the boys turned left and used to hide behind the bushes at the top of the final run-in. That really used to piss me off. We had gone all the way round, and they would join in as we came to the end of it. Mind you, needless to say not many of them went on and made it.

For that first year, George clocked on and off at the electricians', trained obsessively, cleaned the first-teamers' boots ('I used to head for Harry Gregg's'), mopped out the dressing rooms and toilets and played on Saturdays for the A and B teams in front of two dozen zealots. Relaxation, but never distraction in these early days, was provided by his first serious girlfriend, Maria, who had previously been going out with Mrs Fullaway's son, Steve. Maria's aunt owned a cake shop in Manchester, and

George found he could have his, and eat it, in the flat above the shop.

When he wasn't with Maria, nights out with the other apprentices – usually David Sadler, John Fitzpatrick, Jimmy Ryan and Peter McBride – meant sober, innocent expeditions to the snooker hall in nearby Chorlton, or the bowling alley in Stretford. 'The bowling alley was our main hang out,' George says. 'After matches, we went ten-pin bowling. That was our Saturday night. Once in a while it would be the snooker hall, for a change, but the bowling alley was the new "in" place for pulling birds. That was our main reason for going there. We'd have a few Cokes, play a couple of games and pull a few birds. The disco scene came later.'

So did the drinking. At this stage, it was Coca-Cola, coffee, or the occasional half pint of lager and lime. This was George, not Georgie Best, a young man dedicated to the sport that was the love of his life. He was working towards a place in United's vaunted youth team, where competition was every bit as fierce – perhaps more so – than it was at senior level. In the fifties, the Busby Babes had won English football's major youth tournament, the FA Youth Cup, five seasons in a row, and their production line of home-produced talent was the envy of every club in the country. There were rumours of illegal inducements – parents of a promising boy finding money behind the sofa after a scout's visit – but Dickie Best received nothing, and George believes the stories to be exaggerated:

> We all heard about mums and dads getting a new fridge or whatever, but I think that was about the extent of it. And we're not just talking about Manchester United here. Just about all the clubs were doing the same thing.
>
> United were always going to have their pick of the kids anyway. They were the glamour club everyone wanted to join. Because of the Munich air crash, I suppose, even if

United weren't your team, they were everyone's favourite other team. They still have that special aura about them, of course, but now boys may prefer to go to Liverpool, Arsenal or Newcastle. In those days, offered the opportunity to sign for United or someone else, there wasn't really a choice.

Given this easy access to the cream of the country's young talent, there was some concern at Old Trafford at the club's failure to win, or even to reach the final of, the FA Youth Cup between 1958 and 1963, during which time Chelsea overtook United as the dominant force at Under-18 level. George Best's year, as the class of '64 will always be known, would swing the pendulum back the other way.

Johnny Giles may not have noticed it, but there was never any doubt in Matt Busby's mind that the boy from Belfast was going to be something special. He had seen enough to make the decision on whether George should be offered a professional contract on his seventeenth birthday a formality. Dickie, however, was in familiar mode. Worried.

Despite having a terrible time in the League, where they finished nineteenth, United reached the FA Cup Final in 1963, playing Leicester City. Dickie Best had never been to Wembley, and asked George to get him a ticket. It was just as well that he was there for 25 May 1963 proved to be a double celebration for the Best family. United won the Cup 3–1 with goals from David Herd (two) and Denis Law, and young George went to the post-match banquet with his first professional contract in his pocket. His wages had jumped from £4 1s 9d to £17 per week – 'I felt like a millionaire' – yet still Dickie found cause for complaint:

George's seventeenth fell in the middle of Cup Final week, so they signed him three days before Wembley, without me being there, which I thought was wrong. He was a minor. On the Thursday, I'd had a letter from George, saying: 'Your son is now a pro. I've signed.' I wasn't too pleased about how it had been done.

Anyway, when I arrived in London for the final, on the Saturday, the club put me in a hotel across the street from where the team were having their 'do' in the evening. I went to the game, and afterwards Joe Armstrong came to see me at the hotel and asked if I'd like to go to the banquet. He said: 'I hope you don't mind, Mr Best, but we'll have to bring you in by the back door. All the other kids' parents will want to come in if they see you.'

When I got there, George was with Harry Gregg, and Harry said to me: 'Make sure your boy is well fixed up with his contract.' I said: 'But he's already signed, without me knowing.' Harry told me: 'Well, don't worry. They know they've got a good player in this wee fella.' Coming from Harry, that reassured me. After that, I had a few words with Matt Busby, asking him why I wasn't consulted before George signed his contract. He said: 'Well, we knew you were coming over for the final, and we thought you'd be happy enough.' I told him: 'I'd have been happier if I'd been there,' and we left it at that. I also said: 'If he's not going to make it, I'd be grateful if you'd let me know within six months, because I have a position held open for him in the printing trade.'

George did become interested in other positions – inside-right and inside-left, not to mention 'the missionary'. The girls were taking an interest now, and he bought his first car, an Austin 1100, to bolster his pulling power. David Herd, the first-team striker the club had signed from Arsenal, had gone into the garage business, and the Austin was one of his first sales. 'I walked in and paid cash, about £400 I think it was. Amazing. A seventeen-year-old kid from Belfast with four hundred quid in his pocket. I used to get my wage packets at the end of the week and look at the money as if it was a dream. It really was unbelievable to me.'

On the pitch, George Best was always an inside-forward, in tandem with John Fitzpatrick, until he got in the first team, and at this stage that was happening only in his dreams. For the time being, he was content just to be part of the club's other pride and joy, the youth team:

> When you got in that, because it was so important to the club as a source of first-team players, you were treated the same as a first-teamer. From making your own way to matches, on the bus or whatever, suddenly you were travelling in the same coach the first team used. You were having lunch at smart hotels before every game. It was the start of your grooming. You knew you were a little bit special and they looked after you.
>
> All the staff came to the youth team games, whereas before, in the A and B teams, you were lucky if twenty people were there, and you never saw Matt, Jimmy Murphy or Joe Armstrong. The year we won the Youth Cup, Manchester City had a terrific youth side, and were considered better than us, but we met them in the semi-finals and beat them twice, at home and away.

The matches in question attracted tremendous interest, with a crowd of 29,706 present at Old Trafford to see United win the first leg 4–1. Their team that day, 8 April 1964, included Jimmy Rimmer, who was to keep goal for England; Willie Anderson, who, like Rimmer, had a good career at Aston Villa; John Fitzpatrick, who was to play more than a hundred League games for United; Sadler, who played 272; and John Aston Junior, who scored twenty-five goals in 155 senior appearances before transferring to Luton Town. Peter McBride was also in the side, as was Bobby Noble, the captain of the England youth team, whose career was cruelly curtailed by a car accident, after thirty-one first-team games. Man of the match, however, was none of these, nor George Best, but a player who never made the first team at Old Trafford. Albert Kinsey, who had to move to Wrexham to play League football, outshone Best, Sadler and the rest by scoring a hat-trick to leave United with one foot in the final.

Manchester City were fired up for the return twelve days later, which drew 21,378 to Maine Road for an aggregate attendance of more than 50,000. Mike Doyle, a fierce competitor who was to win five caps for England, had good players around him in Glyn Pardoe and David Connor, who were to win Championship medals with City four years later. A City team which also included Bobby McAlinden, who was subsequently to become George Best's team-mate and business partner in America, ran themselves to the point of exhaustion, trying to recover from the three-goal deficit, but again United were too good for them, winning 4–3 with scoring contributions from Sadler (two), Best and an own goal from Doyle.

After those hell-for-leather derby battles, the final itself, against Swindon Town, could only be something of a disappointment. 'I suppose it was,' George says, 'but the club still treated it as a big occasion. We stayed overnight before the away leg, which was unusual.' United drew 1–1 at the County Ground where Don Rogers, the hero of the 1969 League Cup final, scored for Swindon and a goal from Best rendered the second leg little more than a formality. At home, backed by a crowd of 25,563, United won easily, 4–1, Sadler reinforcing his burgeoning reputation with a hat-trick.

George enjoyed the celebrations with his young contemporaries, and by now he was learning how to party. Coca-Cola was a thing of the past. The first step on the road to intemperance, and eventual ruin, was 'innocent enough', he says, and it is true that millions of teenagers have had the same experience without stumbling into alcoholism. 'It started in Switzerland, on a youth team trip to Zurich. I'd hardly had a drink before, nor had John Fitzpatrick, and after three pints of lager we were falling around, drunk. We had the whirling pit, the whole thing. The experience put me off alcohol for a while, but then I started experimenting.'

Now, however, just short of his eighteenth birthday, the demon vodka had yet to put in an appearance. The evil spirit lay waiting, just over the horizon. David Sadler had joined George at Mrs Fullaway's, the sensible influence of the boy who stayed at the bank for an extra six months clearly beneficial. Recalling how they became best friends, Sadler said:

> When I came up to sign pro in February 1963 the club put me in digs near the ground, at Stretford. I didn't like it there, didn't feel comfortable with the people, and towards the back end of the 1963–4 season a spare bed became available where George was. We were already pals, so I got in there. That was how we started to become closer mates. Because we were in digs together, we travelled to and from training together. Before George got his car, we caught the bus, then there was a stage when, because there was two of us, we could afford to get taxis. It was only two or three miles if we were training at Old Trafford. Other times, we would all meet up at the ground and get a coach over to The Cliff.
>
> We both liked it at Mrs Fullaway's. She was a widow who had two sons, one, Steve, who was living with her and one who had married and moved away. We were all pals together. It was a modest, terraced house. George and I shared a room, sleeping in two single beds.

Socially, the Best–Sadler circle took in John Fitzpatrick, Jimmy Ryan and Peter McBride. Sadler says:

> There was a snooker hall in Chorlton that wasn't too far from us, and the ten-pin bowling alley on the Old Trafford cricket

> ground. They had a private members' area at the bowling alley, which was useful because George was starting to get noticed, and the fact that you were United footballers meant you'd get pestered whoever you were. That was our meeting point.
>
> After training, we didn't have much to do in the afternoons, but we used to get passes to get us into the cinema and concessionary things like that. At the snooker hall they would reserve a couple of tables for the lads. I wasn't all that interested in the snooker. It was just somewhere you could go and hang out.

In the early sixties, the Best behaviour meant precisely that. Sadler recalls:

> There was nothing untoward going on. Of course, George was a good-looking lad, and the girls all took to him, but there was no misbehaviour then. Let's take a week when we didn't have a mid-week match. We would probably go out on the Wednesday night, go ten-pin bowling with the lads, and maybe have the odd drink or two down there, but we weren't really drinkers. It was a couple of halves of lager, just to be with your mates. There was none of the hard stuff. On Thursday and Friday I would be at home at Mrs Fullaway's. I'd have my tea, watch the telly and go to bed. George was never really comfortable sitting still, watching television. If he was at home, we'd have to play cards, rather than watch telly. He was a doer, and he would much rather do his relaxing at the bowling alley, or somewhere with his pals. He'd always be in a group. He wasn't boozing it up, or anything like that. He would probably be drinking coffee. But even on a Friday night he would prefer to be out doing that than sat at home in the digs, which is what the club wanted everybody to be doing. He had to be occupied. I don't think

he liked to have time to think: 'There's a match tomorrow, must be up for it at three o'clock' and all that.

To George Best's infinite relief, he was given no time to think about the match he was to play on 14 September 1963, after just four months as a professional. His first-team debut, at home to West Bromwich Albion, was totally unexpected, he says. 'A real bolt from the blue.'

chapter four

The Manchester United George Best joined in the summer of 1961 may have been a great club, but they were not a good team. They were, in the managerial idiom, going through a transitional phase. In Best's first season at Old Trafford, 1961–2, they limped in fifteenth in the First Division. In 1962–3, they fared even worse, nineteenth place representing the worst finish Matt Busby was to experience in more than two decades in charge.

Busby, who had taken over at the end of the Second World War, in 1945, had fashioned two different championship-winning teams. He would have to get the cheque-book out if he was to mould a third. Alex Ferguson, the only United manager to rival the great man's success, has steeped himself in the club's history during his eleven-year tenure, becoming a respected authority on the subject. He admits it is beyond his power to match Sir Matt's achievements:

> Matt built three separate teams, all of them superb. The team that won him his first trophy, the FA Cup, in 1948 was a very experienced one – Johnny Carey, Jimmy Delaney and Charlie Mitten were no spring chickens. They nearly won the League in 1951, when they were runners-up to Tottenham, and did win it the next year, but by that time they were getting old. Matt needed to change it, and that was when the youngsters started coming through. By 1954, Roger Byrne, Duncan Edwards and Dennis Violett were established, and the new

side won the League for the first time in 1956, then again the following season.

Tragically that team was destroyed before it reached its peak, by the Munich air disaster, having had only three or four years together, and Matt had to start all over again, building the next team. That last one will never be forgotten. It won the European Cup.

This final reconstruction was just starting as the fifteen-year-old Best arrived back at Old Trafford, determined to make a go of it after his false start. Dismayed by a 7–3 defeat at Newcastle in January 1960, Busby had begun the process by signing Maurice Setters, a fierce competitor, from West Bromwich Albion for £30,000 to give the midfield some teeth. Before the end of the year he forked out another £29,000 for Noel Cantwell, West Ham's Irish left-back, who immediately became United's captain. David Herd, the Arsenal striker, joined for £32,000 in the summer of 1961, and the *pièce de résistance* was supposed to have been Scotland's flamboyant goalscorer Denis Law, for whom Busby paid Torino a British record transfer fee of £115,000 in July 1962.

Yet still the mix was not right. United won only one and lost seven in a terrible run of nine League matches played in September and October, their erratic form typified in December when they beat Nottingham Forest 5–1, then lost the next game 3–0 to West Bromwich. It was this corrosive inconsistency that Busby was seeking to eradicate when he signed Pat Crerand from Celtic for £43,000 in February 1963.

It was a masterstroke. With Nobby Stiles to win the ball in midfield and Crerand to use it, the lines of supply to Herd, Law and Charlton were now secure. There were minor adjustments still to be made, but United had all the makings again. Distracted, perhaps, by the FA Cup, they won only three of their last twelve League games in 1962–3, and trailed in dangerously close to the relegation places (Manchester City went down, with Leyton

Orient), but the run to Wembley provided handsome compensation.

Law, relieved to be released from 'prison' as he called his unhappy one-year sojourn in Italian football, was an instant hit back in Manchester, where he had played for City before his ill-fated move to Turin. His first season as a United player produced twenty-three goals in thirty-eight League games, and he was no less prolific in the Cup where he opened up with a hat-trick in the third round against Huddersfield Town, with whom he had started his career in England, before scoring the winning goals against Chelsea, and in the semi-final against Southampton. The final was against Leicester City who, having finished fourth in the First Division to United's nineteenth, were the favourites. Leicester had Gordon Banks in goal and were renowned for their 'iron curtain' defence, but at Wembley it looked more like a net curtain, the clever Crerand finding holes everywhere with a man of the match performance which included setting up the first goal, from Law. Herd, a productive partner, had scored nineteen times in thirty-seven League appearances, and outdid the celebrated Scot this time with two more to set the seal on a deserved 3–1 win.

Johnny Giles was in the United team that day, but left soon afterwards, his departure facilitating the promotion of George Best, the tyro whose meteoric progress he had not foreseen. Giles, a Dubliner, had joined United from school seven years earlier at the age of fifteen. Always one to stick up for himself, as many a rueful opponent will testify, he spoke out against perceived injustice when Busby dropped him after the semi-final victory over Southampton, and was never forgiven. Nobby Stiles's absence through injury let him back in at Wembley, but he pocketed his winners' medal with mixed emotions. The little winger who at Leeds was to become the best midfield strategist of his generation knew he was on the way out.

It was United's loss. Busby and his heirs would have given

enough right arms for a fascist convention for Giles's commanding influence when they hit the slippery slope in the early seventies. So how did such a diamond come to be ditched? In answering the question, Giles provides an insight into Busby's treatment of players who fell from favour:

> I think it all went back about twelve months before the 1963 Cup Final. I was playing inside-forward in those days, with Bobby Charlton on the left wing, and we played against the great Spurs Double team in the 1962 semi-finals. It was a big match for us, because we hadn't been going well [United were without a win in five League games going into the tie], and they beat us comfortably, 3–1. I had a nightmare, I was hopeless, but I was only twenty-one, and I was up against truly great players in Danny Blanchflower, Dave Mackay and John White. Anyway, I think Matt and his assistant, Jimmy Murphy, who was very influential, lost confidence in me that day.
>
> It happens, of course. The manager thinks: He didn't do it in the big game, he hasn't got what it takes. In my case, I like to think I proved that was wrong. Anyway, I played on the right wing for most of the following season, and I found that in the eyes of the management, I couldn't do right for doing wrong. I was always a fairly good judge of how I played, I wouldn't kid myself, and sometimes I played really well and was left out for the next game. In the semi-finals of the Cup, for example, when we played Southampton, I was out of the side until Albert Quixall cried off at the last minute. I played as his replacement, and we beat Southampton. The following Monday night we had a match against Wolves, and Matt told me that morning that I wasn't playing. Of course, I didn't like it.
>
> Matt had a way of saying to players: 'How d'you think you're playing, son?' He was looking for the easy way out –

for you to say: 'Not very well, boss', then he could come back with: 'Okay, I agree. I'll give you a rest.' So I gave him a bit of cheek, really. I got in first. I asked him: 'How do you think I played on Saturday?' He said: 'You did reasonably well.' So I said: 'Well, if I did reasonably well, and we won a Cup semi-final, why am I not playing tonight?' He didn't like that. He said: 'I'm putting Quickie [Albert Quixall] in.' I wouldn't let it go. I told him: 'I don't think that's right. Quickie didn't play on Saturday. How can you judge his form against mine?'

That was the beginning of the end. Matt didn't like backchat. For one reason or another, I played in most of the matches leading up to the Cup Final, but I seemed to be in on sufferance. Certainly I wouldn't have played at Wembley if Nobby had been fit. The first match after the Cup Final was the Charity Shield, against Everton. We got a hiding in that, 4–0, and I was left out again, so I went to see Matt and said I'd had enough. He'd had enough, too, but he wouldn't say it to my face. All he said was: 'Well, I'll put your transfer request before the directors.' If I had any doubts before, I was sure then that it was in my best interests to leave. Any manager who tells you that, wants you to go. Most people say Matt Busby kicked me out, but the fact was I wanted to go.

Giles never played for United's first team again. He left on 29 August 1963 to join Leeds, then in the old Second Division, for £32,000, a record fee for the Yorkshire club at the time. There, after two seasons as a right winger, he switched to inside-left when Don Revie's little general, Bobby Collins, broke a leg in October 1965, and went on to become the fulcrum of Revie's dream team which, as everybody's nasty nightmare, was to succeed Manchester United's European Cup winners as the most successful side in the country.

With Giles gone and Albert Quixall in decline, the path was clearing, but the new season, 1963–4, dawned with others ahead of George Best in the queue for first-team places, including a couple of his contemporaries. Ian Moir, a twenty-year-old Scot who was to make forty-five in and out appearances in the League over five seasons before moving on to Blackpool in 1965, was given first crack at holding down the problematic right wing position, with Bobby Charlton on the left. Charlton scored two and Moir the other in a 3–3 draw at Sheffield Wednesday on opening day, but the match was notable mainly for David Sadler's debut as a seventeen-year-old centre-forward:

> I was in front of George in the pecking order at that stage, but I didn't have any expectations of getting into the first team. That seemed a million miles away. All I was thinking was that I might start to get a regular game in the reserves. Anyway, they played in the Charity Shield against Everton, who had won the championship, and got stuffed pretty badly, 4–0, the week before the League season started.
>
> When the teamsheet went up the following Friday, I was in, at centre-forward. Matt left out David Herd, Albert Quixall and Johnny Giles, and I came in, along with Phil Chisnall and Ian Moir. We drew 3–3 at Hillsborough and that was it, I had arrived. I played a dozen games on the trot, scoring three goals, before Matt gave me a rest and brought David Herd back. It was a start. I was up and running.

So were United. After drawing with Wednesday, they won their next three games, rattling in fourteen goals in the process. Law, whose dashing style had established him as the fans' favourite, contributed seven of them, including a hat-trick in the 7–2 rout of Ipswich on their own Portman Road ground. After half a dozen matches United were unbeaten, and top of the League, when Matt Busby had to change a winning team. Denis Law was unfit, and gave way to Phil Chisnall, a Mancunian youth team product who was to make one of those rare transfers, from

United to Liverpool, the following year. Moir was also injured, and out again. The time had come.

George Best remembers being listed as twelfth man, usually little more than a chore in the days before substitutes, but a big moment nevertheless for a seventeen-year-old called up for the first time:

> Ian Moir was supposed to be playing. I didn't know he'd picked up a groin injury, and Matt didn't say anything. Ian had been told to say nothing because Matt didn't want me, or anybody from the press, to know that I was going to play. That was the way Matt wanted it, so that was the way it was.
>
> We used to go to the local golf club for our pre-match meal, and I was there just to make up the numbers, I thought. We left at one o'clock to head back to the ground, and the boss told me on the coach, at about 1.15. He just came up to me and said: 'You're playing today, son.' I thought he meant in the A or B team. I thought they were sending me off to The Cliff training ground for another game in front of three men and a dog. Then he said: 'You're playing against West Brom today, okay?' He had let me eat lunch without knowing, which was clever, because if he'd told me beforehand I wouldn't have been able to eat anything.
>
> There had been no suggestion that I was ready for the first team from anyone at the club. I had no inkling. I was resigned to the fact that I was going to spend the next couple of years trying to get a regular spot in the reserves. To be thrown in at the deep end was a bolt from the blue, to put it mildly. It must have been the same for the public. As far as the press were concerned, I was nowhere close.
>
> As unexpected as it was, I don't remember feeling nervous. When we got to Old Trafford, I started a routine I was to go through for years. As soon as we got to the dressing room I went out and had a cup of tea with some of my pals. There

> was a little refreshment bar outside the big sliding doors at the entrance to the changing rooms, and I'd go there for a cup of tea with my mates until about 2.45. The boss used to send people out looking for me as it got near kick-off time. It was just my way of relaxing.

Young George was thrilled, rather than intimidated, by his big break. 'I wasn't worried. The crowd noise gave me a big buzz, it really did. I like a bit of volume. If I'm listening to the radio and a record comes on that I really enjoy, the first thing I do is turn it up, because good things sound better loud. That's what the crowd atmosphere was like to me. Like a radio playing, the louder the better. I still get a buzz today sitting in a big crowd.' Butterflies would have been normal, but Best always had what they call the big match temperament, and he insists there was no real apprehension attached to his first venture on to the stage they call the Theatre of Dreams. 'I just felt I should go out and play the same as I'd always done, and that's exactly what I did. Mind you, the way I played wasn't appreciated by the likes of Bobby Charlton and Denis Law – keeping the ball instead of passing it to them. I did exactly the same things I'd been doing since I was a kid at school, and in the A and B teams. Every time I got the ball I wanted to beat a couple of players. I didn't realize it wasn't the way you played in the first team.'

If it caused his team-mates occasional frustration, this eagerness to take on and beat his man was appreciated least of all by Graham Williams, West Brom's Welsh international left-back, who had a reputation as something of a hard man, and soon felt the need to live up to it. Left for dead time and again by a skeletal whippersnapper he had never heard of, Williams responded as any self-respecting tough guy would and gave his tormentor what he described as 'a hefty smack'. 'It was quite a bad knock,' George recalled, 'and the boss switched me at half-time, from right wing to left, to get away from Williams. He did give me a couple of kicks, but he was a lovely man. I made my international debut against him, at Swansea, and I've bumped into him many times since, and we always have a good laugh. He usually asks to have a good look at my face, telling people all he ever saw when we were playing was my arse, disappearing away from him up the wing.'

A perfectionist from the youngest age, the debutant found his first taste of First Division football disappointing, and his own performance especially so:

> It wasn't a particularly good game. The massive crowd [57,000] was the thing that turned me on more than anything. Unless you've been through it, you can't imagine what the experience was like. As you came down the tunnel, which was near the halfway line in those days, it sloped, so the crowd could see the first United player coming down, and then the noise just got louder and louder until the hairs stood up on the back of your neck. It was an amazing feeling.
>
> We didn't play particularly well, but we won 1–0, and my mate Dave Sadler scored the goal, which was nice. But I felt a little bit deflated because I wasn't happy with the way I'd played. Perhaps I was expecting a bit too much, but I hadn't found it difficult, and knew I could have done better. The fact that it had seemed quite easy stuck in my mind.
>
> The first thing Matt said was 'Well done', and most of the other players came over to make a fuss of me, which is something which happens with all kids. If it's your first game, everyone tells you that you did well, even if you had a stinker. That's the way it is. The other lads were brilliant about it.

Media coverage of the match tends to support George's contention that his arrival failed to register on the Richter scale. Neither the *News of the World* nor *The Times* found it necessary to refer to the newcomer, who needed to turn to the provincial newspapers – the *Manchester Evening News* and *Belfast Telegraph* – for a mention. 'Boy Best flashes in Reds attack' was the headline in Manchester's Saturday night football paper. The senior players were more impressed by the youngster's start. For Pat Crerand, George's performance merely confirmed what he had known since first marvelling at his skills in a youth team game seven months earlier. Whatever it took, the boy had it in spades:

> I know George felt he hadn't played well, but knowing him, he probably thought he should have been the best player on the field. For me, the things he did in the game marked him out as a certainty to make it. I mean, you don't expect a kid making his debut to control the whole game, but there were certain things he did, like the easy way he beat his full-back, that were top class. Graham Williams was a good, hard international defender, and George gave him a torrid time. Graham was also a nice lad off the field, and a few of us bumped into him in Spain that summer. Majorca was the in place for footballers then. George wasn't with us, but there was a whole gang of us from United, and we met Graham in Palma one day, having a drink. He kept on about what a good player George was going to be, and how he wouldn't recognize him if he walked in. He said all he'd seen was his back.

Denis Law missed the West Brom match, injured, but watched from the bench. 'I sat with the boss,' he says, 'and he loved it. Don't forget George was coming into the First Division at seventeen, which didn't happen so often in those days. The rules favoured the hard guys more, and it really was a man's game. Normally, you had to be in your twenties to be strong enough to get by. Anyway, George was up against the Welsh full-back, Graham Williams, who was a tough lad, and as a skinny guy the kid had to be in for a hard game, but he just pulled poor Graham all over the place. We all knew there and then that he had it.'

Busby knew it, too – better than anyone. George Best remained his favourite player to the day he died, aged eighty-four, on 20 January 1994. Sir Matt said of the rogue who plagued the latter years of his management: 'George was gifted with more individual ability than I have seen in any other player, he was certainly unique in the number of his gifts. He was skinny-looking, but strong and courageous to a degree that compensated amply. Every aspect of ball control was perfectly natural to him from the start, and he had more confidence in his ability than I have seen in any other sportsman.' Busby, then, was sure of this Babe from the outset. He nurtured him carefully, playing him in the A team rather than the reserves to keep him out of the public eye and ward off any campaign for his premature promotion. It was the same sort of pressure-free upbringing Alex Ferguson tried to give Ryan Giggs.

After that first appearance, George went back to the A and youth teams more eager than ever to work on his game. Others may have had no doubts, but he was still far from sure in his own mind that he was going to make it. 'I heard, much later, that Matt had told the coaching staff just to leave me alone, and let me develop naturally because he knew I was a little bit special, but if he knew it, I certainly didn't.' Best would have to be better, he felt, when his second chance came.

He was 'a little bit worried', rather than disappointed, to be omitted from the next game, at Blackpool, where Moir returned in his place. 'Of course, you think: Maybe I'll be in again, but I wasn't confident. I didn't think I played particularly well against West Brom, and with everyone fit again I didn't really expect to be in. Actually, it was quite nice to go back to the youth team and the A and B sides because I'd felt a little bit like a fish out of water in the first team, without any of my pals. I'd had my big break, which was good, but now I was back among the lads I usually mixed with at the snooker hall and bowling alley, and it certainly felt more comfortable. A bit of a relief, I suppose.'

When the second call came, it was almost as unexpected as the first. After their bright start, winning five and drawing two of their first seven League games, United fell back into their bad old ways. When they were good, they were very, very good, but when they were bad, they were horrid. Typically, in November they were impressive in beating Tottenham 4–1, Law netting a hat-trick, then promptly lost 4–0 to Aston Villa. December was worse. In successive matches they beat Stoke 5–2 (Law got four this time) and Sheffield Wednesday 3–1, only to lose the next two to Everton and Burnley, conceding ten goals in the process.

George was at home in Belfast for Christmas when a 6–1 defeat at Turf Moor on Boxing Day persuaded Busby that radical changes were needed. For the return game, at home to Burnley two days later, Best was recalled, and Willie Anderson, who was even younger, was given his debut on the other wing. The first George knew of it was when a telegram arrived at Burren Way, and even then he was counting no chickens:

> I had gone home for Christmas – at that time I was asking to fly home to see mum and dad quite regularly at weekends. In those days clubs played back to back local derbies over the bank holiday, to cut down on travelling. Burnley had hammered us there, and the telegram told me to contact Old Trafford straight away. When I did, they asked me to fly back immediately. I could be a bit cheeky, even then, and I remember insisting that I had to be back in Belfast the same night, had to catch the last flight after the game. They agreed, so that's what I did. Once again, I didn't really expect to play. I thought I was wanted as cover for a few injuries. Ian Moir and Albert Quixall had been alternating on the right wing.

To his great regret, Dickie Best had missed his boy's debut, for want of proper notice. Now he knew it was about to happen again:

Like any parent, I would like to have been there for his first game, but I didn't know about it in time. I had to read about it in the papers. Then, when he came home for Christmas and got the call to go back, I knew he was playing again, but it was too late for me to get time off work.

George thought they wanted him only as cover, but I said: 'If it is important enough for them to send a telegram, you must be playing.' I took him to the airport and then I rang the club and spoke to the trainer, Jack Crompton, who told me: 'Yes, Mr Best, he's playing all right.' I said: 'If I'd known that in time I'd have come across with him.' He said: 'Mr Best, don't worry. There's going to be many more games.' I was happy then.

This time, George was happy, too:

When I got back, they said: 'You're playing today', and, maybe because I had a bit more notice this time and was more prepared, I went out and played a lot better than I had in my first game. We thrashed them 5–1 and I scored my first goal. Someone – I can't remember who – pulled the ball back and I just hit it, right-footed, from the edge of the box. In it went, it seemed so easy.

After the game I flew straight back to Belfast, as arranged. Imagine how I felt. All I wanted to do was get the *Belfast Telegraph*, to see my name in it. They had carried a couple of pieces about my debut, but this was in a different league. I had scored my first goal, and the *Telegraph* had a picture of it on the back page. They had actually snapped the first goal I had scored for Manchester United. I went to see a couple of pals, and they were just freaking out. These were Belfast lads who had grown up dreaming of doing exactly what I had just done. And here was my photo, on the back of the *Belfast Telegraph*, actually doing it. It was literally a dream come true, very emotional.

The following morning, Sunday, was spent poring over the *News of the World*, which referred to the 'predominance' of the two youngest players on the field. 'Willie Anderson, 16, was Matt Busby's latest answer to the wing problem,' the report said. 'He and George Best, 17, who was having his second game, were a pair of wingers who gave the experienced Angus and Elder quite an afternoon. Best got himself on the scoresheet to complete a mature display.' Mature, indeed. Dickie and Ann Best loved that. 'My parents pulled my leg a bit, but they were brilliant about it,' George says. 'They never said too much, but I could tell how proud they were. They were not the sort to say how great I was, or to boast to anyone about me. In fact, mum was just the opposite. She really shied away from all that. It was their happiness, more than anything that was said, that showed me how pleased they were for me. Matt Busby just said: "Well done, son." That was all you ever got from him. And that really was the start of it. I stayed in for the rest of the season, and never looked back.'

Pat Crerand remembers the two games against Burnley better than most. 'I got sent off at their place, so I had good reason to enjoy what George did to them a couple of days later. Their left-back was a good player, Alex Elder, but George destroyed him. Absolutely murdered him. So much so that I actually felt sorry for Alex. George ran him silly for the whole game. It wasn't just the odd occasion, like it had been with Graham Williams. This was total annihilation. George was magnificent, and from then on they couldn't leave him out.'

It was only now that George Best became a winger. Previously, he had always played at inside-forward:

> It wasn't until I got in the first team that they played me on the wing. I think the reason they played me there was because I was still so small and slight. The boss stuck me out wide and told me to stay there to keep me out of trouble, physi-

cally. You weren't surrounded and vulnerable on the wing. Basically, it was just one against one, you and the full-back.

When I scored the goal against Burnley, it was from an inside-forward position, and I was told, quite seriously, that I wasn't supposed to score. I was supposed to stay out on the wing. But that was never for me. Even then I'd go looking for the ball, drifting all over the place. Wherever the ball was, that was where I wanted to be. A bit later, the boss would tell me to do whatever I wanted, go wherever I wanted, but at the beginning I was always stuck out wide, outside right or outside left.

The two wingers from the youth team, Best and Anderson, were retained for a tough third-round FA Cup tie away to Southampton. George recalls their selection causing 'a bit of an uproar', with the world and his wife queuing up to criticize Busby for asking boys to do men's work – shades of Alan Hansen telling Alex Ferguson 'You win nothing with kids' before the 1995–6 'Double' season. Busby's decision to give youth its head was vindicated, *The Times* reporting how his 'fledgling wingers took flight' in the second half, aided by Bobby Charlton's 'kindly nursing', to procure a 3–2 win against a good Southampton team featuring Terry Paine and Martin Chivers.

Yet still the blend was not quite right. Still they could not match Liverpool's consistency. The next match proved it, United returning to Old Trafford to lose 2–1 to Birmingham City. Busby's dissatisfaction was reflected in an ever-changing team. Harry Gregg was replaced in goal by David Gaskell, Tony Dunne was switched from right- to left-back at Noel Cantwell's expense, Phil Chisnall and Graham Moore alternated at inside-right and Nobby Stiles took over from Maurice Setters at left-half. The only constants over the season were Denis Law, who rattled in forty-six goals, David Herd, who backed him up ably with twenty, Tony Dunne and Bill Foulkes in defence and Pat Crerand and

Bobby Charlton in midfield. They were a good side, their unpredictability adding to the thrill of watching them, but too inconsistent, in terms of personnel as well as performance, to win anything.

In fairness, they were competing on three fronts, in the European Cup Winners Cup as well as in the League and the FA Cup, and the sheer weight of matches did them no favours. A sixth-round FA Cup marathon with Sunderland, which took three mud-spattered games to resolve, left them with heavy legs and tired minds, and although they prevailed at the third attempt, courtesy of a hat-trick from Law, they were 'knackered', Best says, when they lost to West Ham in the semi-finals five days later. They had not recovered, and were still in disarray mentally when within four days they had to play another big game.

The European campaign had begun well, the demolition of Holland's Willem II, who were beaten 7–2 on aggregate, setting up a blood and thunder second-round clash with the holders, Tottenham. The first leg, at White Hart Lane, produced a 2–0 win for Spurs leaving the return intriguingly poised, but that nice balance was shattered when Dave Mackay broke a leg at Old Trafford, and United won easily, with two goals apiece from David Herd and Bobby Charlton. Sporting Lisbon should have been no threat after a 4–1 home win founded on Denis Law's second hat-trick of the competition, but the decisive second leg represents the club's nadir in Europe. The Portuguese won 5–0, to Busby's undisguised disgust. Young Best cowered in a dressing room corner, by no means alone, as an apoplectic manager raged at his players, who were, he said, 'an insult to the people of Manchester'. Suitably chastised, they responded by winning 3–2 at Tottenham on their return, but three successive draws followed, and a 3–0 defeat at Anfield put paid to their title aspirations.

It had been a season full of promise, but United were the nearly men in everything – runners-up in the First Division, four points behind Liverpool, losing semi-finalists in the FA Cup and third-round casualties in the European Cup Winners Cup. The team, though improving all the time by process of trial and error, was not quite good enough. George was one of several honourable exceptions, having fuelled his burgeoning reputation with an attention-grabbing run of seventeen League games, illuminated by further goals against West Brom (poor Graham Williams again) and Bolton Wanderers (two). He also scored against Barnsley and Sunderland in the FA Cup, where United's semi-final defeat by West Ham deprived him of an early place in the record books. George Best and Howard Kendall were born on the same day, and when Kendall played for Preston North End at Wembley in 1964 he became the youngest ever finalist, twenty days short of his eighteenth birthday. This historical footnote is of less concern now than it was three decades ago, Paul Allen having rewritten it when he played for West Ham against Arsenal in 1980, aged seventeen years and 256 days. At the time, however, it was a source of regret for George. 'It would have been interesting,' he says, 'to find out whether I was born before Howard. I'm sure my dad would have got his timing right!'

If United ended 1963–4 on the launch pad to great things, George Best already had lift-off. An established first-team player with the biggest, most glamorous club in the country, he was also, at the tender age of seventeen, a fully fledged international. His first cap for Northern Ireland came in April 1964 after just twenty-one appearances for United, when two of the greatest players ever to wear the green made their debuts on the same day. Pat Jennings and George Best both launched their international careers against Wales at Swansea in a match which, by another of the quirks which abound in football, featured two of the full-backs George had just destroyed: Graham Williams of West Bromwich Albion wore number three for Wales, Burnley's Alex Elder was at left-back for Northern Ireland. The unfortunate Williams again had the worst of it, on the wrong end of another chasing, and the 3–2 scoreline, but beyond the result George has little recollection of what should have been a memorable occasion, nor of his home debut, against Uruguay, a fortnight later. The reasons why he came to dismiss international football as a recreational irrelevance are discussed elsewhere.

In 1964, however, playing for his country was a tremendous thrill. It was to be another two years before Manchester United's pre-eminence, and Northern Ireland's make do and mend poverty, made him blasé about such things. Now, half a lifetime on, all he can remember about his debut is that Jennings was also making his first appearance, that the Irish won 3–2, and that their matchwinner was 'a skinny little guy called Jimmy McLaughlin'.

He has clearer memories of how he celebrated his arrival as a rising star on the big stage. An Austin 1100 was hardly the transport of princes. George gave it to his dad and treated himself to the first of a succession of sports cars, a Sunbeam Alpine.

chapter five

Chelsea 0 : 2 Manchester United – 30 September 1964

'The more I wonder when it all began, the more I keep coming back to that game.'

Although still just eighteen, George Best started the 1964–5 season as a fully fledged member of what was to prove the best team in the country, and the confidence derived from the knowledge that he was a first choice, as much as Crerand, Law or Charlton, uncorked a cascade of latent talent. There was a precocious swagger, a cocky hauteur about his play. Under the limelight, the scarlet pimpernel blossomed. Crowds from Leicester to Fulham, Everton to Stoke were suddenly talking about this dazzling newcomer with the mesmeric feet, but nationwide fame, in the days when televised football amounted to no more than occasional highlights, meant catching the eye of the national press. And the real starmakers were in London.

Young George chose his stage well. In the 'Swinging Sixties', no venue was more popular with Fleet Street's finest than glitzy Stamford Bridge, where Chelsea had not only a good young team, attracting the bright young things from the pop and film worlds, but also that most publicity-conscious of managers, Tommy Docherty. It was here, in September 1964, that the George Best bandwagon went into overdrive.

The performance he gave that starry, starry night against the League leaders, who were previously unbeaten, truly deserved an adjective so overused it has become almost meaningless: sensational. Ken Jones, a respected columnist with the *Independent* not given to hyperbole, was working for the *Daily Mirror* at the time. His report of the match ran: 'At the end, they stood and acclaimed him. They gave him their hearts because he had won them with every bewitching swerve, every flick of his magic feet. Not yet 19, the boy from Belfast showed 60,769 fans why he seems destined to become one of the great wingers of our time. Chelsea's manager swallowed the bitter pill of defeat and described Best with one word. Fantastic.' *The Times* was moved to a similar eulogy:

> The company saw as fine an exhibition of wing play as they are likely to enjoy for a long time. It came from Best. He was unstoppable. He even had the Chelsea crowd, it seemed, longing for him to have the ball and float his way past man after man. Shellito, in particular, must have felt that he was trying to push back a genie into his bottle. He failed. The vital stroke came a moment after the half hour, when Best, who has a beautiful balance and low centre of gravity, slid like a wraith through the defence to intercept a backpass by Hinton to his goalkeeper. It was a tiny misjudgement, but wide enough to put Manchester United on their way to victory. In a flash, the ball was home.

Matt Busby, reminiscing much later, said: 'It was one of many great displays George gave at Chelsea. Something about the ground used to lift him. But I shall always remember that first time. After that, whenever we went to Stamford Bridge I thought I ought to phone the police and warn them a murder was about to be committed.'

It was this match that brought the immortal quote from Pat Crerand, who said Best's marker, Ken Shellito, had been turned inside out so often he was suffering from 'twisted blood'. Shellito, who had played for England the previous year, was mauled so badly that he was never seriously considered for international honours again. Crerand says: 'Ken was a tremendous full-back – it wasn't as if George was up against some ageing mug – but he wrecked him. George was still only a slip of a lad, but he had one of those games you just couldn't believe. Playing behind him, as I did, it was hard to get your mind round his ability at times like that.'

Terry Venables, who was to make his England debut the following month, captained the Chelsea team. Without wishing to detract from Best's virtuoso performance, he points out that Shellito had been diminished by a serious knee injury:

> It was just one among many brilliant games George had, and he was obviously a great player, but Ken had just come back from a cartilage operation, from which he never really recovered. George made the most of that. He was in fantastic form and slaughtered Ken who, I think, would have been England's right-back for years, but for his injury. He had played once [against Czechoslovakia in Bratislava in May 1963] and had a blinder, and George Cohen probably wouldn't have got a look in had Ken stayed fit. He was a super player, but he had a horrific injury which wrecked his knee – ligaments, cartilage, everything. He had just come back, and it couldn't have been a worse game for him. He wasn't as mobile as he had been, and it cost him – and us.
>
> I don't want to take anything away from George. He was a superb player, and it wasn't a case of a good young lad having a field day because his marker wasn't 100 per cent. He was doing the same thing to opponents all the time, and might still have done it to Ken even if he had been at his best. In that 1964 game he was out of this world. He played outside-left, but he would wander in and run at anyone and everyone. No one could do a thing to stop him. It was not only Ken

Shellito who suffered. George was doing these mazy dribbles and our players were left strewn on the ground in his wake. He had that fantastic dribbling ability which excites everyone. Even Chelsea supporters were left marvelling at his genius.

Mention the match, and George's father still goes misty-eyed:

I've kept the newspaper cuttings on that one. One of them even says the Chelsea fans were willing George to get the ball. And at the end he got a standing ovation. As he left the pitch, the other players stood and applauded him off. I was working, and I couldn't get there to see it, but years afterwards I met Mrs Fullaway's sister, who lived in London, and she went along to watch the game because George was playing. She said she was overcome, she just sat and cried. They said in the paper – the *Daily Mirror* I think it was – that the two teams applauded him off, and that the little Irishman, as they called him, walked off with head bowed, embarrassed.

Dickie produces a handkerchief and wipes away a tear at the thought. 'I still get very emotional about that,' he snuffles, apologetically.

Denis Law regards that 2–0 win at Stamford Bridge as a watershed. After it, everything flowed United's way. 'Chelsea had a smashing side, and were top of the League, but we murdered them. We started to play really well then. We had struggled to come together, with new players in the team, and all of a sudden it looked like we were going to do something. We were starting to play.'

All the chopping and changing of the previous season having come to naught, Busby accepted that a settled side was a prerequisite of real success. One last signing, made during the summer, would do it. The last piece in the jigsaw, in manager-speak, was John Connelly, an experienced winger who had won both the League and the FA Cup with Burnley. Among United followers of a certain age there is universal acceptance that everything clicked into place when Connelly, an England player since 1960, arrived to play on the right wing, George Best switched to the left and Bobby Charlton withdrew into midfield to complement Crerand's cunning. Swapping wings was no problem for Best, who had been working hard to match Charlton's easy facility with either foot. Today he despairs of a whole generation of top players who put him in mind of the famous Pete and Dud sketch in which Peter Cook says he has nothing against monoped Dudley Moore's right leg: 'The trouble is, neither have you.' George says:

> I believe young players don't work on such things hard enough, or aren't told to. You look at some of the best players in the country, and so many can't do the most basic things. If they had to take an important penalty, how many could use their weaker foot if they had to? Not many. It wouldn't have bothered me, nor did it bother me taking corners from either side, with either foot.
>
> Bobby Charlton was the same. Everyone remembers the amazing goals he scored with his left foot, but Bobby started off naturally right-footed. I think it's terrible to see well-paid professionals who can't use both feet. It's like anything in life, if you work on it, it gets better. My left foot became as good as my right.

Ambidexters both, Best and Charlton were immediately at home in their new roles, and yet for a championship season it had an inauspicious start. United won just one of their first six League games, losing to West Ham and Fulham, and Busby felt compelled to tinker yet again. Dave Gaskell, the goalkeeper, gave way to Pat Dunne, a £10,000 signing from Shamrock Rovers, who had fewer than three seasons at Old Trafford but played thirty-seven of the forty-two games to pick up a champions' medal in 1965. Just as significant was the omission, after the first two games, of Maurice Setters who, ousted by Nobby Stiles, moved on to Stoke City for £30,000.

When it finally came right, it was well nigh perfect. After one victory in their first six, United won thirteen, and drew the other of their next fourteen League matches. Connelly made a big impression on the right wing, five goals in his first nine appearances for the club furthering his international ambitions, and Law was rampant, four against Aston Villa giving him fourteen in his first thirteen games. 'The King', as he was dubbed by the Stretford End, was at his peak in 1964, when his peerless finishing saw him honoured as European Footballer of the Year. At this stage, and for the next few years, he, not George Best or Bobby Charlton, was the fans' favourite. The feeling was mutual. 'What I walked into from Italy,' Law said, 'was the finest football club in the world, with the finest manager.'

Best had been a founder member of 'The Lawman's' legion of admirers. They have become best friends since and holiday together, usually in Portugal, every year, but in the early days the relationship was strictly master and pupil:

> Denis now is such a great pal of mine, but then all the young players looked up to him in awe. I remember going to watch him play, just after he had signed from Torino. I went and watched a game at Blackpool just because Denis Law was playing, and he didn't let me down. He scored a goal with his head that went in as powerfully as any shot. I thought he was great, but in those early days there was no chance of getting to know him. Talk about respect for the senior players – the younger ones didn't dare speak to them. If you passed them in the corridor, or wherever, you didn't speak. That was an unwritten law. Your job was just to clean their boots and look after them.

Law, the definitive sixties striker, a strutting peacock with a gesture for every occasion, came to the job almost by accident:

> People forget I wasn't a front player when I signed. I was an old-fashioned inside-forward, and I didn't like playing anywhere else. Matt said to me: 'We ain't scoring goals, and I need somebody up front.' I told him: 'Well, I don't want to play there,' but you couldn't say no to Matt Busby. I had to do it.
>
> The way the game was played in those days, it was a thankless task unless you had good guys on the wing to supply you. I was fortunate. I was well supplied from both sides, and if the crosses are coming in, like they were, you've every chance of scoring goals. As the years went by, wingers went out of fashion and it became much more difficult to score. I needed someone to get the ball in to me, and Bestie was superb at that, but what really set the whole thing off was John Connelly coming into the side. He was the extra link we needed. It's nice getting crosses from one flank, but much better if you get them from both. The two wingers made a lot of goals for me, but were also goalscorers themselves, which was unusual.

That season, 1964–5, Law scored twenty-eight goals in thirty-six League games, David Herd weighed in with his usual twenty, Connelly contributed fifteen and Charlton (now in midfield) and Best ten apiece. It was a handsome return, but Don Revie's Leeds matched them every step of the way. That barnstorming sequence in which United dropped just the one point in fourteen matches came to an end in December when Leeds, the Second Division champions, who hit the First in rough, tough mode, journeyed to Old Trafford and ground out a characteristic 1–0 win in a match interrupted for seven minutes by a real pea-souper. Brian Glanville, my respected predecessor as football correspondent of the *Sunday Times*, said Manchester United were a fine team, but a fallible one. He wrote: 'At their best, Manchester are the most brilliant side in the country, but they are not remotely the best organized, and if Leeds have one thing, organization is it. Short of ability in striking positions, they are, however, very well supplied with it in midfield, where those two tough little Scottish terriers, Collins and Bremner, are forever busy and inventive.'

Leeds played a cagey game, ceding United territorial supremacy and defending in depth. Most of Connelly's crosses were repelled by Jack Charlton's trusty forehead, and the few chances that came Law's way found Gary 'Careless Hands' Sprake enjoying one of his better days. It was the United goalkeeper, Pat Dunne, who had an attack of the dropsy, his error enabling Bobby Collins to score the only goal ten minutes into the second half. Best, for once, had not lived up to his name. He was 'not himself', Glanville reported, after a 'collision' with Paul Reaney.

For the next few years there would be bad blood between the two clubs. Games between them were 'always acrimonious', Best says. 'Leeds were the only team I found it necessary to wear shinguards against. Questions were always asked about Johnny Giles's attitude when he played us, and Paul Reaney was the toughest full-back I ever came up against.' The two managers did not get on, and there were no prizes for guessing who Busby had in mind when he penned a critique on declining standards. He wrote:

> Without wishing to belittle the achievements of any club, I believe certain methods of attaining success have influenced British football too much, and in the wrong direction. I am thinking of the power game. Results are achieved by placing too much emphasis on speed, power and physical fitness. Such teams now have many imitators.
>
> We are breeding a number of teams whose outlook seems

to be that pace, punch and fitness are all that is required to win all the honours in the game. They forget that without pure skills, these virtues count for precisely nothing. I should like to see the honours in England won by a pure footballing side, the sort of team that concentrates on ball skills, above all else.

It was in an atmosphere of growing antipathy that Beauty and the Beast collided again three months later in a fractious FA Cup semi-final. In the previous round United had beaten Wolves 5–3, with Best among the scorers in a match acclaimed as a classic of the genre. The semi, at Hillsborough, was a case of After the Lord Mayor's Show – a goalless draw notable only for its malevolence. It says much for the nature of the game that Bobby Collins, the archetypal midfield intimidator, and nobbling Nobby Stiles were the star men. United decided that this time they had to match fire with fire, and gave as good as they got in the physical exchanges. What resulted was, as *The Times* put it, 'one long duel at close quarters and an afternoon of unceremonious collisions'. The tabloid press called it 'the X-certificate semi-final', and featured a photograph of Crerand, Stiles and Law in a bout of fisticuffs with Collins, Bremner and a young Norman Hunter. Four days later, at Nottingham's City Ground, an equally grouchy replay was settled in the eighty-ninth minute when Johnny Giles pinpointed a free-kick for Bremner to head home, and United had lost their third semi-final in four years. Giles revelled in putting one over the club he felt had undervalued him:

Manchester United were coming to their best and Leeds were upstarts, really. We'd only just come out of the Second Division, and we didn't have the same ability as United, but we were well organized. Don [Revie] was more modern in his thinking than Matt [Busby], and he had the players organized to defend better than United. In my opinion, United were at their best then. They were a truly great team for about three seasons, 1964–5, 1965–6 and 1966–7. They were already on their way down when they won the European Cup in 1968. But in 1964–5 they were outstanding. Leeds weren't in the same class, yet we beat them in the semi-finals of the Cup and were pipped for the League on goal average.

Manchester United had great individual talent – I had played with most of them. But there was never the same team spirit at United that we had at Leeds where, possibly because no one seemed to like us, our sense of togetherness was much greater. When I was at Old Trafford, the United team didn't get on too well as individuals. I think Denis Law got on with George Best very well, but George didn't get on great with Bobby Charlton and nor did Denis. When they went out and played, they were good pros and pulled together, but I think when we played against Manchester United there was a greater sense of unity about our team, and that was one of the reasons why, after three years, we became a much better side than United.

Like Wimbledon in the early 'Crazy Gang' days, Leeds, on their arrival in the First Division, compensated for any technical shortcomings with a willing, and often excessive, use of brute force. Reaney, a right-back good enough to play three times for England, took full advantage of any laxity in rule enforcement in the days when the tackle from behind was *de rigueur*, interpreting the verb 'to mark' in its fullest sense whenever he played against George Best. George never played well against him. He was never allowed to. 'We were a physical side, there's no getting away from the fact,' Giles says. 'I always felt that George was subdued when he played us. I'm not saying he wasn't brave enough to handle it. George was as brave as a lion, and would always come back for more. But Don recognized that he was a big threat and made provisions accordingly. You could get away with a lot of physical stuff in the sixties, and we probably got away with more than anybody else. There were certain things we did that I'm not proud of today, but that was the climate at the time.'

The League defeat at home to Leeds on 5 December had provoked such a crisis of confidence that United won only two of the next nine games, losing to Spurs and Sunderland. At the turn of the year they were third, behind Leeds and Chelsea, and in March it was still a three-horser, with a short head covering them all. But the thoroughbreds were poised to make their move. On 13 March Chelsea went to Old Trafford seeking to avenge what had been dubbed 'Best's Match', at home in September. Instead, a 4–0 drubbing (George scored again) removed them from contention. Now there were two, and Leeds were to prove the most stubborn of stayers, taking it down to goal average, football's equivalent of the photo finish.

By this time, Dickie Best was into an arduous routine he was to follow for years:

> Once George had made the grade, I used to try to get over to watch him play maybe six or seven times a season. It wasn't easy. I used to go over on the boat overnight on a Friday and come back the same way on Saturday night.
>
> When I was on the nightshift, we worked four and a half nights. That was four normal shifts and then from 4.45 on a Friday afternoon until 8.45 in the evening. I used to collect my wages on Friday at 8.30, before I left. I'd have a change of clothes with me, and I'd pull off my overalls and put them in a bag in my locker and head for the boat. It was a fifteen-minute walk from Harland and Wolff, but if you were lucky you could flag down a car and someone would give you a lift. We'd dock in Liverpool at five o'clock on Saturday morning, and then I'd get the train to Manchester. It was the same, in reverse, coming back. I'd get on the boat back at about ten

o'clock on Saturday night and get back into Belfast at seven on Sunday morning. I've never been able to sleep on a boat, so I went all those hours without a wink. Sometimes I'd book a berth, but even then I didn't sleep. I'd say to the steward: 'Don't call me in the morning until half past five,' but the buggers would be hammering on the cabin door from four o'clock, wanting to clean up so they could get away early. At that time, they didn't have a regular bus service from the docks into the city centre, and you'd have to walk fifteen minutes to the nearest bus stop to get home. I found it hard going, but it was worth it.

In 1965, nobody was complaining. United won ten out of eleven between 27 February and 26 April, but Leeds matched them stride for stride, despite the distraction of a run all the way to Wembley in the FA Cup, and come the final Saturday of the League season it was Revie's roughnecks who led the table, by a single point. Leeds, however, had just the one game left, at Birmingham, while United still had to play Arsenal at home and Aston Villa away.

On the Monday of Cup Final week (they were to play Liverpool in the final), Leeds travelled to St Andrew's while United took on Arsenal at Old Trafford. If Leeds won, the title would rest on United's final game at Villa Park. They didn't. They could manage only a 3–3 draw with Birmingham and United, who beat Arsenal 3–1, were champions with a game to spare. Appropriately enough, Law (two) and Best scored the goals that clinched it. The Villa match being of no more than academic interest, United lost it 2–1 and finished level on points with Leeds, champions by 0.686 of a goal in the days when average, not difference, was the tie-breaker.

The championship was over, but Manchester United's season still had seven weeks to run. They had been making good progress in the old Inter-Cities Fairs Cup, forerunner of the UEFA Cup, beating Sweden's Djurgaarden, the Germans of Borussia Dortmund (10–2 on aggregate), Everton and a French side, Racing Strasbourg. Now, in the semi-finals, they were up against the Hungarian League leaders, Ferencvaros, with the first leg at home on 31 May. After a long, hard League season, the United players were demob happy, and it showed. David Herd scored twice and Denis Law contributed a penalty but the defence, and goalkeeper Pat Dunne in particular, was below par, and a slender 3–2 lead did not bode well for the return. In Hungary, a dodgy penalty awarded against Nobby Stiles (the ball struck him on the shoulder) gave Ferencvaros a 1–0 win and so, in the days before away goals counted double in such situations, a third game was needed to settle the issue. Matt Busby lost the toss for venue and on 16 June, when they longed to be on the beach, United were back in Budapest. To no one's great surprise, home advantage proved decisive, Ferencvaros winning 2–1 to go through to the final where they proved their worth, beating Juventus 1–0.

It had been a big season for United, and a seminal one for English football. George Best had given the game its own pop star, the first of a new breed. 'It was in 1965 that the publicity thing started to spiral,' Best says. 'I'd missed only one game that season, and we'd won the title, so people were sitting up and taking notice. Because I was young, just turning nineteen, and good-looking, the off the field offers started coming in – advertising, modelling, all that sort of stuff. It wasn't massive at that stage, but the club didn't really know how to handle it and neither did I. I needed help.'

Denis Law had just the man. Ken Stanley was one of the first and most conscientious of what has become an increasingly parasitical breed, the footballer's agent. Nowadays, they are more like *agents provocateurs*, fermenting unrest among their clients with an eye on another cut from the next transfer. Thirty years ago, they fulfilled a much less insidious role, handling the commercial spin-offs that were a bewildering labyrinth to players only newly liberated from the maximum wage.

Stanley, a small man with glasses, came to the mercantile world via sports centre management – imagine a cross between Gordon Brittas and Captain Mainwaring and you have it. He had taken his cue from Bagenall Harvey, sport's original agent to the stars, who had made Denis Compton a small fortune as the Brylcreem Boy of the fifties. Stanley, who was running a table tennis hall in his native Burnley, identified a niche in the football market and signed up Jimmy McIlroy and Colin McDonald, two of the local club's best players. Representing these two – one the England goalkeeper, the other Northern Ireland's most celebrated player of the pre-Best era – helped finance the purchase of a cinema, which canny Ken converted into a five-a-side football complex. Yet for all his entrepreneurial enterprise, he was making only pin money, and his next move took him to Huddersfield to work for Mitre, the sportswear company. It was here that he met, and signed up, a pot of gold called Denis Law.

'It was through Denis,' he said, 'that George joined me, and then things started to happen. The phone never stopped ringing, he was in such demand. My favourite saying used to be: "You could put George's name on stair rods and sell them to bungalows."' George Best was a magnet, as well as a money-spinner. Gordon Banks, Jack Charlton, Billy Bremner and Emlyn Hughes joined the stable, and in 1966 it was Ken Stanley the England World Cup squad chose to run the players' perks pool. Four years later, he was the brains (culprit?) behind the 1970 squad's immortal anthem 'Back Home'.

Back in 1965, however, it was all novel – especially to a naïve nineteen-year-old who was as green as the Irish come. Young Best knew little or nothing about maximizing assets through investment, and cared even less. He spent in haste, and was left to repent at leisure. Looking back, ruefully, he says:

> Ken was a nice man, he really was, and he tried to get me involved in the money-making side of things, but I just wasn't interested. I used to go to meetings with accountants and just sit there, gazing out of the window. They could have ripped me off left, right and centre, but they didn't. Well, Ken didn't, anyway.
>
> I know what happened was my own fault, but I think the club could have done more to help. They protect the players now, making sure they invest wisely, in the right pension plans, and look after their money, but I had none of that advice. I was earning terrific money, £125 per week [the equivalent of £2,400 today] at eighteen, but I was spending it as fast as I was getting it.

These days, the players' union, the Professional Footballers' Association, are commendably pro-active in such matters, promoting pension plans, advising on wages and representing members in contract negotiations, but back in the sixties the PFA had a much lower profile, in every sense. 'It was a very different organization then,' Best says. 'Cliff Lloyd was in charge, and while you could go to him for advice, he wouldn't offer it unless he was asked. To be fair, if he'd given me any I probably wouldn't have listened. I was young and stubborn. It was my money, and I wanted to spend it. But I do think more help should have been offered.' It was not until later – too late – that Ken Stanley was able to make his headstrong client appreciate the need to make some provision for an uncertain future. 'I did take out a couple of pension plans eventually, but they are only small. I should have put a lot more into them. They should be massive, because I was earning big money.'

That, too, could have been more. At his peak, Best discovered that Denis Law was being paid considerably more than him. Again, however, he had only himself to blame. 'Ken Stanley handled all the other things, but not my wages. I negotiated those with the club myself. That was never a problem. Whatever they offered me, I said yes to. I never went in and asked for more money. All I wanted to do was train, play and enjoy myself.'

In 1965, George Best enjoying himself was still a long way short of the Bacchanalian binge it was to become. A fully integrated member of the first team on the pitch, he was in something of a halfway house socially, still mixing mostly with his mates from the youth and reserve sides. David Sadler was in much the same position:

> The Laws, Crerands and Charltons were married, with families, so they had different lifestyles, and the young players were not accepted in their social circle. It was a different environment, away from the pitch. But then, as George got more and more certain of his place in the team, he did start to mix, with Denis Law in particular.
>
> You can train and play well with people, but that doesn't mean you are going to be great pals off the field, because your individual temperament, and what you want to do, might be totally different. But George was on the same wavelength, had much the same nature if you like, as Denis and Pat Crerand, and he started to get a bit more involved with them. By this time, we were still in digs together, but I'd be doing different things. I was courting, and would be going out with my girlfriend. Bestie didn't have a girlfriend, as such. He was going out to clubs, where he was always very popular with a lot of girls, but he wasn't 'walking out' with anyone, as we used to say.

The man himself was increasingly happy with his lot. 'It helped that some of my pals had started getting into the first team. John Fitzpatrick was the main one – he was my snooker-

Above: Bestie beats the Fulham full-back Mark Pearson in one of his early matches for Manchester United at Craven Cottage, September 1964.
Popperfoto

Right: George gets to the ball ahead of Denis Law to score against Liverpool at Old Trafford. The Liverpool player challenging George for the ball is Tommy Smith, the beaten goalkeeper Tommy Lawrence.
Popperfoto

George gets away from Neil Young in a Manchester derby. Popperfoto

Lining up another shot, 1965. Times Newspapers

Footballer of the Year, 1968. George Best with his family. Times Newspapers

George and Matt Busby in 1968, with the European Cup and Footballer of the Year trophies. Popperfoto

George and Denis Law flanking the Old Trafford groundsman, Joe Royle.
Popperfoto

By 1970 George had a chain of mens' boutiques . . .

. . . and a Swedish fiancée, Siv Hederby.
Times Newspapers/ UPI

Sent off at Stamford Bridge, 1971 . . .

. . . and on his way to appeal to the disciplinary committee.
Central Press Photos/Sport & General

Left: At a Manchester fashion show in 1972. PA

Below: On his return to Manchester United, after going AWOL, George undergoes a medical, supervised by Malcolm Musgrove (left) and Laurie Brown, the club physiotherapist. The year is 1972. Popperfoto

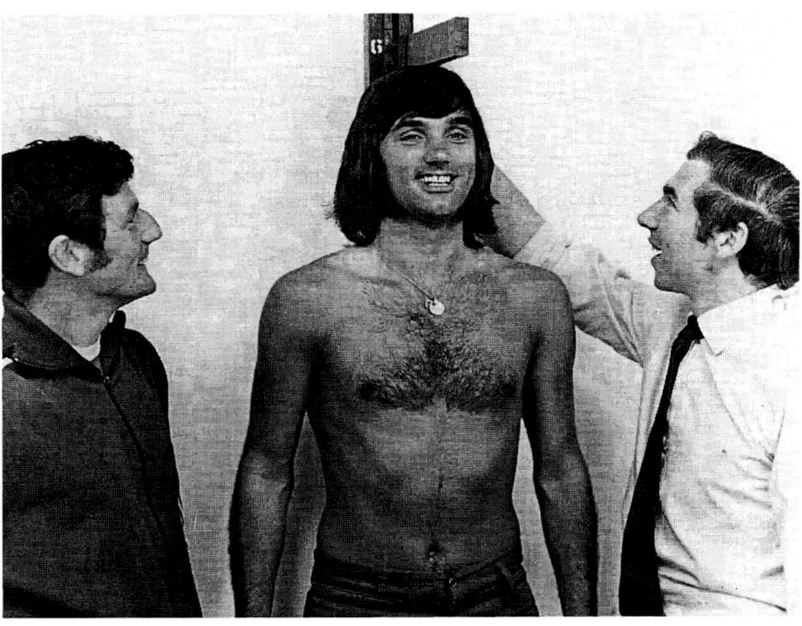

Right: In the money. Best outside his Cheshire house in 1972. PA

Below: With Tommy Docherty in 1973. PA

The pin-up, training with Denis Law, 1973. Times Newspapers

playing partner. He had a couple of games in 1964–5 and Jimmy Ryan got his chance the following season. David Sadler was also in and out of the side, so the mate I was in digs with was playing, or at least in the squad, and the lads I hung around with were getting in as well, so it was a nice situation. And at the same time, I was getting closer to some of the senior players, and getting to know them a little bit better.' As he did so, George's post-match routine changed:

> I still used to go bowling in the alley which had opened in Stretford, just around the corner from Old Trafford, but not as much, and certainly not on a Saturday night. When I went, a bunch of us would go, to hang around and pull the birds. There would be a couple of us from the first team, maybe me and David Sadler or Jimmy Ryan, and the rest would be a mixture from the reserves and A and B sides. I was in the first team regularly, but I'd still want to be with lads of my own age, and not too many of them were playing in the First Division. But on a Saturday night, I was starting to go to the clubs.

At that stage, there was a marked 'us and them' divide between the senior players and the young tyros who were coming into the team, threatening to lay permanent claim to the old sweats' places. It would take another year, Best said, before he was welcomed into the inner sanctum on a social basis. 'It took quite a while. Some of the senior players – Paddy Crerand, Denis Law and Noel Cantwell mainly – had a routine on Saturday nights whereby they would go to an Italian restaurant for a meal, with their wives. Gradually, as I played more and more games, I started to go. I went on my own – not with a girlfriend – just to say hello and have a quick chat, really. Then I'd go off to the local discos to meet up with the boys. I was getting a little bit closer to the senior players, but still keeping in touch with the younger lads.' Recalling the restaurant ritual, Crerand says:

> About five or six of the older players, with our wives, used to go to a place called Arturo's, in Faulkner Street, Manchester. It's not there any more, which is a shame. It was a great place – the food was brilliant and nobody pestered you, wanting to talk about football when you were there to relax. There was a little guy called Charlie who used to play the piano in the Ritz, over the road, and when he finished work there, at about half past midnight, he'd come over and play for us. We'd have a sing-song and a good laugh. George would bugger off to a club somewhere, and the rest of us would sit with Charlie until about two o'clock, when they'd sling us out, and we'd go home.
>
> It was a bit late, I suppose, but it was just a bit of harmless fun. Matt Busby knew all about it, and saw nothing wrong in it. The players going out together helped to foster good team spirit. As long as we behaved reasonably well, Matt wasn't bothered. Mind you, he always drilled into us that we were representing the club wherever we went, so we had to behave in a manner befitting. And he'd know immediately if we didn't. There was nothing going on in the city of Manchester that Matt didn't know about. It's not like London, it's a big village, and village people gossip. If you asked Alex Ferguson, he'd be able to list what all his players did over the weekend, because people tell – and they can't wait to tell the manager of Manchester United.

At this stage, George Best had the tittle-tattlers on starvation rations. It was to be another couple of years before famine turned to feast. 'George wasn't doing anything wrong,' Crerand says. 'He was pretty sensible then.' Maybe so, but the warning signs were there, for anyone prepared to read them. After their 5–0 humiliation in Lisbon, some of the players had gone out to drown their sorrows, and were fined for breaking curfew. Best, still only seventeen at the time, had been among them. And now his circle of friends – and influences – was widening to take in bookmakers and nightclub owners. If Matt Busby was not yet worrying, he would soon have reason to start.

chapter six

Manchester United were back in the European Cup in 1965–6 and, by common consent, this should have been their year. Everyone concerned agrees that they, like another famous team, were at their peak in 1966, and a better side than when they finally got their hands on the Holy Grail two years later. 'We should have won it three times,' Denis Law says. 'In 1966, 1968 and 1969. But we were definitely at our best in 1966.'

What 1966 did produce was the definitive Manchester United performance, and a display of scintillating individual virtuosity that catapulted George Best to international celebrity. But that came towards the end of the season, in March. You would scarcely have guessed it was on the way as the defending champions won just one of their first five League games.

It was hardly the most auspicious of starts, for United or for George Best, who was formally disciplined by Matt Busby for the first time and dropped for three matches after a string of late nights was deemed to have had an adverse effect on his performance. The *Sun*, under the headline 'Busby Axes Boy Best', reported: 'The reluctant axe of manager Matt Busby fell yesterday on George Best, who last season emerged as the wonder boy of British soccer. Best, the 19-year-old Irishman, who dresses in Edwardian style, and likes to dribble in the old-fashioned style of football, sits it out as substitute for the First Division match with Chelsea at Old Trafford today.' The 'reluctant' Busby was quoted as follows: 'George needs a rest. He's been running into trouble.

People forget that he's just 19. I'm sure the lapse is only temporary.' Best said, ominously, 'I'm finding it difficult to concentrate on the game.'

One of the matches he missed while on 'jankers' was the first in the European campaign, away to HJK Helsinki of Finland, where United won 3–2, with John Connelly and John Aston on the wings.

At nineteen, however, late nights meant nothing more dissolute than a few drinks and a dalliance with one of the many girls (and older women) who were increasingly keen to share his company, not to mention whatever else might be available. This was the era of 'Free Love', and George Best was hardly alone among teenagers in taking advantage of the offer. Like his football, it was just that he performed more often, and in better company, than most.

At this stage, a managerial rebuke was enough to persuade him to give due attention to more weighty matters. An international, against Scotland in Belfast, allowed him the chance to show United what they were missing, and to remind the Ulster public that his temporary fall from grace at Old Trafford had nothing to do with ability. Best, at his most impish, inspired the Irish to a 3–2 win. When he was restored to the United side four days later, he scored twice as HJK Helsinki were routed 6–0.

It seemed that normal service had been resumed, both individually and collectively, but this was a strange, switchback season in which a team widely acknowledged to be the most talented in the country never won more than three League games in succession, and after beating the eventual champions, Liverpool, 2–0 at home, the same players took a fearful 5–1 drubbing at Tottenham next time out.

By this time a new and enduring friend was on the scene. Towards the end of August 1965, Manchester City paid Swindon Town £30,000 for Mike Summerbee, a combative right winger who was to play for England eight times. Summerbee, who comes from Cheltenham, was twenty-two, and three years older than Best, but George was the precocious type and they were kindred spirits who hit it off at once. They were soon pretty much inseparable 'after hours', sharing a penchant for fast cars, and women to match. Both in digs, where they were required to keep 'respectable' hours, they soon acquired a flat for extra-curricular activities.

Summerbee, whose son Nicky followed the same route into the Manchester City team, is a successful businessman, manufacturing and selling made-to-measure shirts. A dry wit with an endless fund of football stories, he is also, like Best, much in demand on the after-dinner speaking circuit. On the day we met to mull over old times, he was en route from his Cheshire home to Essex to take the dimensions of David Sullivan, the soft porn king and owner of Birmingham City, who is among his clients, and then to entertain the denizens of a chicken-in-the-basket nightclub. Still recognized, and fêted, as one of the stars of the game's golden era, Summerbee is given the full deferential treatment when he arrives for our meeting at Manchester's Four Seasons hotel. When the noise in the lounge threatens to drown the interview, he commandeers a table in the restaurant, which is closed. There, invasive background muzak is silenced immediately, at his request. 'Of course, Mr Summerbee. Will there be anything else?' Finally settled, the man who was George Best's closest friend in the halcyon years recalled how they met, and the ratpack routine into which they fell:

> Before I signed for City, and came to Manchester, all I knew about George was what I had read in the newspapers. I think everybody realized that Manchester United had a truly outstanding young player, and people were delighted about it. There wasn't the jealousy and dislike of United then that you come across today – just the opposite. Because of the Munich disaster, which was still comparatively fresh in the mind in

the sixties, there was a lot of sympathy for them. If you didn't actually support them, you had a soft spot for them as your 'second team'. I certainly did.

I had been living in Cheltenham, and travelled to Birmingham quite often to watch the big games at Aston Villa, West Brom and Birmingham City, so I'd seen George play, and knew how good he was. Even before that, I realized he had to be special to break into a team as good as Manchester United's at seventeen.

The first time I met him, I had been in Manchester three or four months and I went into a coffee bar called the 'Can-Can'. George was in there and we introduced ourselves, had a coffee and just got on like a house on fire from the start. There was not much talk about football as I remember. We had other things in common. We liked a drink and we liked to go looking for a bit of skirt. The 'Can-Can' was in the back streets, Booth Street, I think. It isn't there now, it was demolished. Funny that, everywhere we used to go was knocked down, even our old flat. There were no blue plaques put up. There is no lasting monument to us – unless the Child Support Agency knows different!

In those early days, in 1965, we probably spent more time in coffee bars than nightclubs. There were a couple of places in King Street where we used to go for lunch, but at night we'd go to a coffee bar until late on, then slip into a club for a while before going home around midnight. George never drank much then, and I was on Mackeson at the time, which is hardly a big drinker's tipple.

We were both pretty naïve when it came to nightclubs and the entertainment scene that was going on in the sixties. There was a club called 'Le Phonographe' where it was wall to wall miniskirts. Well, they weren't really skirts, more like strips of cloth that went round the tops of the thighs. It was a difficult club to get into – a bit like Tramp in London. The guy who owned it was very fussy about who went in. If you weren't flavour of the week, you'd get turned away, but eventually Bestie and I used to get in there quite regularly. We used to sit and gawp at the young ladies – slaver as they went by. George was a bit shy then, and I was, too, because I spoke like a farmer. To be honest, the girls weren't really interested in a skinny lad with a Belfast accent and his mate from Wiltshire who sounded like Farmer Giles, so we had to take our time. We sat and watched before we moved in. We were never bull-at-a-gate pullers. We chose good spots, at the end of the bar, by the ladies' toilet, because they'd all have to go in there eventually, so you could clock what was around.

Within a year or so, when City were doing well and George was getting in the newspapers quite often, it would be different. The girls would be looking at us, paying a bit of attention. In some places there would be ten or fifteen hovering, waiting for George to make his decision. I'd be saying: 'Hurry up George, once you've had your pick there's thirteen for me to have a go at,' but that was later.

On the field, it was becoming apparent that the knockout competitions represented United's best chance of success. In the League, typically, they exacted full revenge on Spurs, beating them 5–1 at home in December, only to win just one of their next six games.

That special, titillating atmosphere peculiar to Cup football seemed to bring out the best in them. In the fifth round of the FA Cup they were 2–0 down to Wolves after only nine minutes, but came charging back to win 4–2, with goals from Law (two), Best and Herd. George's was the pick of the four, according to the then England manager Alf Ramsey who attended the match just three months before the World Cup, and mused over dinner on the train back to London how 'I wish that lad was born in England.' It is an intriguing thought that had George Best been English, there might have been no 'Wingless Wonders', no 4–4–2.

For Manchester United, the European Cup was the big one of course, and here, after routinely disposing of Vorwaerts of East Germany (5–1 on aggregate), they came up against the team that had superseded the fabled Real Madrid as *la crème de la crème.* Real had monopolized the European Cup in its first five years to 1960, but then Benfica, under a shrewd Hungarian coach by the name of Bela Guttman, took over. Winners in 1961 and 1962, losing finalists in 1963 and 1965, they had a trinity of their own as revered as Best, Law and Charlton: Eusebio, Torres and Simões. In Portugal, they had eclipsed Sporting Lisbon, who had been good enough to beat United 5–0 in 1964. This, then, was the acid test.

It was one England's champions seemed destined to fail when they could only win the first leg, at home, 3–2. A fragile one-goal lead was unlikely to be enough in one of the great cathedrals of the game, the Stadium of Light, where Benfica had never lost a European tie. There, playing mind games some thirty years before Alex Ferguson perfected the art, the hosts stoked up the temperature by presenting Eusebio with his European Footballer of the Year trophy on the pitch immediately before the kick-off, which had to be delayed until after ten o'clock. The referee, Italy's Concetto lo Bello, had been caught up in a gridlock, and during what was a tense, nervy wait in the dressing room, Pat Crerand horrified team-mates of superstitious bent by breaking a mirror.

Nevertheless, had Benfica but known it, the atmosphere generated by a crowd of 90,000-plus was counter-productive. It might have intimidated ordinary players, but there were not too many of those in United's Class of '66, and George Best was truly inspired by this most dramatic of backdrops. The hairs stood to attention on the back of his neck, a signal that always meant: Beware. What followed was fabulous fiction made fact. Eusebio ought to have handed over his award after the first twelve minutes. By then, Best had turned the tie on its head, scoring twice. Not for the first or last time, he opted for the Nelsonian approach, turning a blind eye to managerial instructions:

> We'd been slaughtered in Lisbon two years before, and we were only one up from the first leg, so as far as the public and the press were concerned, it was all over. We knew it wasn't. The situation was a bit dodgy, but we felt we had a chance. Before we went out, the boss said: 'Take it easy, keep it tight for the first fifteen or twenty minutes, and we'll see how it goes.' He had never said that before, ever, and we didn't know how to keep a game tight. We just knew how to batter teams, which is what we did. I scored twice in the first twelve minutes and that was that. Basically it was all over. I had one of those nights when you can't do anything wrong.

At half-time, exacerbating Portuguese dismay, laughter rang out from the away dressing room. Crerand had enquired if anyone had another mirror to drop.

Best had opened the scoring after six minutes, all those levitational hours in the gym rewarded when he dispatched Tony Dunne's free-kick with a soaring header. Another six minutes and the noise in 90,000 throats became a death rattle as Snakehips slalomed between three bewildered defenders and stroked the ball into the corner for a goal well up in his personal top ten. Benfica were nonplussed. Briefed to expect opponents in backs-to-the-wall defensive mode, they were still trying to adjust when their tormentor in chief laid on the third, for John Connelly. An own goal by Shay Brennan was of no more than statistical note as Crerand and Charlton made it 5–1 for an historic 8–3 aggregate win.

The Italian newspaper, *Corriere dello Sport*, marvelled at the performance. Their report ran: 'The myth of Benfica collapsed in

15 minutes, destroyed by the powerful, irresistible Manchester United, who showed themselves as the great stars of European soccer.' Geoffrey Green of *The Times*, the late, lamented doyen of British football writers, waxed lyrical about: 'The most inspired, inspiring and controlled performance I have seen from any British side abroad in the past 20 years.' Of Best, he wrote:

> With his long, dark mop of hair, he is known in these parts as The Beatle. Now he was the Best of All, as he set a new, almost unexplored beat. Best seemed quite suddenly to be in love with the ball, and the whole side followed his lead. Before our astonished eyes came the disintegration of a great Benfica side.
>
> In the sixth minute Charlton was checked, Dunne curved a free-kick into the penalty area and Best, rising on spring heels, headed beautifully past everybody. After 12 minutes Charlton passed back to Gregg. The goalkeeper cleared straight down the middle of the field, Herd headed backwards and downwards and there was Best, gliding like a dark ghost past three men to break clear and slide the ball home – a beautiful goal.

The players had ignored his game plan completely, but Matt Busby had nothing but praise for their performance, and told them in the dressing room afterwards that they had given him the proudest moment of his life. Reflecting on it later, he said: 'I told them to play it tight for a while, for twenty minutes or so, until we got their measure, but George just went out and destroyed them. I couldn't believe it, and Benfica most certainly couldn't until it was too late. They were also prepared to play it tight for a while – that is what always happens in European games. Then out comes this kid, as if he's never heard of tradition, and starts running at them, turning them inside out. I ought to have shouted at him for not following instructions, but what could you say? He was a law unto himself. He always was.' Disobedient of Belfast insists he had been prepared to do as he was told, but changing circumstances had dictated another approach:

> Matt told us to take it easy and see how it went, and it went so well that there was no need to take it easy. In those days my starting position was well forward, on the wing, but if the other team had the ball I always chased back as a matter of course. This time, Matt wanted me to start deeper, to hang back instead of chasing back. But it started so well for us that all that went out of the window.
>
> We got that early free-kick which Tony Dunne crossed from the left for me to score with a header from a fair way out, near the edge of the penalty area. Three of us went up for it, the 'keeper came out and I just got above everybody. My extra work, heading the ball in the gym, had paid off. People forget, I scored quite a few goals with my head. For my size, I was good in the air. When I played rugby I always had spring, as well as power in my legs, and when we had line-out practice I could get up above lads who were a lot taller than me.
>
> So that was a hell of a start for us, a goal after six minutes. Then we got another break, David Herd flicked the ball to me and I knocked it past a defender and when the 'keeper came out, I knocked it past him too, and into the net. I might have had a hat-trick, but the referee disallowed the third, saying I was marginally offside. Still, the game was effectively over. At 5–2 [on aggregate] they had to score four to beat us.

Brennan's own goal caused 'a bit of the jitters', conjuring memories of the five conceded to Sporting Lisbon, 'but then we stuck another two in, and that was that'.

In terms of all-round performance, individual and collective, this was the absolute apogee. Winning the European Cup two years later had to be the highlight of Best's career, but that magical night, when he played ringmaster to the Lions of Lisbon, was perfection, and as such could not be bettered. 'That night,' Best says, 'we knocked it about as well as any of the great sides I've ever seen. That night, at least, we were as good as the Real Madrid of the fifties, the Spurs Double team – anyone you care to mention.' Best had all the adulation, but he recalls Crerand playing particularly well:

> Paddy was our engine room, he really was. If there was one player in that team we didn't want to be out injured, or suspended, it was him – more so than me, or Denis [Law], or Bobby [Charlton], or Nobby [Stiles]. We missed him more than anyone. He controlled the game so well from midfield. His influence and importance was like Eric Cantona's. People like them make it a different team, they pull the strings and make everything happen. Paddy wasn't the quickest, but he didn't need to be. He knew how to make the ball work. His passing was in the highest class, and he got stuck in as well.

More than thirty years on, Crerand says he remembers the Benfica game as if it were yesterday:

> I can still see Matt telling us to keep it tight. Anyway, the game had been going six minutes when we got this free-kick on the left, which Tony Dunne was going to take. Now Tony didn't have a particularly long kick, and I said to George: 'Try to get in at the near post, because Tony will never reach the far post with a cross.' When Tony played it in, George went towards the near post, and headed it straight into the back of the net. George ran amok after that. Poor Matt had told us to keep it tight for twenty minutes. Some chance. It was just one of those nights. It reminded me a great deal of the Real

> Madrid v. Eintracht Frankfurt European Cup Final [1960], which finished 7–3. I mean everything was just perfect on the night. We should definitely have gone on to win the cup.

Bobby Charlton agrees that the performance in question was United's, and George's, best:

> Benfica had never been beaten at home in a European tie, we only had a one-goal lead from the first leg, and everybody assumed that we were going out. On the coach, going to the game, I remember their fans putting five fingers up, going 'Five, five, five', to remind us that we'd been beaten 5–0 in Lisbon a couple of seasons before. They can't have dreamed that it would be five the other way. But it happened. We had a good team, strong in defence as well as attack, and if someone like George really turned it on, then we were always going to score goals.
>
> It was probably George's best game, largely because it wasn't a selfish performance. Sometimes he could be a bit selfish. If he thought 'this is my stage', and the crowd were loving him, he would do a few tricks and the rest of us would sit back and say: 'All right, we'll leave him to it.' Sometimes it was all a bit unnecessary, but in the match against Benfica we saw him at his peak because he wasn't trying to be clever and torment people, he was just doing the best that he could. His control, his speed, his heading – his whole game was as good as anyone could get.
>
> That night George was just so fast and so direct, and his control was exceptional. Where other players would get into a good position and check to set themselves, George just struck the ball instinctively, and it was in the back of the net. Suddenly we were three up – four on aggregate – and it was just a fantastic experience. I would say it had to be George's greatest game. There were probably occasions when people

> enjoyed watching him more, when he sold a few dummies and did all the tricks, but to the professional that's the icing on the cake. Your bread and butter is what you do as a team man, and in that respect it was definitely George's best.

Denis Law says:

> The best we ever played as a team, and the game when George gave his consummate performance, was against Benfica. That was the best football he ever played, and the start of all the hype. It was Manchester United's finest performance in my time there, without a doubt. To score five against them on their own ground really was something. We'd played Sporting Lisbon two years before and lost 5–0, so the Portuguese fans were all giving us five fingers, and secretly you thought: Christ, it could be. But we just went out there and slaughtered them. Bestie was magnificent that night.

Everyone acclaimed the brightest new star in the European firmament, the Portuguese included. Their sports paper, *Bola,* headed its report of the game 'A Beatle called Best smashes Benfica', and suddenly George was 'El Beatle.' Today, teams playing abroad fly home straight after the match, but in those days they stayed overnight, and the morning after found the man of the moment fêted like John, Paul, George and Ringo rolled into one. 'The girls all wanted my autograph, some wanted a lock of my hair, and the men were almost as bad. I was having my first real taste of adulation, and I'd be a liar if I said I didn't enjoy it.' Playing up to the 'El Beatle' image, Best went out and bought the biggest sombrero he could find. He was still wearing it when he got back to Manchester, a heaven-sent picture for the phalanx of photographers awaiting him on his return. For the first, but by no means the last, time he was on the front and back pages simultaneously on 10 March 1966. A star was born.

It was post-Benfica that George Best's popularity mushroomed to pop star heights, unprecedented for a footballer. He had made his debut the week The Beatles went to number one with 'She Loves You', now he was matching them fan for fan. His agent, Ken Stanley, was inundated with offers to promote everything from sausages to haute couture. 'Everything we were touching was turning to gold,' George says. 'I was in the papers almost every day, and not just on the sports pages. I had ghost-written columns in national newspapers on fashion, music, clothes – everything. The publicity thing was becoming a monster. I never sought it, and Ken Stanley wasn't going out of his way to get it. It just came, regardless. We had three girls working full-time, just answering the mail. That's how big it got.'

Just six days after the Benfica game, a mob of schoolgirls of Beatlemania proportions turned up when George, still only nineteen, opened his first business venture: Edwardia, a male boutique in suburban Sale. His partner, who had suggested the venture, was Malcolm Mooney, a Mancunian entrepreneur who started in the rag trade and went on to own a celebrated restaurant in Knutsford, the Belle Epoque. Best says: 'We were six miles out of town, stuck in a suburban shopping area between a betting shop and a small jobbing printer, yet two hours before the official opening there were three or four hundred fans, mostly schoolgirls, hammering on the plate glass window.' Was he put off by all the attention? Hardly. A ladies section of the George Best boutique opened in October 1966, and two more shops were to follow. George says:

> I ended up having a stake in three. There was the one in Sale, another just off Deansgate, and we opened a third one in the Arndale precinct in Manchester. Mike Summerbee and I were partners, but it was Malcolm Mooney who ran the whole set-up. Mike and I didn't really have much to do with it. We used our names to promote the business and popped in once in a

while. It was just another way of pulling birds, I suppose. You'd finish training, have a bit of lunch and hang about the shop in the afternoon, waiting for all the girls to come home from college. A lot of them had to pass the shop to get home.

Back at the football, it was a case of riches to rags. Best, and United, returned from their Lisbon triumph to play Chelsea at Stamford Bridge, and experienced the sort of hangover (metaphorically speaking) that has been a constant problem down the years. They lost 2–0. The championship was all but a lost cause. Distracted by Europe and the FA Cup, United won just four of their last twelve League games to trail in fourth, ten points behind the champions, Liverpool.

There was another good reason for their decline. Playing in a sixth-round FA Cup tie at Preston on 26 March 1966, George Best sustained a cartilage injury which was to trouble him for the rest of his career, and which still causes the knee to swell to twice its normal size today. He was rested for a week but then, with Busby naturally reluctant to lose the jewel from his crown, he tried to play in the first leg of the European Cup semi-final, away to Partizan Belgrade. It was a gamble that failed. The pain returned, and although Best was again better than the rest, he was clearly hampered, and underwent surgery on returning home. He did not play again that season.

Denis Law was also restricted by a knee problem which was to need an operation, and he, too, was well below par in Belgrade, where United lost 2–0. Law says: 'I missed a couple of chances over there that, fully fit, I'd never have missed in a million years, and we got stuffed. That was definitely a year when we should have won the European Cup, but perhaps we were too confident. We thought all we had to do was turn up to get the result we needed. We were wrong, of course.'

Willie Anderson took Best's place for the decisive second leg, but Partizan defended like the wartime guerrilla army they were named after, and United could manage only a 1–0 win courtesy of a scruffy own goal. Not enough. Crerand, sent off for retaliation, was appalled. 'They were an ordinary team, and should never have beaten us,' he says. 'It was a disaster. If George and Denis had been fit, it would have been a different ball game. But after Benfica, teams in Europe were wary of us. We had lost the element of surprise. Partizan knew George was a potential match-winner, so he got a lot of stick over there. Partizan weren't what you'd call a gentlemanly team. I mean, we could look after ourselves, but they kicked lumps out of us.'

Matt Busby took elimination hardest of all. This was to have been United's year, the European Cup his swansong. There were tears in his eyes after the second leg, and he was to describe the result later as 'The lowest ebb since the Munich air crash.' It had been in his mind, he said, to turn his back on football altogether. 'I remember telling Paddy Crerand: "We'll never win the European Cup now."' Crerand, the senior pro who had become the manager's dressing room confidant, confirms that the conversation took place, that Busby had spoken of standing down: 'I think Matt was broken-hearted when we went out. He was talking about retiring there and then. I said: "Don't do it. We'll win the League next season and go again."' Wilf McGuinness, the Busby protégé who was eventually to succeed him, was on the coaching staff in 1966. He corroborates the story that management's first knight was thinking of calling it a day at the end of that season: 'He spoke about it, but the players didn't want him to go, and the board talked him round. Louis Edwards, the chairman, wasn't ready for a change then. Matt's disappointment was understandable. We all felt, and still feel, that the 1966 team was the best of that era.'

To compound the sense of under-achievement, United promptly fell at the same penultimate hurdle in the FA Cup. Three days after going out of Europe they went to Burnden Park, Bolton, to play Everton for a place at Wembley, and lost 1–0.

Fourth place in the League behind Liverpool, Leeds and Burnley was not good enough in those days to qualify for Europe, so the team that thrashed mighty Benfica, and which Busby regarded as the finished article, ended the season empty-handed.

Not so some of the players. Bobby Charlton, rising twenty-nine, was at the peak of his majestic powers in 1966, and was a deserving and popular choice as European Footballer of the Year. Scoring sixteen goals in thirty-eight League games from midfield was a considerable achievement, but it was not so much what he did for United, of course, but his swaggering form in England's World Cup-winning team that saw him honoured as Europe's finest – just as Denis Law had been two years earlier.

George Best was third in the domestic Footballer of the Year poll behind Charlton and another of England's heroes, George Cohen. Still recuperating after cartilage surgery in those pre-keyhole days, Best drove Summerbee and Sadler to Wembley for the World Cup Final in his new white Jaguar Mark Two. The fourth member of the party was Danny Bursk, a fur trader and United fan who was one of the first non-footballing friends George had made in Manchester. As early as the summer of 1965 they holidayed together in Majorca. Living life in the fast lane by this time, Best was booked for speeding for the second time in three months on the way to Wembley. 'We stayed overnight in north London, in Holloway I think it was,' Summerbee says. 'We went to the game, and afterwards we went out on the town. We ended up in a club called Tiffany's, in Shaftesbury Avenue. I remember there was a black dancer, wearing a mask. We just wandered in there and had a couple of drinks. Nothing came of it, so we went back to this council flat which belonged to Mrs Fullaway's sister, and drove home to Manchester the next day.'

This was a rare expedition for Sadler. He still shared digs with Best at Mrs Fullaway's, but by now he had a steady girlfriend, and he was with her more often than he was in George's company. Times were changing, and Summerbee and Bursk had replaced the old youth team clique on the social scene. Sadler says:

> Bestie had become a star, and those of us in his age group had been left behind. We were struggling to get into the first team, playing mostly in the reserves, and he was in to stay. We were still good friends, and would always remain so, but George was opening his boutique and getting into the night-club scene, and he'd got very pally with Mike Summerbee. There was nothing wrong with that. They got on well, and knew the places to go in Manchester. They even had their own flat, for use at weekends.
>
> 'I was doing the normal thing, if you like. I was courting – going to the cinema and going out for a meal with my girlfriend. That way you establish friendships outside football. You meet people, they become friends, and suddenly you find yourself moving in a different circle. George was very much the bachelor type. He was going around with all sorts of girls, generally having a good time. So while we still got on very well, there was always a parting of the ways when it came to 'Where are we going tonight?' I would say: 'I'm meeting Christine, and we're going to the cinema,' and he'd be off clubbing it somewhere.

Between the good-time drinking sessions, there was real cause for celebration that heady, flowers-in-their-hair summer of 1966. Not in England's World Cup triumph, for as an Irishman George had little time for that. But back home in Burren Way there was a new arrival. At the age of twenty, George had a brother. Ian Busby Best (no prizes for guessing where the middle name came from) weighed in on 19 July. George recalls, with amusement, his father's embarrassment when he first broke the news that there was to be an addition to the family. 'Dickie called me and said: "Son, I've got something to tell you." I could tell from the tone of his voice that it was serious, and I was a bit worried until he finally got to the point and blurted it out. I remember laughing and saying: "Congratulations. That's great news." My dad was so relieved. It was as if a great weight had been lifted from his shoulders. "You don't mind, then?" he said, as if I was going to say it was disgusting or something.'

Ann Best was forty-three when the sixth, and last, of her children came along. It is a difficult age for a woman to give birth, and the new arrival would add to the stresses and strains building within the family home. Bringing up five children on a shipyard worker's modest wage had been hard enough. A sixth would make it tougher, despite the financial help the dutiful George was providing. To make ends meet, Ann worked in an ice-cream factory during the day and in a fish and chip restaurant in the evenings. She was not seeing much of George, whose trips home were becoming increasingly infrequent, and she missed him to a painful degree. It made the yearning worse that people around her were now talking about 'Geordie' Best, the pride of Belfast, all the time.

Ann, who had not taken a drink until she was past forty, was to die an alcoholic at fifty-four. It is only with the benefit of hindsight, however, that Dickie and George can recognize the origins of the problem. Then, it seemed that their beloved wife and mother, like everyone else in the Swinging Sixties, was just trying to have a good time.

chapter seven

By the time he was twenty, in May 1966, George Best had played his best match for Manchester United, against Benfica, and was settling into the lifestyle that was to unravel his brain at twenty-seven. Already he was out on the town almost every night, either with a girl on his arm or in the company of Mike Summerbee or one or more of the older, non-footballing friends he had met in his favourite Manchester nightclub, Le Phonographe.

Matt Busby was sufficiently worried to contact George's father, Dickie Best, to discuss the hours the young tyro was keeping, and his penchant for older women of the sort a twenty-year-old does not take home to mother. One in particular was causing acute concern – the wife of a prominent local business-man. George smiles at the memory:

> I was seeing a married woman whose husband was well known locally. We weren't keeping it too much of a secret, and it was getting quite heavy. I was getting threats from the sort of people you don't cross: stay away from her, or else. Sir Matt knew all about it – he always knew what everyone was up to – and he called me in to see him. He knew everything – names, places, the lot. He said: 'You are a young, single man and there are plenty of girls out there. Find one who is less trouble.'
>
> I found out a lot later that he had called my dad and asked him to speak to me about it, too. I got a serious talking

to from Dickie, but the relationship was dying a natural death anyway. It was fairly typical of what was happening at the time. I was forever getting threats to stay away from people's girlfriends, wives or daughters. My reputation was starting to get a bit hot, and I was definitely one the women were told to stay clear of, which only made them all the more interested, of course.

At this stage, the precocious sybarite could handle it. The really heavy drinking which was to undermine his constitution and his career had not yet started, and he could easily run off the after-effects of the late nights. Any fears Busby may have had were eased by the sight of the nocturnal carouser training harder, and longer, than any of the other players. By common consent among his peer group, Best's diligence on the training ground was second to none. Much as he liked to party, football was his *raison d'être.*

Bobby Charlton says: 'Nobody ever complained about George's attitude when he was at work, not at all. He loved his training and he really applied himself when he was at it. It was when he started missing training, later on, that the rot set in.'

Using Charlton, who had made himself genuinely two-footed as his role model, Best worked assiduously, and by the 1966–7 season he considered his left foot to be virtually as good as his natural one, the right. For Charlton, the dual facility was born of necessity:

> When I started out my right foot was the stronger, and then, just as I was hoping to break into the first team, I injured my right ankle playing against Manchester City reserves. The centre-half caught me, and I thought: Well, that's your first-team chances gone for a bit. Three weeks later the Old Man [Matt Busby] asked: 'How's your ankle?' and I said, 'Yeah, it's great.' It wasn't at all, but I wanted to play. Anyway, the Old

Man said, 'You're playing tomorrow,' and I did. I carried my right foot, didn't use it at all for a couple of weeks, and I got away with it.

For me, it was enforced practise really. I probably wouldn't have done it without the injury, but it did improve my left peg a lot. My 'other' foot was never that bad, but it's amazing how, when you've only got the one to use, your whole technique – your timing, your positional sense and your thinking – has got to change. The experience was really good for me. George wasn't forced to do it, he chose to. With him it was entirely voluntary and self-motivated. Practise, practise all the time. You had to admire his dedication.

Brian Kidd, now United's assistant manager, was an apprentice at Old Trafford at the time. He remembers watching Best in awe, mostly for his extravagant skills but also because of what he calls his 'phenomenal appetite' for practise:

In everything he did in training Bestie was always a top three man. His fitness was tremendous – second to none – but he also worked hard on his technique. When the other first-teamers had finished training and gone, he would come out in the afternoons with a bag of balls and practise taking corners, left- and right-footed. He would try to score direct, and he could do it quite regularly.

I remember after one of those sessions on a Friday afternoon he went out and did it in a match on the Saturday. He scored direct from a corner. Everybody said it was a fluke, but I knew it wasn't. He'd worked on it. He had God-given talents, but he worked hard on the training pitch to improve them.

The natural gifts Best was embellishing were superlatively singular, so much so that United were forced to amend their training to prevent him from monopolizing the ball. David Sadler says:

> Our training in those days used to include a lot of physical work – hard running, which was boring, but necessary to reach and maintain the required level of fitness. They used to starve us of ball work, really, and we always looked forward to the game at the end of training, when we'd have an eight-a-side match, or something similar.
>
> It's an amazing story, but they had to adapt those games to compensate for George's skill. If we played a free, open game, Bestie would get the ball, and you'd need another one for the rest of us. No one could get it off him. So they introduced a maximum of three, then two touches. That was the most one player could have, so that the ball was passed around. The trouble was, Bestie was so good that when we were playing two-touch, the ball would be passed to him and he would take one touch to control it, then with his second he would play it against an opponent's legs and get it back, so now he had two touches again. And so it would go on.

Wilf McGuinness, one of the coaches who supervised these practice matches, confirms the story:

> We started playing two-touch to stop him dribbling, so that the others could have a game, because he used to keep the ball and take the mickey. He wanted that ball all the time, so we said: 'Right, two touches only,' but still he kept it because he'd control it, someone would come at him and he'd knock it against them and control it again. That way he'd run right through everyone and smack the ball in the back of the net. So then we decided to play one-touch, just to stop him hogging the ball, but even then it was the same. As it came to

him, he'd play it against somebody with his first touch and he'd be off again.

There was nothing we could do to stop him. He was utterly exceptional. You see gifted players now who have the speed of a racehorse and the brain of a rocking horse. You look at the Paul Gascoignes and wonder about their intelligence. George was a very intelligent player. George was a footballer with a brain.

Having failed to secure a place in Europe, Manchester United went into the 1966–7 season with tunnel vision. They were going for the championship, free from distant distractions. They began well enough, with four wins in their first five games, but then the old fallibilities surfaced in a way that demanded drastic action. After successive defeats in the First Division at Stoke and Tottenham, United went to Blackpool in the League Cup and were thrashed 5–1. The malaise clearly needed urgent treatment, and a transfusion of new blood.

The goalkeeping situation had been unsatisfactory for years, with Harry Gregg, whose effectiveness had been impaired by a recurring shoulder injury, Dave Gaskell and Pat Dunne all unable to hold down the job for any length of time. All three were now offloaded in the space of six months, Busby grasping the nettle and paying Chelsea £50,000 for Alex Stepney to solve the problem. At the end of the season the grateful manager was to say that Stepney's arrival was the biggest single factor behind the winning of the title. 'I don't think we would have won it without him.'

The new goalkeeper was by no means the only significant change. John Connelly was still only twenty-eight, but his level of performance had declined in his second season from fifteen League goals in 1964–5 to five in 1965–6, and just three months after winning his twentieth, and last England cap in the first of the World Cup ties, against Uruguay in July 1966, he was deemed surplus to requirements at Old Trafford and sold to Blackburn Rovers for £40,000. George Best was switched from the left to the right wing to replace him.

George's contemporaries were beginning to come through, and the autumn of 1966 found four players from the FA Youth Cup-winning class of 1964 making their mark in the senior side. John Aston junior, son of the United and England full-back of the same name who was on the coaching staff, was introduced on the left wing, Bobby Noble, whose career was to be cruelly ended in his debut season by a car crash, came in at left-back with Tony Dunne switching to the right, and David Sadler, after thirty-five appearances spread over three in and out seasons, gained a regular place at last, albeit as a jack of all trades.

Four losses in the first ten games did not bode well, but the 4–1 defeat at Nottingham Forest at the beginning of October, which left United eighth in the table, proved to be a watershed. The team Busby now freshened with new faces won seven and drew one of their next eight matches to establish a platform from which they were to launch a buccaneering and ultimately irresistible charge.

By the season's mid-point it was a three-horse race between United, Liverpool and the dark horses, Forest, whose formidable forward line included four England players of varying vintage in Alan Hinton, Joe Baker, Frank Wignall and Ian Storey-Moore. Two goals from Best were not enough to see off the defending champions, Liverpool, who fought with Shanklyesque fervour for their 2–2 draw at Old Trafford in December, and United dropped another valuable home point against Leeds on New Year's Eve. They still had a two-point lead going into 1967, but their rivals scented blood.

What they could smell was the whiff of cordite. Busby and his dressing room adjutant, Paddy Crerand, rallied the troops, and when they came over the top there was no holding them.

They withstood a staggering body blow in March, when David Herd broke a leg in the act of scoring his sixteenth goal of the season, at home to Leicester, and another in April when, returning from Sunderland, Bobby Noble was involved in the car crash that was to terminate his career at twenty-one. A lesser team would have been fatally undermined, but United regrouped and came back all the stronger. The big push began in mid-January when a 1–0 victory at Tottenham was the catalyst which produced the classic, championship-winning formula. Eight home wins and eight away draws later, Liverpool had been burned off, and only Forest remained in contention.

By 6 May it was all over, with a game to spare. United went to West Ham needing a point to be sure of the title, and produced a display which George Best rates among their top six in his decade as a first-team player. West Ham, who had won the European Cup Winners' Cup in 1965, had a good team featuring three players – Bobby Moore, Martin Peters and Geoff Hurst – who had been World Cup winners the previous summer, but United routed them 6–1. 'It was one of the great performances of my time,' Best says. 'When we clicked like that, no one could live with us. We could have settled for a point, as we'd done in every away match since the New Year, but there was something about going to London. You felt you had to show you were the best.' Crerand smiles at the memory. 'We only needed a point, and it was another of those rare occasions when Matt told us to keep it tight. Some chance. Bobby Charlton scored in the second minute, and it was 4–0 at half-time. During the interval, we were all a bit puzzled when Matt kept talking about us shutting up shop at 3–0. He'd been late taking his seat, and when he saw West Ham kicking off he thought it was the start of the game – he didn't realize we'd scored. For a while he sat there thinking it was 0–0 and we were 1–0 up!'

One short or not, Busby cannot have been concerned for long. After Charlton's fulminating first goal Crerand quickly added a headed second and the old warrior, Bill Foulkes, thumped in Aston's corner to make it 3–0 before the game was ten minutes old. Best, after a typical piece of trickery to bemuse John Charles, added the fourth after twenty-five minutes, and the only question in the second half was whether Law could join in the fun. It was a rhetorical one. The most acquisitive of finishers was not about to miss out, and Law it was whose two goals rounded off the biggest away win of the season in the First Division.

Crerand says: 'West Ham had a bloody good side then, and it was always a difficult place to get a result. We won there the following year, and I don't think United won at Upton Park for twenty years after that. But once we got that goal so early, there was no stopping us. We knew we had the championship tied up.' In the end they won it comfortably with sixty points, four clear of Forest and Tottenham, both on fifty-six. Busby said: 'The FA Cup defeat by Norwich [2–1 in the fourth round] was a bitter disappointment at the time, but it proved to be a blessing in disguise. With only the League to worry about, we have been better equipped, physically and mentally. Ability is no longer enough, although there is still no real substitute for it. You need a combination of ability plus work-rate.'

Geoffrey Green of *The Times*, was left pondering the relative merits of the teams Busby had built. He wrote: 'I still believe the 1956 to 1958 side would have developed as the best of all, but if a composite team were to be chosen, my vote would be: Stepney, Carey, J. Aston snr, Coleman, Blanchflower, Edwards, Best, Law, Herd, Charlton, J. Aston jnr.' Commenting on the 1967 champions, Green said: 'Certainly in Law, Charlton and Best, backed by Crerand, United now possess men who bring the sort of artistry and invention to their game which can make them so exciting, and such a magnetic draw wherever they play. Here, indeed, was a scholarly lecture on what the game is all about.'

Magnetic draw was right. For United v. Forest in February 1967 the gates were locked on a crowd of 62,727, and the average attendance at Old Trafford, where United were unbeaten that season, was 53,800 – a post-war record. Law, with twenty-three goals in thirty-six First Division games, was still the fans' favourite, but Best, the great entertainer, now enjoyed cult status and was to overtake his old hero in the popularity stakes. George had been one of only two ever-presents in the League (Bobby Charlton was the other), contributing ten goals as well as countless 'assists' in his forty-two games.

In 1967 George Best was making the acquaintance of greatness. When Busby acclaimed him as 'a world class footballer', and said he 'had the lot', there were few, if any, dissenting voices. Beautiful balance was the bedrock of his lovely, lyrical talent, enabling him to evade or withstand the most brutal of challenges and drift past the hit men on either side. Once past there was no catching him – his sprinter's pace saw to that – although when the devil was in him, he would deliberately allow an opponent to recover and draw level, in order to make a monkey of him a second time. He was blessed with adhesive close control (the product of all those childhood hours making a tennis ball answer his beck and call) and a mesmeric mastery of that most crowd-pleasing of arts, the dribble. Unable to stop him by fair means, most resorted to foul, but that stick insect frame – throughout his career, Best's height and weight were given as 5 ft 9 in. and 10 st. 3 lb – concealed a tough, resilient physique, and he could not be buffeted out of the game. He was the target of all the chopping, leg-biting hatchet men who had *carte blanche* in an era when the scything tackle from behind was *de rigueur*, but he had the bullfighter's knack of drawing the beasts on, then skipping away at the last moment to leave them charging off in the wrong direction. On the odd occasion when he did take a goring, bravery and pride kept him coming back for more, and his significant absences, through injury could be counted on the fingers of one hand. 'It seems impossible to hurt him,' Joe Mercer, the manager of Manchester City, marvelled at the time.

Above all, of course, George Best was the scorer of celestial goals. Examples abound, but one against Tottenham (George always did well against Spurs), which was fairly typical of the genre, had even the most hard-bitten of press-box cynics nonplussed. Britain's foremost sports writer, Hugh McIlvanney, was a witness, and recalls it thus: 'George Best had come in along the goal-line from the corner flag in a blur of intricate deception. Having briskly embarrassed three or four challengers, he drove the ball high into the net with a fierce simplicity that made spectators wonder if the acuteness of the angle had been an optical illusion.' When sagging jaws started working again, a cub reporter enquired as to the time of the goal. 'Never mind the time, son,' came McIlvanney's Caledonian growl. 'Just write down the date.'

Unlike some of the other great wingers (Stanley Matthews springs immediately to mind), Best was a goalscorer. A deadly finisher. This attribute, even more than George's dexterity with either foot, points up the stupidity of likening Ryan Giggs to George Best. Bobby Charlton told me in February 1997:

> I was talking to Alex Ferguson the other day after Giggs had missed a couple of chances, and we agreed that he was trying to score great goals, instead of doing the simple thing. He was getting into great positions, but not putting his chances away. If you put George in a good position, he would score. He could finish better than any of us. He could score just as easily with either foot. How the ball came didn't matter to him. A congested area, like the eighteen-yard box, was made for him. You'd think: Bloody hell, there must have been a dozen people around him – how did he finish up getting in a shot, let alone score? Alan Shearer is a different type of player, of course, but he has that same ability to work in tight areas.

> To George, it didn't matter how close a defender was, he would create that little bit of space that was all he needed. He didn't score goals from a long way out – unless he was chipping a 'keeper. It was mostly close stuff, and very clever.

In retirement, Busby said:

> George Best was gifted with more individual ability than I have ever seen in any other player, certainly he had more ways of beating a player. He was unique in the number of his gifts. He remained deceptively skinny-looking, but he was strong and courageous to a degree that compensated amply. Every aspect of ball control was perfectly natural to him from the start. He even used his opponents' shins to his advantage by hitting the ball on to them so accurately that it came back to him, like a one-two pass.
>
> He had more confidence in his ability than I have ever seen in any other sportsman. He was able to use either foot, and his heading could be devastating. If he had a fault, it was that he wanted to beat too many opponents when he could have passed the ball to better advantage. You could see him beat two, three or even four, then lose the ball, and you would all be having apoplectic fits and saying: 'Why the hell doesn't he pass the ball more?' Then he would beat four men and score the winner. What do you do about that?

This tendency towards go-it-alone greediness became a source of frustration to his team-mates as Best made the metamorphosis from second fiddle to virtuoso. It was no coincidence, Denis Law maintains, that his own goals-per-game ratio declined as his provider's improved. In 1966–7, Law rattled in twenty-three goals in thirty-six League appearances to Best's ten in forty-two. Over the next two seasons, Law scored a modest twenty-one goals to Best's forty-seven. Law says:

In the early days, George was superb at getting the ball into the area for me. Later on, he got a bit greedy, and I was getting into position and the ball wasn't coming. We had a lot of arguments about it in the dressing room. It was a case of: 'Excuse me, but that ain't right.' Bestie's reputation was becoming very big, and he was trying to live up to it by beating an extra guy instead of crossing the ball, which was the winger's job. We had a lot of barneys about it, on and off the field. He started scoring more goals than me because he wouldn't give me the ball. It's as easy as that.

When I told Bobby Charlton of the complaint, there was sympathy for Law's case:

There may be a little bit of jealousy there. For a few years Denis was like greased lightning and the crowd loved him, then George took over. But I know what Denis means about George's greediness. He used to sell me dummies!

When I was learning the game, changing from an amateur to a professional with United, Jimmy Murphy always used to say to me: 'When any of our players gets the ball, make yourself available. We're all in it together, it's a team game, so be there for the man on the ball, in case he wants to use you.' That was ingrained in me, and I used to do it all the time. If anybody got the ball and I was within range, it was: 'Here I am,' and if he didn't bother, it didn't matter. But George would never give it to me. Never. Off he'd go, and I'd think: Jesus, not again. So many times I'd say: 'Here I am, George, use me,' and off he'd go, in another direction.

There's a nice story that sums it up. We're playing a match against Nottingham Forest, who had a little full-back called Joe Wilson, and George gets the ball on the touchline. I say to myself: 'Go and support George, he's got the ball,' but he's been so frustrating over the years, not passing to me, that I've often thought: One day I'm not buying it. To hell with you. Anyway, we're three goals up against Forest with two minutes to go and George gets the ball. This is my chance. My instincts say: 'Show for him,' but my brain says: 'No, you promised yourself this little luxury. Stand still.' So I've stood still, and I'm watching George doing one of his dribbles. Little Joe Wilson is weaving after him, trying to kick him, but he can't catch him. George weaves from one side of the pitch to the other, and I'm saying to myself: 'Don't go, Bobby. Stand still.' But by now he gets so close to me that I can't keep it under control, and I start to yell: 'Give it to me, you greedy little bugger,' only to end up saying: 'What a fantastic goal, George!'

Yeah, he was frustrating. We all used to argue in that forward line. We would be bollocking one another right, left and centre. It was commonplace at that time. I was a midfield player, and I never really criticized anyone for having a go at goal and missing, but Denis would. It was his business to score goals, and if a pass would set him up to knock one in, he'd expect to get that pass. David Herd was the same. All he wanted to do was score. So if George was being greedy, or one of the others, there would be big arguments. I think it was fair enough, really. You can't be a good striker unless you have that single-minded attitude.

Later, there would be more sinister reasons why a pass to Charlton would always be Best's last option. In their declining years they fell out so badly that they were both well into middle age before mutual friends, such as David Sadler who runs the United ex-players' association, could get them back on speaking terms, but in 1967 they were comrades in arms, if not exactly peas from the same pod. George says:

When things are going well on the field you don't have many problems off it. They came later on. I wouldn't say Bobby and

I were ever mates, but that was because we were so different. He was married, and didn't mix socially. After matches, I'd be out and about while he went straight home to his wife, and if we were training at The Cliff he'd finish, hurry off to his car and that was it. But it would be wrong to say we didn't get on when the team was successful.

On the days when we trained at Old Trafford, and not The Cliff, half a dozen of us would go up and sit in the tearoom afterwards, and a lovely old lady called Mrs Deeley would keep us topped up with tea while we talked for ages. There would be Bobby, Denis, myself, Shay Brennan, Nobby Stiles and Alex Stepney, and we'd sit there for ages, just chatting.

At night, George kept different company. The United players were either married or stay-at-home types, and Mike Summerbee was his only nocturnal partner. The only male one, that is. By now, George had what he calls his first 'serious' girlfriend, a statuesque Mancunian by the name of Jackie Glass who worked for a film director from France, where she now lives. George has always liked a Glass, of course, and they had a stormy, on–off relationship which waned and was revived over a matter of years, continuing when Jackie moved to London. George says:

The first time I met her was in Le Phonographe. She was with the comedy actor Kenny Lynch, who over the years has become a great pal. He introduced me to her, and I bumped into her once or twice after that. Jackie was living in Manchester at the time, and I started going out with her regularly. Then she moved to London to write scripts for a French film director called Gérard Brach, and every time I went to London, which was quite often, I stayed at her place in Wandsworth.

It was a fraught relationship, always a bit frantic. When we were together, we were bickering and arguing twenty-four hours a day. There was nothing physical. We never beat each other up, or anything like that. It was all verbal. Because I was living in Manchester and she was in London it was all jealous accusations. 'What are you doing when I'm not there?' That sort of bullshit. On a couple of occasions I nearly got arrested, turning up at her place. I remember climbing a wall which had broken glass set into it and getting my hands cut to pieces. Another time I threw a milk bottle at her upstairs window.

Later on, when it was all over between us really, I'd go to Tramp and if I didn't pull in there I'd go round to her place at three or four o'clock in the morning. I'd go out for a night on the town and then turn up on her doorstep and try to get in. I had no chance. She was a pretty strong character, that one. After we finally split, we kept in touch for a while, then she moved to France to be with the film director.

A wistful, lustful look came into the old roué's eye. 'Some looker, Jackie. She was the first serious one, yeah.'

Mike Summerbee, a spikily competitive winger, was a key member of the Manchester City team that won the League in 1968, when he was good enough to be capped in an England side generally held to be even better than the '66 World Cup winners. There was professional respect, as well as shared recreational appetites, at the root of a friendship which is undiminished today, and, having witnessed it all, Summerbee is able to provide a first hand insight into Best's behaviour in the halcyon years of the late sixties.

What was their weekly routine? 'On Monday night we would go out, Tuesday night we used to go out, Wednesday night we went out, Thursday night we'd go out but get in early, and Friday nights we would keep it low-key because we had a game to play on Saturday. The real late nights came at the weekends. But we were fit, and we weren't making fools of ourselves. Through the week and on Sundays we'd be home by half past midnight because we'd be training the next day. And on the Monday we knew we had heavy training, to get out of our systems what we'd put in over the weekend.'

Best and Summerbee, and some of their non-footballing friends and acquaintances, congregated at a spit and sawdust pub called the Brown Bull near the Granada TV studios in Manchester. It was an unprepossessing place, but one which became George's favourite haunt because of its bohemian attitude to the licensing laws. In his cups, he knew he could get a drink there any time of day or night. In the mid-sixties, however, it was little more than a meeting point, or a late-night stop-off for 'one for the road'. Summerbee says:

> We flitted from club to club, place to place. They tended to become more downmarket as the night wore on. George didn't drink pints of bitter or Guinness, he drank vodka and lemonade. It doesn't smell and there's no real taste, but if you're not careful it's a dangerous drink for anyone, because it goes down so easily. From the time George was twenty or twenty-one, we always used to drink vodka. I'm not talking about bottles of the stuff. Through the week we'd have a few, but nothing stupid. I mean, we weren't staggering out of places blind drunk. We were sober enough to enjoy ourselves and get home unaided.
>
> On Saturday nights it could be different. We'd played our matches, the tension was off, so we smartened up, got suited and booted, and we were ready to roll. We'd worked hard through the week, and if one of us hadn't played well, we'd want a drink to drown it out. If we had played well, it was even better. A cause for celebration.

Le Phonographe had 'the best birds in Manchester', according to George, who was probably the leading authority on the subject, and as such it was the favourite venue for the 'two amigos'. But if they didn't 'pull' to their satisfaction there, there were plenty of other places. Summerbee says:

> We used to start off in the posh clubs and end up in the doss houses. There was a place called 'Phyllis's' in Whalley Range, that was famous in Manchester in those days. It was where the casino croupiers and all the late-night people used to go. It was just a private house, really – a big Victorian building. There was a big lounge with very thick, velvet curtains which were always kept closed. There were no clocks, so you didn't know whether it was day or night outside. You lost track of time. The croupiers from the clubs – really good-looking girls – looked after us in those days, because they were streetwise and we weren't entirely. Not yet.
>
> That part of Manchester, Moss Side and Whalley Range, was different then. A fabulous place. It was all terraced houses – there were none of the blocks of flats that created the ghetto effect – and people of West Indian origin and the white locals all mixed together really well. There was the Nile club, which became infamous later because there were a few shootings there, but in our day it was nice. You'd get West Indian cricketers like Clive Lloyd, Keith Barker and Charlie Moore in there, passing round the Cockspur rum, and we were all welcome in the 'shebeens' [unlicensed, late-night drinking dens].

George remembers Phyllis with particular affection:

> Phyllis was the mother of Phil Lynott, from the Irish band Thin Lizzy. She ran this marvellous late-drinking place where you could turn up, any time of day or night. It was always open and she was always there. She never seemed to sleep. You could turn up there at five in the morning and the place would be heaving. It was a big, old house, and downstairs it

was just like walking into your own front room. There were nice couches, some stylish bric-à-brac around the walls and a little bar in the corner. The atmosphere was amazing – just like Las Vegas. There were no clocks and the thick curtains kept out the daylight. Phyllis's boyfriend, Dennis, kept watch from a window upstairs, to check who was coming. If the police came by, all the lights went out and the music stopped.

It was the place to go if you'd been out elsewhere and hadn't got lucky. The croupiers from the casinos would finish work at three o'clock, and you knew that they'd be coming in, so from three until seven in the morning, if you were still inclined, you had a chance. There was a choice. You could sit there, get absolutely pissed and crawl home, or if you were capable, you could pull. It was a nice little hideaway. There were always 'faces' in there, and a few villains as well, but there was never any aggro.

I still keep in touch with Phyllis today. She's living in southern Ireland. Her son, Phil, bought her a hotel, and every time I work over there she tries to come and say hello. When I was in Dublin to do the Gay Byrne show, she came to see me and gave me her address. She said, 'It's just like the old days, we never close. Just jump in a cab after the show.' I was going to go, but when I checked I found the place was a three-hour drive from Dublin, and the cab didn't seem quite such a good idea. I didn't get there.

On signing for Manchester City from Swindon Town in August 1965, Mike Summerbee had been put up in the Grand hotel for three months. During that time he became friendly with one of the receptionists, Sandra Cargill, and when the club required him to find accommodation of his own, he moved in with Sandra's parents in Sale [Sandra lived elsewhere]. 'It was a bit chaotic,' he says, smiling at the memory. 'I used to come in on a Sunday morning after a Saturday night out, and there would be people out in their gardens mowing the lawn as I drove my sports car into the gatepost!' George's style was similarly cramped, in digs with Mrs Fullaway, so they rented a flat together in the Manchester suburb of Crumpsall. 'We needed somewhere we could take birds back to,' Summerbee says, 'so we got this one-bedroom place in a big Victorian house.' One bedroom? 'Yeah, well the lounge was big!'

To the disquiet of Matt Busby and the staff at Old Trafford, George's circle of friends outside football was widening all the time. Apart from his partner in the boutique, Malcolm Mooney, and the fur trader Danny Bursk, they included an entrepreneurial hairdresser and nightclub owner, Malcolm Wagner, and Selwyn Demmy, bachelor son of the wealthy Manchester bookmaker Gus Demmy. Summerbee says:

> George would have been twenty or twenty-one when we both met Selwyn at the same time, at Le Phonographe. He was a regular in there – in fact it was there one Sunday night that he introduced me to my wife. He's a millionaire bookmaker, very well known around Manchester. He's not really football-oriented at all, but he became a good friend to both of us. We met him in the club, and he invited us round for afternoon tea on the Sunday. He had a luxury flat in a place called Riverside Court in Didsbury. We weren't used to invitations to tea, and we didn't really know what to expect, but when we got there it was wall-to-wall women. Models. Top quality stuff. After that, needless to say we made a habit of going round there on Sundays. There would be afternoon tea, with smoked salmon, cream cakes and all the trimmings, and loads of girls there, so you always had a good time. It was a great way of killing a Sunday afternoon. We'd all been out on the town the previous night, so we'd meet up at Selwyn's at three o'clock and sit around chatting to all these model types, then go on to the Phonographe in the evening.

Selwyn is still around. He has never married, but he's got a big house now near Wilmslow. He's got the lot there – swans, ducks, cows, and the model girls, of course. There's still plenty of them about.

If Sunday afternoon meant birds at the bookies, Friday night was bagels with the barber. Another ritual was centred on the Wagners in Prestwich, and kosher food. Summerbee says: 'Malcolm Wagner had a hairdressing shop, called The Village Barber, next to George's boutique at the back of Deansgate. Malcolm is a nice person, still a close friend of George's and mine. He's Jewish, and every Friday night, if we were not staying overnight somewhere for an away game the following day, we'd go round to his mother's for salt beef sandwiches or whatever she was cooking. Malcolm has got a hotel out at Ramsbottom now. He has always been involved in bars and nightclubs. He first went into that business with George, when they had a couple of clubs called Oscar's and Slack Alice's.'

Nightclubbing wheeler-dealers are hardly the sort of company Matt Busby, or any other football manager, would choose for an impressionable young player, but Summerbee and Best strongly reject suggestions that Demmy, Bursk, Wagner and Mooney were bad influences. 'Selwyn was always around,' Summerbee says, 'but he was never a hanger-on. He was a genuine friend, and still is. Danny would go thirsty rather than take a drink off anyone if he couldn't buy them one back, and Malcolm Wagner was a sensible, well-to-do businessman. I don't think these people were a problem at all. At this stage, George had a close unit of real friends, and he soon identified and got rid of any hangers-on. There were bad influences, of course, but they came later.' Best echoes this assessment of his inner circle:

It used to annoy me when the boss talked about hangers-on, because even at an early age I knew who they were, and I knew who my real friends were. Selwyn Demmy never took advantage of me, or Mike. It was the other way round, if anything. Sunday was dead in Manchester, as it is in most places, so we used to go round to Selwyn's in the middle of the afternoon. We'd maybe go somewhere for Sunday lunch, and then on to his place. He would always have ten or twelve girls round there, all beauty queens or actresses or whatever. He did a lot for charity, and these were girls he met at those functions. At that time all the Miss Englands, Miss UKs and Miss Great Britains seemed to come from the north-west, and Selwyn would meet them, and a lot of footballers, through his charity work. Selwyn would invite them all round for tea and they'd bring their friends. It could get pretty weird. Occasionally he would bring out song sheets, and we'd all sit round singing whatever rubbish was on the sheet. We went there for a laugh, I suppose – and in the hope that we'd get lucky with one of the girls.

Danny Bursk became one of my best pals. He was Manchester United nuts. His boss was a guy called Michael Edelson, who is a United director now. Danny started off as a tea-boy and worked his way up in the fur trade. He is still a big United fan, but we lost touch when I left the club. In the mid- to late 'sixties, though, we'd go out together every week. He was a bit older than me, as most of my close friends were, and I think that was another thing that worried Sir Matt. But Danny was lovely. When I first met him, and we became friends, I was earning a lot of money and he wasn't. We'd go out for the night and I'd be buying drinks for the company, but Danny would always refuse if he couldn't afford to buy one back. He would stand his round and then, when he knew he couldn't afford any more, he would say goodnight and shoot off home. He has done well for himself since, but in those days, when he didn't have a lot of money, he could easily have hung around and had a good time at my expense, but he never did.

Malcolm Wagner had the hairdresser's next to Edwardia. It was originally his father's old-fashioned barber's shop, and I used to go in there to have his dad shave me with a cut-throat razor. We became friends, Mike Summerbee got on well with Malcolm too, and together we had this regular routine. Religiously, every Friday, Malcolm went to see his mum and dad. We'd go with him, and it was always a real Jewish family occasion. We had the same meal every Friday night for as long as I can remember – always the same soup. Malcolm used to drink about two gallons of Coke. His drink when he was with us was scotch and coke, but at mum's it was always Coca-Cola. That was our way of relaxing before a game on Saturday. We'd go round there and take it easy.

It was on a less abstemious night out with Wagner that George discovered the Brown Bull, the pub that was to become the bane of Matt Busby's life. George's local, a place called the Grapes, had been pulled down, and he was on the look-out for a new haunt. 'We discovered the Brown Bull, which was the most ridiculous location for having a drink you can imagine. It was under a railway bridge, so every time a train went by the whole bloody place shook. It was the filthiest, tattiest place I'd ever seen, and that first night I went in, with Malcolm Wagner, there was nobody in the place. It was a real dive, but Billy Barr, the guy who was running it, was such a lovely man that we kept going back.'

Old Billy had hit paydirt. George Best was to turn a grubby morgue of a place into the hottest spot in town. The effect on trade was such that when he retired, a wealthy man, Billy Barr handed George an envelope containing £6,000 as an expression of his gratitude. 'I started taking friends and girlfriends there,'

George says, 'and it became the in place. It was another one that never closed. I mean, you couldn't get out of there. Right from the start you'd go in and Billy would say: "Do you guys fancy something to eat?" and he'd shout upstairs to his wife: "Leila, the boys are here, put on four T-bones." She'd come down with these steaks a foot long and Billy would never charge us a penny.' No wonder. Thanks to George Best and friends, the *Marie Celeste* of Manchester's licensed trade was suddenly heaving. 'It was like a who's who in there,' George says. 'Apart from the footballers, all the television personalities from Granada were going. It was a perfect place for a single lad because there were a dozen bedrooms, and all the young actresses who were working for Granada started staying there. I ended up having my own key. Billy said: 'If I'm in bed one night and you want a drink, let yourself in and take what you want. Just make sure you lock up after you.'

Hugh McIlvanney recalls one memorable evening in what Matt Busby came to know as the hostelry from hell. 'After a European Cup match at Old Trafford, a bunch of us gathered in the Brown Bull. No one had given much thought to dinner, but by the time the after-hours session was under way, hunger was a problem. At least it was until Best went round taking fish and chips orders from everyone in the bar, then disappeared. He returned half an hour later, not merely with all the orders accurately filled, but with plates, knives and forks for everybody.' The waiter, McIlvanney observed, 'seemed less like a superstar than the appealing boy who had worked small miracles with a tennis ball on the streets of the Cregagh housing estate in east Belfast'.

chapter eight

On 22 April 1997, Manchester United were preparing for the decisive home leg of their European Cup semi-final against Borussia Dortmund, a match Alex Ferguson billed as the club's biggest since the 1968 final. As the players turned in for an early night, George Best booked a room at the Travel Inn, Hereford (rooms £36.50, two-course lunch £5.15) at the start of another late one. As a favour to the Bass-Charrington Brewery, who were talking of setting him up in his own sports bar within a longish goal kick of Old Trafford, he had agreed to open O'Neill's Irish pub (formerly the Hop Poles). It was not to be the most salubrious of evenings.

George and his wife, Alex, are driven to Hereford from Manchester by Alan Platt, a middle-aged United 'nut' who runs the Manchester United Luncheon Club – a nice little 'earner' for George and many other sporting celebrities, active and retired, who ply the after-dinner circuit. We meet in the Starting Gate pub next to Hereford racecourse before the gig, George sending Alex to check in at the Travel Inn next door while he fortifies himself with a baked potato and copious draughts of white wine.

The venue is unprepossessing, a working man's 'drinker' on Commercial Street trying to move upmarket, but George's brief is undemanding. We sit in the corner, studiously ignored by the cool and the macho, our conversation, and the flow of drink, interrupted only occasionally by gushing drunks and autograph anoraks. We join in with the sounds of the Dubliners drifting out from the back of the bar, but the rebel songs tend to grate second time around, and near closing time I decide to head for home. George, just getting his second wind, takes on ballast at a fish and chip shop, and is then directed to a pool hall just a few doors from O'Neill's.

Pool has become something of a passion in recent years, and he regularly takes on, and usually beats, all comers in the Rat and Parrot pub, near his Chelsea flat. It is a source of wonder to all who witness these marathon sessions how he casually makes the most problematic of pots after the sort of consumption which would render most of us comatose, never mind exemplars of skilled hand-to-eye coordination. These sessions, however, do have a habit of causing confrontation, and this is to be one of those nights, the sort which periodically decorate the front page of the *Daily Star*. George slaughters the local champion, winning frame after frame, and it turns nasty. The young bucks don't like it, the atmosphere becomes distinctly unfriendly, and when George, who is about to break again, sees a punter sit down next to Alex and whisper something in her ear, he assumes the worst. Liberties are being taken. Intensely jealous by nature, he reacts aggressively, warning off the intruder. Alex, anxious to defuse a potentially explosive situation, insists nothing improper has happened, but George can see nothing but red mist and tells her to shut up and keep out of it. Alan Platt intervenes, also in placatory vein, but is told that he can mind his own effing business too, and when a bystander asks George to moderate his language and behaviour in front of a lady, it is all off at Hereford. George, who sees nothing untoward in any of this, takes up the story:

> I'd won something like twenty-six games of pool on the trot and they didn't like it, so they tried to wind me up. It happens all the time. This big guy with a shaved head told me to mind my manners in front of Alex, and I wasn't having any of that.

I said: 'You can fuck off and mind your own business. She's my wife, not yours, and if I want to have a pop at her, or give her a slap, I will. It's got fuck all to do with you.' The fella then said: 'Do you know who I am?' which made me smile. Apparently he was in the SAS and well known locally, but I didn't have a clue who he was. He got a bit aggressive, telling me what he could do to me, but when I got hold of the cue the wrong way round he backed off, and then the guy who owned the place came over and asked me to stay behind when he closed and have a drink with him. I said: 'Not with that arsehole around,' and they threw him out. He went saying he'd catch up with me later. I told him: 'If you do, you'll be sorry.' I never saw him again. As usual, it was all talk.

The Bests eventually get to bed at about three a.m. and the following, or rather later the same day, we meet up again in Manchester's Holiday Inn, minus Alan Platt who is still nursing the feelings bruised the night before. George has been commissioned by the *Daily Mirror* to write a 'ghosted' verdict on the semi-final for a fee of £500. For reasons known only to themselves, the *Mirror* drop the idea in mid-afternoon. When I arrive for our rendezvous at four o'clock, George and Alex are in the lounge enjoying a livener or six in the company of Shay Brennan and his wife Liz, and Noel Murphy, the former Ireland and British Lions rugby union international. Alex, feeling 'fragile', is drinking champagne. George, button-bright but still wearing last night's clothes, sticks to the white wine.

Brennan joined United as a sixteen-year-old in 1953 and played 355 games for the club between 1958 and 1970. He might easily have been on the plane at Munich, and has been living each day as if it was his last ever since. On leaving United he joined Waterford, where he is now the proprietor of a small hotel. As befits an Irish landlord, he enjoys a drink, and his generosity in convivial company is such that Liz feels compelled to keep a firm hand on the family purse strings, doling out beer money as if paying for a child's school dinners. Here she gives him twenty pounds, but at Holiday Inn prices (£6.50 for Alex's champagne, £4.60 for Liz's vodka and tonic) it is spent long before Shay's thirst. The inevitable request for more, reminiscent of Oliver, meets with a Dickensian response, and George is left digging so deep that Alex is dispatched to enquire about cashpoints.

That task accomplished, she retires to change from jeans into something more appropriate for the match. Leather trousers. 'It would be nice if I could put something else on,' grumps George. Alex, who always packs for him, has forgotten not only a change of clothes but also his toiletries, an irritation exacerbated when a button is found to be missing from his shirtfront.

As the kick-off approaches, and the question of transport is raised, it becomes apparent that the party to travel may not be at full strength. Brennan is having second thoughts about going to the match. Once ensconced at the bar he is notoriously difficult to move, and to no one's great surprise he says: 'I think I'll watch it on telly.' In Hereford the previous night George had forecast that this would probably be the case, and now he decides not to go either. 'I'll stay and keep Shay company.' Attempts to persuade these legends of 1968 to change their minds get nowhere, but at least good sense prevails when someone suggests that Brennan might swell his beer fund by selling his match ticket on the black market.

'How much will it fetch?'

'You'd probably get £250.'

'Bloody hell, as much as that?'

'Don't be daft,' says George, all too aware of the field day the press would have with such a story. Alan Platt can have one of their tickets, as a peace offering, the other is to be returned to United.

Brennan and Best go in search of a television, and a refill, their wives and Noel Murphy join me in my taxi for the short ride to the 'Theatre of Dreams'. In the cab, I express surprise that the two celebrated alumni have chosen to stay behind. The response from their wives provides an interesting insight into the ex-player's psyche. Shooting a knowing look, Liz Brennan says: 'What happens if United win?' Before I can say anything, she answers her own question. 'Shay and George are forgotten. Yesterday's men. They don't mind United winning everything else, but they don't want them to win the European Cup because they're afraid of losing their place in history.' Alex Best nods in agreement. 'Deep down, I know George doesn't want them to win it.'

At the match, Paddy Crerand is disappointed but not surprised when his old team-mates fail to show up. 'They should be here, but we all know what they're like,' he says. 'Bloody unreliable, the pair of them.' Wilf McGuinness, who was Brennan's best friend in their playing days, gets it in one. 'Where are they, in the bar at the hotel?' he asks me, knowing the answer.

Mutual friends doubt whether Best would actually want his old team to lose a European Cup Final, but there is a telling glimpse of his true feelings on Sky Television a couple of weeks later when, after United have retained their Premier League title, Bobby Charlton is quoted as saying that Alex Ferguson's four championships in five years had to be the club's 'best achievement of all time'. George won't have it. 'I have to disagree with Bobby, which I don't normally, but I think the greatest achievement was our European Cup success.'

chapter nine

If the 'El Beatle' game, against Benfica in 1966, was George Best's finest individual performance, the *annus mirabilis* which assured him of a permanent place in the football pantheon came two years later. Their fortunes indivisible, as they were to remain to the bitter end, Manchester United became European champions in 1968, and George, at twenty-two, was the European Footballer of the Year.

It has become a cliché that the European Cup is United's Holy Grail, but clichés tend to be true, and this one was even truer thirty years ago than it is today. The full dimensions of the historical context have become blurred by the mists of time, so it is worth stating that the magnificent obsession pre-dates the Munich disaster, and goes all the way back to the competition's inception.

Not for the first time (it kept us out of the World Cup until 1950), sniffy conservatism, fuelled by self-interest and undertones of xenophobia, delayed England's participation. The European Cup was inaugurated in 1955, some twenty-eight years after the concept was first mooted by Henri Delaunay, the secretary of the French Football Federation. Like Martin Peters, Delaunay was years ahead of his time, and it was 1954 before the French again, this time in the influential shape of the sports paper, *L'Equipe*, persuaded UEFA (itself only six months old) that the idea really was a good one.

In April 1955, sixteen clubs attended the draw for the first round, Chelsea among them, but by the time the greatest club competition of them all began, the Football League had ordered England's champions to withdraw on the specious grounds that European excursions might cause them problems when it came to fulfilling their domestic fixtures. Matt Busby was appalled. With visionary insight, he said: 'This is where the future of the game lies,' and when United won the League that year, he was determined that they should take part in 1956–7. Backed by a staunch chairman, Harold Hardman, and by the secretary of the Football Association, Stanley Rous, he defied the League to break new ground on 12 September 1956, when the 'Busby Babes' went to Brussels and beat Anderlecht 2–0. The return, played at Maine Road because the newly installed Old Trafford floodlights were not ready, saw the Belgians thrashed 10–0, and England's participation in the Champions Cup was off to a barnstorming start. United went on to beat Borussia Dortmund and Atlético Bilbao before going out in the semi-finals to the fabled team which was to monopolize the cup in its early years, Real Madrid.

The following season, they had put out Shamrock Rovers and Dukla Prague, and had just completed the elimination of Red Star Belgrade when tragedy struck on an icy runway, imprinting the headstone 'Munich' deep in the Mancunian psyche. Eight players, not so much the nucleus as the very essence of the team, were among the twenty-three passengers who died in that third, abortive take-off, and Busby, whose condition was critical for a time, was scarred for ever, in body and mind.

Like many who survive dreadful accidents where others perish, he was left with an irrational but unassuageable sense of guilt. The European odyssey had been his idea. Why, then, should he be spared when so many good men died? It was against this deeply emotional background that winning the European Cup, as a memorial to the fallen, became an impassioned crusade. In 1966 Busby had been distraught when United, for the third time, went out at the semi-final stage. The board, and senior players, had had to persuade him to stay on for one last try. This, in his twenty-first season as manager, was it.

A sentimental man as far as his beloved 'Babes' were concerned, he could be ruthless with lesser mortals, and he was anxious to replace David Herd who had broken a leg in March 1967, at an age, thirty-three, when players used not to recover match fitness. Brian Kidd, a precociously powerful eighteen-year-old who had been with the club on schoolboy forms since he was fourteen, was given first crack, and quickly made the position his own. Kidd's father was a bus driver whose route took him past Old Trafford, and Brian was a Mancunian from the same school (St Patrick's) as Nobby Stiles. Taken on the pre-season tour of Australia in the summer of 1967, he was deemed ready to make the quantum leap from youth to senior football and played in the FA Charity Shield at Wembley, where United drew 3–3 with Tottenham. He kept his place for the first League game, at Everton, and went on to score fifteen goals in a debut season good enough to see him capped by England at the old Under-23 level. Kidd was not the only young man to catch the eye in Australia that summer. Francis Burns, captain of the Scotland Schoolboys side, started the season at left-back, with Tony Dunne switching to the right at Shay Brennan's expense.

Neither United nor George Best made the most auspicious of starts. Their first League match, at Goodison Park, was lost 3–1, and August also saw George convicted of driving without due care and attention – the first of a series of minor offences which left him dependent on a Spanish chauffeur, more of whom later. This time, for knocking down a woman who suffered a fractured pelvis, he was fined ten pounds and had his licence endorsed. Best's fortunes, and United's, improved quicker than the pelvis. That opening-day defeat was followed by an unbeaten sequence of eleven League games, seven of which were won. George was surrounded by his mates now with David Sadler, Jimmy Ryan,

John Fitzpatrick and John Aston from the 1964 youth team all joining him in the senior side, and in congenial company he went from strength to strength. When Sadler, Ryan and Kidd all scored at West Ham, George was determined not to be outdone and put together a run of five goals in seven games.

United were five points clear at the top of the League in January, with Best, Charlton, Kidd and Aston all scoring freely. The old warhorse, Herd, was hardly missed, and there was ample compensation for Denis Law's diminished effectiveness due to knee trouble. Going out of the FA Cup in the third round to Tottenham was a disappointment, but only a minor one. When it came to the cups, United had bigger fish to fry.

The European campaign had a low-key start, against Hibernians of Malta. The minnows were coached by Father Hilary Tagliaferro, a priest who doubled as a sports writer, but there was no divine intervention and precious little to inspire the pastoral muse with Law and Sadler filling their boots with a couple of goals apiece. While the Maltese prayed for success, United felt it was preordained. Best says: 'For all of us, the European Cup was the really big deal, and it was always in the back of my mind that we were destined to win it. You almost felt that it was inevitable. We knew we were good enough, and it was just a matter of time. That was the feeling in the dressing room.' Munich was a powerful, if unspoken, motivation:

> I joined the club in 1961, three years after the crash, when it still hung over the place. It was a shadow we were always under, if you like. No one ever said anything about it, and in 1967–8 it was certainly never mentioned, but we all knew what a terrible experience people like Matt, Bobby and Bill [Foulkes] had been through, and we all marvelled at the guts it must have taken for them to fly again. I used to think about that whenever we got on a plane. I found it utterly amazing that there were people on that plane who had been through

> such a terrible ordeal, and were still prepared to fly. Flying has never bothered me, but I would never have got on a plane again after going through that. No way.
>
> There was definitely a feeling that we had to do it for Matt, and also for one or two of the senior players, who were running out of time. A lot of us felt that this was the last chance for this particular team. If we hadn't done it that year, I don't think we would ever have won it.

This last chance theory is one that has been trotted out so often down the years that it has become set in stone, but it is one that does not bear up under close analysis. Of the eleven United players who contested the final in 1968 only one, thirty-six-year-old Bill Foulkes, could be said to be well past his prime. The next oldest was Shay Brennan, at thirty-one, followed by Bobby Charlton who, at thirty, was to be one of the stars at the Mexico World Cup two years later. Seven of the players were twenty-six or younger, and the average age of the team was 25.8. For purposes of comparison, the United team that won the championship in 1996–7, when they were generally held to be a young and improving side, were older, with an average age of 26.4.

That United were not going over the hill in 1967–8 is evident from their results. On returning from Malta, they went to Maine Road and beat a strongly resurgent Manchester City 2–1, Charlton scoring twice, and if Europe was the priority you would hardly have known it in the first half of the season as they piled win upon win. Five in succession culminated in the 4–0 thumping of Coventry at the end of October.

In the middle of November they went into the second round of the European Cup, against Sarajevo, on a new high, having just beaten Liverpool 2–1 at Anfield, where Best provided both their goals. United were without Law and Nobby Stiles, but George teased and tormented Ron Yeats, Shankly's defensive 'colossus', and embarrassed the formidable Tommy Smith to score with a header and a darting run through and rolled shot. Sarajevo was a difficult trip, in every sense. Nearly ten years on, it was the first time after Munich that the club felt able to ask Busby and his players to travel by air again. For almost a decade, European excursions had been made by rail. It was not the most relaxing of journeys, for obvious reasons, and the Bosnian hosts made the arrival even less enjoyable, kicking and niggling their way to a grim goalless draw. Best, singled out for special treatment by the hatchet men, kept his cool in the first leg but was provoked into lashing out at the Sarajevo goalkeeper in the return. His punch missed, but a defender, Fahrudin Prljaca, retaliated so blatantly that he was sent off. With ten men, the Yugoslavs had no chance. Already trailing to John Aston's eleventh-minute goal, they were removed from contention when Best, more accurate with legitimate boot than furtive fist, made it 2–0 midway through the second half. Sarajevo did manage to score three minutes from the end, but it was United who deservedly went through to the last eight.

Back in the First Division, they were still going like trains. Between claiming their place in the quarter-finals and the first leg against Poland's Gornik Zabrze on 28 February, they played eleven League games, winning eight and losing only one. Best, the brightest star in a coruscating firmament, burnished his reputation by scoring in five successive matches.

For Gornik, then, United were bristling with confidence. Law was to miss both legs, but they had proved that they could win, and win well, without 'The King'. The Poles, however, had a good form line behind them, having knocked out Dynamo Kiev, who had themselves caused a stir by putting out the holders, Celtic. For the first leg, at Old Trafford, Jimmy Ryan deputized for Law and led the applause as Best put United in front with a pulverizing shot to remind everyone that he had brute force in his armoury as well as subtlety. Kidd, receiving from Ryan, completed the scoring, and 2–0 was considered a satisfactory, if not conclusive, result.

For the return, it was Ice Station Zabrze. Snow and ice evoked unwelcome memories, and Busby approached the referee seeking a postponement, only for the Italian, Concetto lo Bello, to rule the Arctic conditions playable. He was probably right, but the surface was problematic for both sides, and against a stubborn United defence augmented by the inclusion of John Fitzpatrick, Gornik could manage only the one goal, which was not enough. Geza Kaloscai, the Polish coach, had no doubt as to the major difference between the two sides. 'If there is a better winger than George Best,' he said, 'I haven't seen him. He could have got into any of the world's greatest teams.'

Manchester United were in the semi-finals for the fourth time, familiar territory upon which to renew old acquaintance with the most evocative of all the game's famous names, Real Madrid. Father Time having deprived them of Del Sol, Di Stefano and Puskas, the Castilian bluebloods were not the irresistible force that won the European Cup in each of its first five seasons, but they were still a match for anyone on their day, and Busby rated them stronger than Benfica or Juventus who were contesting the other semi-final. United versus Real would have made the perfect final, he said.

By this stage, United's preoccupation with Europe was beginning to undermine their defence of the domestic title. Before the decisive away leg against Gornik they lost 3–1 at home to Chelsea, and straight after it they were beaten 2–0 at Coventry. Now, distracted by the European semi-finals, they lost successive home games to Manchester City and Liverpool. Already out of the FA Cup, where Tottenham had eliminated them in the third round, it was beginning to look like Europe or bust.

For the first leg against Real, at Old Trafford, the Spanish champions were without their most dangerous forward, Amancio. United gambled on the fitness of Law, who was in need of a cartilage operation, and preferred David Sadler at centre-half to the ageing stalwart Bill Foulkes. The 'Theatre of Dreams' was packed to the rafters, more than 63,000 dappled in spring sunshine and scarcely daring to draw breath as two well-matched teams sought to set themselves up for the decisive second leg. Real, at variance with their cavalier tradition, were in cagey, defensive mode, sitting deep and challenging United to break them down. They might have done so early, and gone on to win conclusively, but from Best's cross Aston was denied by a top-notch save, and from the consequent corner Crerand shot powerfully against a post. Kidd should have scored after a lovely sweeping move in which Crerand, Best and Charlton were all prominent. 'I raked a shot over the bar and into the Stretford End from twelve yards,' he says. 'It was a bad miss.'

And so, after dominating the game territorially and in terms of chances, United had just the one goal to take to the Bernabeu for the return. Its scorer? George Best. A glorious one it was, too. Kidd's long pass released Aston on the left, and when the winger cut the ball back from the byline, Best met it with a thunderous left-footed shot of the sort which brooks no argument. Old Trafford exploded, relief mixed with exultation, and a scared cat bolted from one end of the pitch to the other. Crerand, the king of the one-liners, said afterwards that George had set it among the Spanish pigeons. Cometh the hour, cometh the Best, but if George was the hero, the Russian referee picked out another man of the match. It had been 'a splendidly sporting contest', he said, adding: 'I have never had more pleasure from taking a match. And the number one footballer, and gentleman, on the field was Bobby Charlton.'

A win is a win, Busby insisted, in the way of managers the world over, but even his own players queried whether a 1–0 lead was enough to take to Madrid and one of the great bullrings of the game. With three weeks separating the two legs, United went back to the League where the scrap for domestic supremacy was being fought out in their own back yard. Under the avuncular management of Joe Mercer, and Malcolm Allison's innovative coaching, Manchester City had developed into a formidable force. They never quite made the heart sing, as United would on the days when it all came together, but they were well drilled and sustained their form with a higher level of consistency than their Mancunian rivals could muster. If the mercurial Best characterized United, Colin Bell was the personification of City – immensely proficient at all aspects of the game, but truly brilliant at none.

What happened next was typical. Between the first leg of the European semi-final against Real and the return, United had to play their last three League games. They lost the first, away to West Bromwich Albion, 6–3, then thrashed Newcastle at home 6–0, Best scoring a hat-trick. That left the two Manchester clubs level on fifty-six points going into the last round of matches. United, to the dismay of their huge following (the average attendance at Old Trafford in 1967–8 was a British record 57,696) lost 2–1 at home to lowly Sunderland while City won 4–3 at Newcastle to take the title by two points.

United had a good excuse. The European Cup was a considerable distraction, and they had to play Sunderland with the second leg of the semi-final only four days away. When it came it was billed, inevitably, as the most important game in the club's history, and the tension was almost tangible. Matt Busby decided not to risk Denis Law, whose knee injury had kept him out of the championship denouement, instead using Best alongside Kidd in attack. Bill Foulkes, the old stalwart, was recalled in defence, where Shay Brennan took over from Francis Burns at full-back.

On the morning of the match the squad had more butterflies than Kew Gardens, and two of the players, Nobby Stiles and Pat Crerand, thought a visit to the local Catholic church might help. When the collection plate was passed round, Stiles scorned the usual loose change for a folding contribution, horrifying his

Scottish companion. 'Bloody hell, Nobby, that's bribery,' exclaimed Crerand, in a stage whisper that might have been heard back in Manchester. George Best, never the nervous type, preferred more orthodox preparation, lingering late in bed. He was in a minority, but he was quietly confident. 'A lot of people thought we wouldn't do it, that we couldn't defend a 1–0 lead, but my mind kept going back to Benfica two years earlier when we had a one-goal lead from the home leg and went out there and scored five. If we could do it once, we could do it again.'

For a time it seemed United might need five. Real, as bold at home as they had been cautious away, smoothed the ball around with arrogant artistry, and soon turned deficit into profit with a headed goal from Pirri, and a second from Gento. An own goal by Zoco, panicked by Dunne's long shot, restored the balance, but only briefly. By half-time Amancio, who had missed the first game, had put Real 3–1 up on the night, and 3–2 on aggregate. United were on their way out, but Busby had other ideas. Good ones, too. He used the interval not only to rally his troops, but also to redeploy them. In the first half he had opted for a 5-3-2 formation, with Sadler supporting Foulkes in central defence and Best a wandering foil for Kidd up front. Now he pushed Sadler all the way forward, the defensive auxiliary becoming an extra attacker. 'That might surprise them,' Busby said. It did.

Best's face lights up, the years dropping away, as he savours the memory. 'We were struggling, 3–1 down to a good team in front of a hostile 120,000 crowd, but just like in Lisbon the boss was brilliant. He said: "Go for it. Just go out and enjoy yourselves. We're only 3–2 down overall, so if you get a goal the whole picture will change. Don't worry about anything. Go out there and have a go at them."' Kidd remembers the players being roused and yet put at their ease at the same time. One or two with an aversion to blame had been looking for excuses, but Busby rounded everyone up and pointed them in the right direction. 'Sir Matt was fabulous that night. I never saw him lose his cool in the dressing room, he never swore. The excuse merchants – the rubber dinghy men I call them – were looking for a way out, and started to shout the odds, but Matt just cooled everything down. There was this impressive calmness about him. He wasn't panicking, so why should we? When we went out for the second half, I was confident that we'd go through.'

Busby earned his corn as a tactician, as well as a leader, the change which sent Sadler forward proving to be a masterstroke. The defender-turned-attacker glanced in the goal that put the sides level on aggregate, setting up the most romantic and emotional of finales. With twelve minutes left Crerand took a throw-in on the right and sent Best corkscrewing his way up the touchline. His genius took him past one man, Sanchis, and then a second, Zoco, before he reached the byline and looked up to pinpoint his centre. George takes up the story:

> Big Bill Foulkes had charged out of defence and was the nearest man. God knows what had got into him because it was totally out of character, and everyone on the bench was screaming at him to get back where he belonged. Anyway Bill was there, so I gave him the ball. As I did so I thought: Here we go. In training, whenever Bill had a shot he always blasted it over the bar, and I was sure this one was going to go into the stand. What happened amazed us all. Coming in at the far post, Bill calmly sidefooted the ball into the corner of the net. I couldn't have done it better myself.

What a finish; what a story. The thirty-six-year-old centre-half, who had joined United as a schoolboy nineteen years earlier, had put them through to the final with his first European goal. Foulkes, who amassed nearly 700 appearances in his eighteen seasons at Old Trafford, made his debut in 1952 and was capped once by England, two years later. Come 1968 he was the sole survivor of the semi-final between United and Real eleven years earlier. Still coaching, in America, at the age of sixty-four, he nurtures vivid memories of the match. 'I was lucky to be playing,' he said. 'I had missed the first leg with a knee injury, and I think Matt went for experience for the return because I wasn't really fit. My knee was strapped up, and I was hobbling a bit. I still don't know what possessed me to go forward and score the goal. After so many games with no thought of scoring, it seems unbelievable.'

In the dressing room afterwards, traditional English reserve gave way to unbridled emotion as Busby and Bobby Charlton embraced each other, the tears flowing as freely as the champagne. 'I can't help it, I just can't help it,' Busby kept saying, as if an excuse was necessary.

For the final, United held the aces. For a start it was being played at Wembley in front of a predominantly English crowd. And the opposition, Benfica, came with disconcerting memories of their Best-inspired 5–1 humiliation in Lisbon two years earlier. On the downside, and to his eternal regret, Denis Law would miss the match, laid up in hospital after undergoing surgery on his troublesome knee. His absence was a blow, but United had been playing well without him in a season in which 'The King' had been dethroned by George Best. Law was restricted to twenty-three League appearances which yielded just seven goals. George was the First Division's leading scorer with twenty-eight from forty-one games. Law or no Law, United were supremely confident as 29 May, their date with destiny, approached. Best recalls:

> For all of us, this was the big one, the really big deal. Everyone – management, players and supporters – was so committed to winning the European Cup that there was a feeling it was inevitable. I know I had it in the back of my mind all season that we were going to win it. We had been disappointed twice, in the Cup Winners Cup in 1964 when we lost so badly

> to Sporting Lisbon, and in the European Cup in 1966, when we went out in the semi-finals to Partizan Belgrade. We had been so close, and we weren't going to miss out again. There was a feeling that it was now or never. A few of the players were coming towards the end of their careers, and Sir Matt certainly was. We felt that this was probably our last chance to win it for him.

Bobby Charlton remembers thinking along the same lines: 'We'd been close, and I felt it was only a matter of time before we won it. But winning the European Cup is never easy. First you have to win your domestic title to qualify, and there were some great teams around at that time – Leeds, Liverpool and Spurs – so that was hard enough. I always thought we were going to win it in 1968, but some of us weren't getting any younger, there was no guarantee that we would win the League again, and there was definitely a feeling that this could be our last chance.'

The final was to be played on Brian Kidd's nineteenth birthday, and the baby of the team spent the build-up telling all and sundry how keen he was to repay the man who had given him his chance so early: 'I want to win it for the boss.' Nearly thirty years on, he said: 'Every player wanted to win it for the Old Man, no doubt about it. It had been his dream, his was the first English team to enter the European Cup, and when you think of what he'd been through, seeing so many perish at Munich, it's only natural that we were emotionally committed to winning it for him.'

Pat Crerand recalls Portugal's finest 'whistling in the dark', and drawing specious encouragement from the result of a friendly match between the two sides. 'We'd hammered them in 1966, but the following year we went on a tour of America and Australia after winning the 1967 championship, during which we played Benfica in Los Angeles. They beat us 2–0, but they took the game a lot more seriously than we did – probably with that 5–1 in mind. They were a good side, but we always had the opinion that we were better than them, and after 1966 I think we had the Indian sign on them.' Busby, too, was confident. On the eve of his ultimate fulfilment he said of his players' state of readiness: 'Their heart is right, which is the important thing.'

There were solid grounds for optimism. Benfica were a good, star-studded team, but past their best in 1968. In the early sixties, inspired by Eusebio, they had superseded Real Madrid as the dominant force in European club football, reaching four European Cup Finals in five years. But after carrying off the cup in 1961 and 1962 they lost to AC Milan in 1963, and again to Internazionale in 1965. If the sell-by date was creeping up on some of the United players, a few of the opposition were past theirs.

After an intensely emotional build-up, the match itself was something of a slow burner, taking what seemed like an eternity to do justice to the occasion. Bobby Charlton says: 'It was a poor game for ninety minutes, and only caught fire in extra-time. It was a case of both teams being afraid to lose, rather than trying to win.' George Best agrees that it was no classic. 'When the team had a reunion on the twenty-fifth anniversary of the final, we sat through a video of the whole match and were not exactly riveted. For a long time our performance was disappointing. We were so confident – quietly confident – that it came as a surprise to us when we didn't kill them off straight away. The memory blurs over the years, and it was interesting to see that although we played some good stuff in the first ninety minutes, we were never at our best.' Geoffrey Green, in *The Times*, drew a veil over the first half, which was 'episodic' and 'dull'. Using imagery of which Best would have approved, the scribes' doyen wrote: 'A waiter might well have dropped a tray of glasses, such was the clatter, the crash and the bang of it all, with football secondary and both teams clearly out of humour with each other.'

Understandably, after the chasing they had from him two

years earlier, Benfica were obsessed with shackling 'El Beatle', and Humberto was booked early for interpreting the verb 'to mark' much too literally. Always shadowed by two defenders at least, George struggled to make much of an impression during normal time. Bobby Charlton says:

> I don't remember George's contribution being greater than anybody else's. He played his part, but you wouldn't call it the George Best Final, not by any stretch of the imagination. I think the game was disappointing from his point of view. George loved the big stage, and you could hardly get a bigger stage than the European Cup Final. I could see in everything he did that he wanted to use it as a platform for a great virtuoso performance, but it didn't quite happen. There were reasons for that. Benfica defended well, and it was a hot, humid night. The conditions weren't right for individualist stuff, you had to pass the ball around and share the load because the heat sapped your energy, and that didn't really work for George.

Instead it was Charlton, with a rare header, who opened the scoring. Geoffrey Green put it thus:

> When the untidy, often ugly, baggage of that first half had been brushed out of the way, the match at last began to find its stature as the blue shirts of Manchester United finally found rhythm, pattern and purpose. Sadler, put clean through by Kidd, shot past the post to miss a dolly, and it seemed that United could pay the price, for Eusebio was constantly prowling, like a caged, hungry animal, threatening danger when he almost splintered Stepney's crossbar with a thunderbolt from 20 yards. Yet when Dunne and Sadler worked a movement down the left, and over came Sadler's cross for Charlton, rising on spring heels to glide the ball home off his thinning

head, it seemed that United were heading for their long-awaited glory.

A goal to the good, Busby and his players were more confident than ever, and there would surely have been no need for extra-time had Sadler not spurned his second straightforward chance after a mesmeric dribble and a shot from Best which the goalkeeper could only parry. George, too, was culpable when he danced past a couple of defenders before trying, extravagantly and unsuccessfully, to dribble round the 'keeper.

Reprieved, Benfica hit back with a sucker punch after eighty minutes when the giant Torres, who had been nullified by Bill Foulkes, won the ball in the air for once for Jaime Graca to thump in the equalizer. As is so often the case, one goal was enough to transform the game and, suddenly inspired, the Portuguese would have prised victory from the incisors of defeat but for the gallantry of Alex Stepney beneath the United crossbar.

In those far-off days, before the advent of cheque-book management, Stepney was one of only two United players in their Wembley twelve to have cost a transfer fee (Crerand was the other), and the £55,000 Chelsea received was repaid in the instant the twenty-three-year-old Londoner denied Eusebio what would surely have been the winning goal. There were just three minutes of normal time remaining when the man from Mozambique eluded Nobby Stiles in a way he had never been able to do in 1966, and sliced through the United defence to leave himself one on one with the goalkeeper. Wembley held its breath. The 1965 European Footballer of the Year was deadly in such situations. But not this time. Uncharacteristically, he opted for power rather than precision, and in so doing he gave Stepney a chance. The ball was close enough to his body for the 'keeper to make a stunning reflex save, one so good that Eusebio stood and led the applause.

Galvanized by their goal, Benfica assembled a withering last ten minutes, and Stiles, for one, believes that if normal time had gone on for another few minutes they would have won. Instead, Busby had the break between normal and extra-time in which to rework the oracle which had turned the semi-final in Madrid. Best says:

> We could easily have lost it, and we all knew it. Now we had another chance to go and win it. All the staff came on to the pitch to gee us up – the boss, Jimmy Murphy, Jack Crompton and John Aston senior – all giving various players a bit of a rub down and saying things like: 'They're tired, you've got them. You've just got to keep going. Keep going.' I had no problems. I still felt fresh and full of running. Looking at our players and glancing across at theirs, I knew we had it. We had real competitors like Paddy Crerand and little Nobby Stiles shaking clenched fists to get us going. They were like that in practice matches, so you can imagine how fired up they were with thirty minutes to win the European Cup.

Crerand has more reason to remember Busby's exhortations:

> We'd had a bit of a fright in the last ten minutes, and Matt wasn't happy about the way we were giving the ball away. He wasn't upset, or anything like that, and he was still telling us that we were going to win it, but he made the point to me, and to Bobby Charlton, that it was our job to keep possession in midfield. 'Keep the ball,' he said, 'don't give it away.' He went through all the usual stuff about Wembley being a big, tiring pitch if you didn't save your legs by keeping possession. It was true, mind. It was a great surface to play on, it always had a bouncy spring to it which I loved, but it did take a toll on the old legs.

In Best's eyes, Crerand was United's most important player:

> Paddy was very good to have in the dressing room. He was madly competitive. Every team has different characters, with different ways of doing things. Paddy was the aggressive one – before, during and after the match. He was my 'minder.' If anyone threatened me on the pitch, he was the first man there to take care of it.

In extra-time, Crerand, with his proud, combative nature, came into his own, the man from Celtic contesting the midfield as if it were an 'Old Firm' derby. 'We were much stronger,' he says, dismissively. The coaching staff had been right, Benfica were tiring. With a matador's instincts, George Best sensed it, and within a minute of the restart he had them on their knees, ripe for the kill. The goal was straightforward in its inception, deft in its execution. A long clearance from Stepney was transferred expertly by Kidd to Best, who wriggled past two defenders before drawing and rounding the goalkeeper, Henrique, and knocking the ball into the vacant net. Benfica's heads dropped, and almost at once Kidd turned the knife that rendered the Portuguese moribund. The initial header with which he met Charlton's corner from the left was brilliantly repelled by Henrique, but when the ball came back to him, Kidd rose majestically to score via the crossbar. As nineteenth birthday celebrations go, it would take some beating. Before the first period of extra-time had ended, Charlton, with typical dexterity, had flicked in Kidd's cross to make it 4–1, and that was that. The last, fifteen-minute period was notable only for another top-notch save by Stepney, again at Eusebio's expense.

His long, pioneering crusade finally complete, Matt Busby was in tears again. Fittingly, after their trail-blazing entry twelve years earlier, Manchester United had become the first English club to win the European Cup. 'The players have done us all proud,' Busby said. 'After Munich, they came back with all their hearts to show everyone what Manchester United are made of. This is the most wonderful thing that has happened in my life, and I am the proudest man in England. The European Cup has been the ambition of everyone at the club, and now we have it, at last.'

George Best had contributed in handsome measure, scoring the first all-important goal in extra-time, but double-marking succeeded in subduing him for long periods, and Bobby Charlton and the comparatively unsung John Aston were more influential on the night. Geoffrey Green wrote of 'Best being chopped, harried and bruised from start to finish as he tried to bring his artistry to full flower. Trying to dominate his ruthless opponents, he began to play with a kind of fury which overstretched itself as he attempted to beat the hoards of Benfica off his own bat.' Frustrated? It is not the way George chooses to look back on 'the highlight of my career':

> Benfica must have been pig-sick of me, because it was much the same story as when we beat them 5–1 over there. I can still see my goal, clear as anything, in my mind's eye. I get really annoyed when they replay it on television because they only ever show me going past the goalkeeper. There was more to it than that. When 'Kiddo' knocked the ball down and I picked it up, the centre-half came in to tackle me and I stuck it through his legs first, before going on to take it round the 'keeper. We knew then we'd won it. 'Kiddo' scored one that tends to be forgotten and Bobby knocked his second in with his natural right foot, instead of the old flying left, and that was it. We might as well have come off then. We still had the second period of extra-time to play, but they were gone. Out for the count.
>
> Afterwards, all I can remember is seeing Matt's face when

he came on the pitch at the final whistle. I can still see it, as if it were yesterday. He wasn't crying – that came later – but he looked as if he should have had a halo over him. He had one of those faces that lights up, like the pictures you see of saints. Of course the first person everyone ran to was the boss. He had achieved something which had almost cost him his life.

That achievement soon received formal recognition when Matt Busby became Sir Matt, knighted for his services to sport.

After the match, United had a reception and a celebration dinner at the Russell hotel in London's West End, but Best can recall nothing of it, his evening having dissolved into a boozy haze. It is impossible to pinpoint when his drinking became a serious problem, but for want of a precise date, his finest hour appeals to the perverse side of his nature as a convenient hook. 'That might have been the start of it,' he says, 'because I can't remember anything after the final. I don't remember where I went, it's a total blank. I couldn't tell you where we had the reception, the banquet, or where I went after that. I don't know who I went with, or where I ended up, nothing. I can't even remember coming back to Manchester. I can only remember the game.' Pat Crerand recalls seeing George at the Russell hotel, and the reception at which the Joe Loss Orchestra welcomed the players with the Cliff Richard hit 'Congratulations', and Kidd was presented with a giant birthday cake, but says the great maverick had gone his own way by the time the party moved on to Danny La Rue's nightclub. Malcolm Wagner believes he has the answer to his best friend's whereabouts. 'George's mates from Manchester had all gone down to Wembley as a crowd, but we weren't in on what he got up to after the function. I think he went to see Jackie Glass.'

In 1968 George Best was the hottest property not just in the English First Division, but in the whole of Europe. The youngest ever European Footballer of the Year, he was also voted Player of the Year in more than twenty countries across the globe. If there was anyone around blessed with his sublime talents today, the mind boggles at what he would be worth. The bonus for winning the European Cup added roughly 50 per cent to George's basic wage, which was £150 per week (the equivalent of £2,500 thirty years on). That figure was doubled by his earnings outside the game where, apart from his boutique, he was well paid for television advertisements, ghosted newspaper columns, and a menswear modelling contract with a shopping catalogue, Great Universal Stores.

> The commercial side had gone mad. I was involved in something nearly every day. In the papers I wasn't just appearing on the sports pages, I was doing columns on music and fashion too, and I was advertising everything you could think of, from sausages to Brut aftershave. The publicity thing was a monster. If I went to the cinema, the place came to a standstill and the film had to wait while I was mobbed. I never sought that and I certainly didn't want it. It wasn't really down to Ken Stanley, either. He wasn't going out of his way to get me publicity – it just came. I tried to keep a level head, but how could you, at twenty-two? It had never happened to a footballer before, I was the first, so I wasn't prepared for it, and there was no precedent to learn from. I had to handle it as best I could, with no real help from the club.
>
> All the stuff I was doing outside football was crazy. I didn't want to do it, and had to be talked into it. I didn't want to make television commercials, I found it boring, and the modelling side of it, for the catalogue, I hated. I had to go to their headquarters in Manchester where they had set up a studio, and hang around for hours. Hour after hour, just standing in front of a camera. I really didn't want to be there.

> Even today, I don't like having my photograph taken, but then I absolutely loathed it.

There were compensations, of course. In a good week in 1968, Best's total earnings from football and extracurricular activities would top £2,000, an astronomical sum at a time when the average weekly wage was £23. 'At United,' he says, 'apart from the usual win bonuses, the players were on a bonus for every thousand spectators we drew over 30,000. We were averaging crowds of nearly 58,000, so it doesn't take a genius to work out that we were getting a lot more than our basic wage. I was making big money, and I didn't know what to do with it really. I helped my mum and dad to buy a fish and chip shop, which was sensible enough, but I was changing cars every few months. I had a soft spot for Jaguars, and in 1968 I had two or three – always white, they were.'

In the absence of good investment advice, either from his employers or from the players' union, Best frittered away a small fortune. 'I was naive,' he says. 'Without someone to advise you properly, you can only learn by experience, and I thought, in my naïvety, that if you earned £2,000 a week, you spent £2,000 a week. I should have been a rich man, like the top players are today. I was still living in digs, paid for by United, and when I was on club business, playing wherever, they picked up the bill for everything. It is difficult now to see how I got through so much money, but I suppose it was a case of easy come, easy go.'

Apart from his nocturnal activities, holidays knocked a big hole in the Best bank balance. Every year, from 1965, he spent the whole of the closed season – nearly two months in those days – in Majorca with a gaggle of friends, acquaintances and hangers-on:

> The routine was always the same. As soon as the season finished, it was the first flight out to Spain. A whole crowd of

us would spend the summer in Majorca, in the days before it became Costa Blackpool. Mike Summerbee would come, until he got married, 'Waggy' [Malcolm Wagner] was always there, so was Johnny Prescott, the boxer, and a friend of his called John 'Chalky' White, who I still see today. There were some lads from London – cab drivers, mostly – a couple of guys from America and two or three from Switzerland. There must have been twenty of us gathered there every year, without fail. Same time, same place. The ritual was to lie on the beach all day and go out and party all night. We were all single lads, and in those days, before Aids, we didn't have to worry too much about catching anything too serious. They were two months of pure madness.

It was on the fourth of these Bacchanalian breaks, in the summer of 1968, that George met Felix Izquierdo-Moreno, a Spanish barkeeper he was to bring to England to run his two restaurant-nightclubs in Manchester, Slack Alice and Oscar's. Felix is still a close friend today. It was in Majorca, too, that George first bumped into Tommy Docherty, who is anything but.

chapter ten

If 1967–8 supplied the highlight of George Best's career, it also produced a haven of contentment in a field of constant frustration. International football. By universal agreement, George would have been much less likely to reach for the self-destruct button had he sensed even the hint of a chance to prove himself on the stage where true greatness is measured, the World Cup. Instead, by accident of birth, a player on the same plane as Pele and Cruyff was condemned to scratch around with the no-hopers of Northern Ireland, and missed out on all the major tournaments. To his eternal regret, George Best never played in a European Championship or World Cup. 'Recreational football' is how he describes an international career in which he could be bothered to turn out thirty-seven times between 1964 and 1977. Only once, he believes, did he really do himself justice – against Scotland at Windsor Park in October 1967. 'My game for Belfast' was how he put it.

George Best was a coltish kid of seventeen, who had played just twenty-one first-team games for Manchester United when he was given his international debut against Wales at Swansea on 15 April 1964. It was something of a red letter day for the Irish: not only did they win 3–2, but another newcomer, Pat Jennings, also took his first step on the road to a record 119 caps. George recalls next to nothing of what should have been an occasion to remember. His impressions typically sketchy, he says: 'There was a big build-up in the newspapers back home.

The fact that the two of us, myself and big Pat, were making our debuts gave them their angle. Wales weren't a bad side then – I think Mike England, Ron Davies and Cliff Jones played [they did] – and it was a great result for us, because we didn't win many.'

An understatement, this. Northern Ireland had lost their previous match 8–3 against England at Wembley, an embarrassment which spelled the end for one of Best's boyhood heroes, Harry Gregg, who was replaced, permanently, by Jennings in goal. They had also been beaten 4–1 by Wales in Belfast in 1963, so expectations were none too high in the squad young Jennings and Best joined at their Swansea hotel. 'We won, so I suppose we must have played well,' George says, 'but all I can remember of the game is a skinny little guy called Jimmy McLaughlin scoring the first goal. I don't know where he was from [he had just joined Swansea from Shrewsbury, so he was playing an away game at home], but he wasn't a bad little player, and he got a few goals. He was typical of the Northern Ireland team. We always had four or five decent players from the top clubs, but had to make up the numbers with lads from the Second or Third Division – sometimes even the Irish League.'

One of the cadre of 'decent' players was Terry Neill, the Arsenal centre-half, who won fifty-nine caps between 1961 and 1973 and managed Northern Ireland from 1971 until 1975. George once described him as the worst manager he ever played for, but if there is any ill feeling, it is all one way. Neill, who celebrated his fiftieth cap by scoring the winning goal for the Irish against England at Wembley in 1972, also managed Hull City, Tottenham and Arsenal. He now runs a successful sports bar and brasserie in the centre of London. An established member of the team in which Best had his baptism in 1964, he is blessed with near-total recall (not to mention the gift of the gab), and is a reliable witness to call on to fill in some of the gaps:

The first time I ever heard Bestie's name was from Harry Gregg. I was very fortunate to come into the Northern Ireland team at a time when there were still quite a few of the 1958 World Cup squad around – people like Danny Blanchflower, Jimmy McIlroy, Peter McParland, Billy Bingham and Harry Gregg – and at one of our get-togethers I remember Harry saying: 'We've got this kid from Belfast at Manchester United called George Best.' Now Harry was a very proud man, and a good goalkeeper, for whom the term 'custodian' meant 'over my dead body', so everyone sat up and listened when he told us this story of what the kid had done to him in training. Harry said Matt Busby had played this sixteen-year-old in a practice match with the first team and that he'd 'done' him not once, but twice.

Harry said: 'This skinny little kid came through on me and I thought I'd dummy as if I was going to dive one way and fool him easily.' Instead, Harry said, the boy rolled his foot over the ball, like an old pro, and calmly knocked it into the corner of the net. The kid had taken the piss out of Harry, and Mr Gregg was not pleased. He told us that he thought: No one is going to take the mickey out of me, but that a bit later in the same game the same thing happened again. Harry dived one way and George put the ball in the other corner. Knowing Harry as we did, George was lucky to be able to walk again after that. We were all aware of him from then on.

When the 'skinny little kid' arrived in the international squad less than two years later, the old hands were not disappointed. Neill says: 'Bestie only needed five or ten minutes in his first training session to make his mark. I remember he was first out on to this quagmire of a pitch and the last back in. He just loved playing football, and no wonder. No one I know of has ever had the natural talent George had. I don't use the word genius lightly, but that's what he was. We were all looking at each other, raising our eyebrows, within those first few minutes. The looks said it all. Here was something special.'

Best's second game for Northern Ireland, and his much trumpeted home debut, came just two weeks later, against Uruguay. Again he remembers very little apart from the score (the Irish won 3–0). It is left to others to fill in the details. Wilf McGuinness, reserve coach at Manchester United at the time, recalls it being the sort of spell that is now deemed to 'burn out' young players and which, consequently, would not be allowed today:

> George was still seventeen – it was two months before his eighteenth birthday. He played in a First Division game at home to Nottingham Forest on the Saturday, in the first leg of the FA Youth Cup Final at Swindon on the Monday, and then he went off to play for Northern Ireland against Uruguay on the Wednesday. The following day I picked him up at Manchester airport and took him to Old Trafford to play against Swindon in the second leg of the Youth Cup Final. In the space of six days he played four games – a First Division match, an international and a two-legged cup final. He could do it because he had the appetite, you see. It wouldn't be allowed now, and if it was you'd be lucky to get two decent performances out of four. But George could keep a peak in those days. He played well in all four games – you can take my word for that.

Dickie Best has mixed memories of his son's early days in international football. 'After George's debut,' he says, 'the local paper said they couldn't understand what all the fuss was about over this boy Best. Then, when he played against Uruguay, he had a good game against a rough, tough side, and the papers were full of him and what a good player he was. After that, there was no looking back – no one here doubted him.' Terry Neill vouches for the fact that young George stood out against Uruguay, in difficult conditions:

> I remember we were all in the dressing room getting ready, and me, being the conscientious pro who had to work at everything, had my boots polished, with lovely, new, clean white laces in them. I was admiring myself in the mirror and then I spotted Bestie, shaking his boots and banging them on the floor to get the mud off from the last game. I'd done everything right, had my proper rest, trained hard and looked after my gear, and here was this kid who looked as if he'd just woken up after a night out, with kit like a tramp, and he was the one who went out and played like a star.
>
> George was playing on the right, and the Uruguayan left-back was intent on tackling him anywhere from the eyebrows down. The League season was over [it finished on 25 April that year], the match was only a friendly, and I couldn't see the point of anyone getting hurt unnecessarily when we were just about to go off for our summer break. So I sidled over to George and said: 'He's trying to "do" you, drop deep and stay out of trouble if you like.' I was wasting my breath. George was in the mood, completely irrepressible, and played the guy like a matador. We stuffed them 3–0, and although he didn't score, I'm sure the rest of the team that night would agree it was all down to Bestie. He totally destroyed that full-back.

After a winning start, George came up against England, in Belfast, in his third game, and although the Irish put up typically spirited resistance, they lost 4–3. That was to be the way of it down the years, too many honourable – and a few dishonourable – defeats. When he scored his first international goals, away to Switzerland and Scotland in successive games in November

1964, it was to no avail. Northern Ireland lost both matches, a 2–1 defeat in Lausanne ruining their chances of qualifying for the 1966 World Cup. Asked once how a certain Irish manager motivated so many make-do-and-mend teams, Danny Blanchflower said: 'He never mentioned tactics. He simply sat us down in the dressing room and told us of the heroic deeds and legendary performances of Irish sides in the past. We'd look up the results later and discover that Ireland had lost!'

Playing for Manchester United, losing was not something to which George Best was accustomed, and it was definitely not an experience he enjoyed:

> In the sixties I'd be coming off a high with United almost every time and when I went and played for Ireland we were always struggling. We did win a few games, but we were always up against it, and the results, and lack of expectation, made it difficult to take the whole thing seriously.
>
> The trips away with Ireland became like holidays. The matches, obviously, were taken seriously, but the days leading up to them were just a bit of fun. We'd have a drink and a laugh, and there was quite a lot of activity 'after hours'. That's what I mean by recreational football. It wasn't easy for me to take it as seriously as perhaps I should have done. I'd be turning it on and coming off the pitch losing almost every game. It might sound a bit cruel, but I wasn't playing with the calibre of player I was used to at club level, so if I made a run, the man on the ball often didn't spot it, or if I passed it inside the full-back, the winger wouldn't make the run. That was difficult, three days after playing with Denis Law and Bobby Charlton. There were *some* good players, like big Pat Jennings, Johnny Crossan and Derek Dougan, but we always had to make up the eleven with five or six rag, tag and bobtails.

After playing in twelve of Northern Ireland's thirteen matches between his debut and the 1–1 draw with Albania in Tirana in November 1965, George started to miss internationals which were not to his, or his club's, liking. In 1997, much was made of the fact that Ryan Giggs had never played in a friendly for Wales, and suspicions were aroused when some of the Manchester United players who were said to be unfit to play for their countries in mid-week made near-miraculous recoveries come the weekend. It was ever thus. George says:

> A lot of times it was suggested to me that maybe it was better if I didn't go and join up with the Irish squad, that I would be better off staying at home. It was common knowledge that the clubs preferred you to stay as fresh as possible, and frowned on international football. No one ever admitted it. You just didn't say those things about Manchester United, or Matt Busby in particular, but yes, there were times when Sir Matt would say: 'Well son, it's up to you.' He didn't actually say 'remember who pays your wages', but you knew what he meant.
>
> I think he was right. I loved playing for Ireland, and going home, but if it was a choice of playing for Manchester United alongside the great players I played with week in, week out, or going and having a laugh with the Irish lads, there wasn't much choice from the football viewpoint. The club v. country thing is the same today, even more so with the fabulous wages the clubs are paying and their reluctance to risk having £5m players injured.

In such circumstances, Northern Ireland rarely saw the jewel in their crown in its best light. The shining exception was on 21 October 1967 when George destroyed Scotland almost single-handed. 'Genius of Best beats Scotland' ran the headline in *The*

Times, and in Belfast they still talk about it today. The Scots had a strong team, fashioned around the Celtic club side that had won the European Cup in Lisbon five months earlier. The Irish were the usual mixed bag, with Jennings, Neill, Dougan and Best supplemented by Billy McKeag and Arthur Stewart, both part-timers, from Glentoran. The result should have been a foregone conclusion. Scotland had just beaten England's World Cup-winning team 3–2 at Wembley while the Irish had struggled to draw 0–0 with Wales in Belfast. But George Best on song was capable of turning any form book on its head, and this time George was in the mood. 'It was just one of those games when everything was right,' he says. 'I could have scored four or five, and would have done but for Ronnie Simpson, who was absolutely brilliant in the Scottish goal. Some of the saves he made were phenomenal. It was one of those games when every time I got the ball something was going to happen. On occasions like that, you get a real buzz, and I had it every time I was in possession. It was my best game for Ireland by a mile.'

As usual, others have a clearer recollection of events. Terry Neill says:

> We won 1–0, but the score was irrelevant really. Because of Simpson, who was in heroic form, George didn't score, but he made the goal for Dave Clements of Coventry. It was the usual bog of a pitch at Windsor Park. I had always prided myself on my fitness, but I was glad I played at the back and didn't have to do the running of a midfield player or a forward. I can remember very late in the game, when I was feeling knackered, big Pat Jennings bowled the ball out to me on the edge of the box, just as we were all starting to think: Christ, we're 1–0 up at home, we might just have a sensational victory here. Let's not do anything silly. I think Pat probably thought I'd hold on to the ball for a few seconds, then maybe whack it into touch to waste a bit more time, but

the next thing I hear is: 'I'll have it, I'll have it.' Who is there, on my shoulder? Bestie. Even at that late stage I thought: Here you are George, do what you want. He was just twenty-one, but already the rest of us were prepared to play a subordinate role to his genius. Anyway, I gave him the ball and off he went again on another of those marvellous runs.

The nice thing about playing at the back is that when someone is playing like that in front of you, you get a great view of it. George was murdering them. It started off with Tommy Gemmell, a super full-back, being run ragged. Then a midfield player – I can't remember who it was – provided double cover. Eventually one of the forwards started to drop back, so they had three people trying to mark George, and still he took them to the cleaners. George was in his element, he wanted them all queuing up to have a go. It was too easy, beating just the one man.

It was the same when we trained. Like most teams, we would finish our training with a game, seven or eight a side. Everything would be going normally, and then Bestie, being Bestie, would decide: 'Right, I'll take you all on. I'll play individual keep-ball,' and we'd all end up running around after George. I'm talking about the entire squad, chasing after him. I think he almost beat the fifteen of us a couple of times! He just loved it, and we all enjoyed it as a bit of fun.

In that Scotland game our team really turned into George Best and ten supporting players. Bestie had one of those days. It was a case of: If you lot play half a role here, I'm in the mood. Just give me the ball every time. After the game, I remember vividly sitting just inside the dressing room door with Bestie just to the right of me. I looked over at him with such admiration. It was then that I realized, fully, that I was a journeyman footballer. I thought to myself: You might make a living at this, but if you live to be 200 you won't be able to play the same game as him. And there he sat, looking like a young kid who had just come off a school pitch on a Saturday morning. There were no airs and graces about him, no outward sign of euphoria. He was just one of us, one of the boys.

Pat Crerand's international career with Scotland had ended the previous year but, always the gregarious sort, he was still in touch with all his old team-mates, and found them shell-shocked by Best's performance. 'Talking to some of the lads afterwards, they admitted it could easily have been much worse than 1–0. The two full-backs were Tommy Gemmell and Eddie McCreadie, and the story goes that Tommy said to Eddie at half-time: 'I'm having a bit of trouble with this kid. D'you mind swapping sides?' Eddie laughed and said 'Go fuck yourself!'

The Times said of Best's display: 'His genius was matched only by his courage, and he deserved the victory all on his own. He caused as much trouble as three men with some exhilarating runs and shots of quite remarkable force from such a slight frame.'

Northern Ireland's hopes of capitalizing on a morale-boosting result were undermined when George missed their next three games, the European Footballer of the Year returning, to a hero's welcome, for the World Cup qualifier against Turkey at Windsor Park in October 1968. For the first time, George played alongside Eric McMordie who, after that abortive visit with Best to Old Trafford in 1961, had taken another three years to cross the Irish Sea and try his luck in the Football League, with Middlesbrough. After that false start with Manchester United, McMordie, too, was to enjoy a rewarding professional career, playing more than 200 League games for Boro before moving on to Sheffield Wednesday, York and Hartlepool. He won twenty-one caps for Northern Ireland between 1968 and 1972 and, along with Pat Jennings, was George's constant companion on international duty. McMordie, fondly remembered by the Irish players as their 'social secretary', settled in Middlesbrough, where he runs a successful fruit and vegetable business.

Turkey's 4–1 defeat at Windsor Park is another match Dickie Best, who took the family along to watch, remembers well. 'In the first few minutes,' he says, 'George had dropped deep, and a fella sitting just in front of us said: "Aw c'mon glamour boy, get into the game." That went on for a bit and I could see my daughter, Barbara, who was sitting alongside me, was getting angry. I told her: "Say nothing, just leave it." Anyway, George got the first goal, a cracker from a fair way out, and I couldn't resist it. I leaned forward and said: "Hey mate, the glamour boy all right for you now?"'

In a team that was ordinary at best, George found motivation easiest to come by when he had the chance to pit his wits against high-class opposition. Apart from Scotland in 1967, he recalls being 'up' for games against Uruguay (1964), the old Soviet Union (1969) and, of course, every crack at England. 'I think there was an order to it,' he says. 'We wanted to beat England first, then Scotland, then Wales, but England were definitely the enemy, the number one target. We always wanted to "do" them. Unfortunately, we never did when I played.' George crossed swords with 'the enemy' six times, and the Irish lost every game. He scored only one goal against England, in a 3–1 defeat at Wembley in April 1970, but he will always insist that it should have been two. Playing in Belfast in 1971 against a team which included his great *bête noire*, Peter Storey, he nipped in when Gordon Banks threw the ball up and dexterously hooked it away from the startled goalkeeper before heading it into the net. To Best's chagrin, the goal was disallowed by the Scottish referee, Alastair Mackenzie:

> I used to study goalkeepers' kicks, because in those days you could put them under a little bit of pressure. Nowadays you can't go near them, but then you could harass them a bit, and

> I used to watch how they cleared the ball. Banks always threw it high in the air and volleyed it when he wasn't throwing it. Pat Jennings, on the other hand, kicked it on the half-volley.
>
> If the ball was in the air, which it was when Banks threw it up, I was entitled to play it. When the referee disallowed the goal I asked him why, and he didn't know. Later, when he'd had time to think, he said it was for dangerous kicking – my foot had been too high. I said if my foot was too high, and we were going for the same ball, Banks's must have been high too. I suppose it was just something the referee hadn't seen before, but to this day I maintain it was a goal. I did something similar not long after, against Pat Jennings. He went to half-volley a clearance and as the ball hit the ground I tackled him and it broke free. I got up and knocked it in the net and the referee allowed it. Like most decisions, it boils down to the individual's interpretation.
>
> England were always a superior side, by a long way, but we never seemed to get the break of the ball. I know it must sound like sour grapes, but even the referees made it difficult for us.

Storey, the Arsenal hard man who won the second of nineteen England caps in the Irish match in question, is one of very few contemporaries to whom Best took a real dislike. 'Every time I played against him he would tell me that he was going to break my leg. I took particular pleasure in turning him inside out. I had nothing but contempt for the so-called hard men. For hard men, read men who couldn't play. If you have the skills, you are going to play football.'

Results were never better than moderate, but the Northern Ireland squad made up for any disappointments on the field by ensuring that they always enjoyed themselves off it. 'It was good fun,' George says. 'Big Pat Jennings became a great pal, we always roomed together, and the two of us and Derek Dougan were drinking partners. There were a lot of characters in the team. Eric McMordie was a total nutcase, organizing all sorts of outrageous goings-on to make it one big party. We tried to keep the games as serious as possible, but the behind-the-scenes activities were riotous, and away trips were just total madness.' Female company figured prominently in the 'madness', with George always prepared to play up to an audience, in every sense of the phrase. McMordie's habit (in which he was not alone) was to secrete himself in wardrobes to witness the fun.

The thought occurs today, as it must have to the management at the time, that with fewer high jinks and more application the results might have been better. Maybe so, Best says, but not significantly. 'The football sometimes seemed to be incidental, which obviously isn't the way it should be, but that was because we were never going to win anything. We just weren't a good side. We had players who weren't even close to the standard required, and so those who were got frustrated. We were doing the right things on the pitch and the others were making us look silly. You could play a lovely pass, one of the makeweights wouldn't run on to it and you'd get booed for what the punters thought was a bad ball. I suffered from the same thing when I played in America.' Terry Neill shared George's frustration, yet always managed to apply himself with due diligence. It would be easy for him to criticize the self-indulgent maverick who let him down more than once during his Irish managership, but instead he expresses only sympathy for Best's under-achievement at international level:

> If you were to ask any of us who played with George in the Northern Ireland team I think you would find, to a man, that we would have loved to have got to the World Cup for our own personal satisfaction, but just as much so as a willing vehicle for George. We all knew, in our hearts, that we weren't

> going to get there, and it left us with a feeling of sadness that each of us, as individuals, was not good enough to provide the platform for someone who could have got into any country's national team, including Brazil. It was like a guilt thing you carried around with you when the big championships came around. You felt: Shit, I'm letting this guy down.

Inadequate they may have been on the field, but off it the Irish delighted in providing a haven for their star player when the pressures of playing, or not playing, for Manchester United threatened to overwhelm him. 'We were an escape,' Neill says, 'a refuge from all that was going on around him in Manchester. There was a terrific camaraderie in our squad, and I think he enjoyed a few days away from it all with his old mate Eric McMordie and Pat Jennings. We could all talk about Ulster Fries [transport 'caff' fare], the glory hole, which is the cupboard under the stairs, gutties instead of plimsolls – all the old Ulsterisms. He was at home with that.'

The most notorious occasion when George Best pulled out of an international squad may well have cost him, and Northern Ireland, a place at the 1970 World Cup. In 1969 the Irish, after beating Turkey twice and drawing at home to the old Soviet Union, needed a good result in Moscow to win the three-team qualifying group and book their place in Mexico. They were taking no chances with their potential matchwinner. Billy Drennan, secretary of the Irish FA, attended United's League Cup replay at home to Burnley on the Monday and stayed over in Manchester to ensure that Best joined up with his international team-mates the following day. Instead, to Irish dismay, the key to their World Cup aspirations withdrew, injured. Best's absence brought furious complaints from Harry Cavan, president of the Irish FA: 'It is a scandalous situation that allows a footballer to play in a club game forty-eight hours before an important international. The four British associations met last year and changed the pattern of the game to stop this sort of thing happening. We agreed to keep eight dates free [of club games] for internationals, and this was one of them. If Best had been required by England there would have been no possibility of his having to play a club fixture forty-eight hours before. Surely a club of Manchester United's stature could have done without him for a match in a subsidiary competition.' George himself did not escape criticism, Cavan adding: 'Danny Blanchflower used to tell his club he was playing for his country and that was that. Full stop. You can do that if you are good enough, and George Best is very, very good.'

To no one's surprise, the injury had cleared up by the weekend, when Best played for United against West Bromwich Albion. Without him, Northern Ireland lost 2–0 in Moscow and finished runners-up in the group, with five points to the Soviet Union's seven. To this day, George wonders what might have been. 'Would we have qualified if I'd played? It's something I'll never know.'

Bitterly disappointed, the Irish went downhill fast, losing their next four games, and bad was to become infinitely worse when the onset of the Troubles in Ulster meant it was unsafe for the team to play in Belfast, and they were left staging home games in Hull, Coventry and Liverpool. The nadir, from George Best's point of view, came in November 1971 when threats on his life caused the cancellation of the European Championship qualifying tie at home to Spain. An anonymous caller had told police that George would be shot if he played for Manchester United at Newcastle at the end of October. Not only did he play at St James's Park, he scored the winning goal. But when the threat was repeated, United refused to allow him to play against Spain in Belfast, where the bombings and shootings were escalating on a daily basis, and after his withdrawal FIFA, world football's governing body, stepped in and called the game off.

Northern Ireland eventually played Spain at Boothferry Park, Hull the following February, but any chance they might have had of getting to the European Championship went with the loss of proper home advantage, and by the time the qualifying stages of the 1974 World Cup came around George was in crisis. He played in the qualifier against Bulgaria in Sofia in October 1972 and was sent off for punching an opponent in retaliation, then missed the next four games. When Terry Neill, who had taken over as manager, picked him to play against Scotland in Glasgow in May 1973, Best failed to turn up. Neill says:

> George had done a runner from Manchester United, and nobody knew where he was. There was a national hue and cry and I had the press and television cameras virtually camped in my bedroom at the team's hotel in Troon. It wasn't something the players talked about, but we all loved Bestie, and we put up a protective wall and held on, saying nothing. The rumours were coming in on a half-hourly basis. George had been spotted here, George had been spotted there. As far as the squad was concerned, he was one of us, whatever he did, and we were on his side. We hoped that he was OK. We would rather he had been with us, but we weren't annoyed that he wasn't. We were worried about him, each of us in his own way.

When George left Manchester United a few months later, it was generally assumed that his international career was over too, but he was to have one last hurrah, as a Fulham player. In 1976, when he had just turned thirty, Northern Ireland were striving to qualify for the World Cup in Argentina and after five games without a win Danny Blanchflower, as manager, needed a lift from somewhere, and was sufficiently impressed by George's renaissance at Craven Cottage to welcome the prodigal back into the fold. It was hardly the easiest of comebacks, away to the Total Footballers of Holland who were to get to the final two years later, but George's personal performance always varied in direct relation to the quality of the opposition, and the presence of Johann Cruyff inspired him to roll back the years. The Irish drew 2–2 in Rotterdam, a highly creditable result, but it proved to be no more than an oasis in a desert of defeats. They lost five and drew one of their next six matches and the World Cup was again beyond them by the time George won the last of his thirty-seven caps, in the return against the Dutch on 12 October 1977. It was hardly the way he would have chosen to say goodbye, in a 1–0 home defeat.

The end of the story, in terms of international football? Not quite. There was a postscript in 1982, when Northern Ireland finally succeeded in qualifying for the World Cup. George was thirty-six by this time, but still playing, for San José Earthquakes in the North American Soccer League, and there was talk of the Irish taking him to the finals in Spain, if only to play cameo roles as a 'supersub'.

> I had half a chance to go, I suppose. Billy Bingham was the manager, and the Irish media, and general public, put him under a bit of pressure to take me with them – sentimental stuff, really. I was getting towards the end. I was still reasonably fit, but I was playing in a bad side in America, and it was just about time to come home. Anyway, San José came to Europe on tour, and when we played an exhibition game in Scotland, against Hibernian, Billy Bingham came to watch me. It was a disaster. We were well beaten [3–1] by Hibs, who weren't a good side themselves, so you can imagine what we were like. Bingham said afterwards that he thought I had lost my enthusiasm – I think that's how he put it. It was not true. If I had got in the squad for a World Cup I would have trained like a lunatic and given absolutely everything.
>
> Quite a few of the Irish players said to me: 'We thought he might have picked you, not to do the ninety minutes, but to come on if we needed you, or to start and see how it went.' It would have been nice, but it wasn't to be. In fairness to

> Bingham, it did come a bit too late, which was sad. I had played all those years, and then when I was just about finished they qualified for the World Cup. To be fair to them, they did really well without me.

It is the unshakeable belief of everyone who knew him, especially those who played with him, that George Best would have applied himself with a greater sense of purpose, and resisted the temptations of the flesh rather longer, had international football provided the stage – the big tournaments – that he craved. Bobby Charlton says:

> I think that grates with him all the time. Every time the subject of international football comes up he will mention that he never played in the World Cup. It is obviously a source of enormous disappointment to him, and it was a great shame. In global terms, people always judge you on what you did in the World Cup. In 1970, after the tournament in Mexico, I went to Australia to do some coaching. On the way back, I stopped over in Fiji and I remember meeting this little lad who couldn't get over the fact that I was there. He had seen me on television, playing in the World Cup, and couldn't believe that now he had met me. The point I'm making is that this young kid from Fiji knew all about Bobby Charlton, but he couldn't tell you anything about George Best, because George hadn't played in a World Cup.

David Sadler recalls conversations in the digs they shared in which George expressed envy that he, Sadler, could play for England, as he did for the first time against Northern Ireland (minus George Best) in November 1967. Sadler says:

> It was a real joke for George, playing for Ireland. He had fantastic matches, like when they played Scotland and it was

> George Best against eleven Scotsmen, but the fact of the matter is that Northern Ireland were never going to qualify for the World Cup, and that definitely got to him. At Old Trafford we had a few people who were involved in England's triumph in 1966, and George was very envious of that. Those of us who were fortunate enough to play with him would never question that he was world class, but if you don't do it in the big tournaments there will always be someone who says 'You didn't prove it,' and you don't have an answer if you never played in the World Cup, with and against the best players in the world.

In his book *How Not to Run Football*, which has a shocking portrayal of George Best crucified on the cover, Derek Dougan puts it thus:

> His erratic behaviour was sometimes caused by frustration. Here was a brilliant player, an absolute genius, without the international showcase he needed. Had he been born English, he would have excited the world. In a Northern Ireland jersey, he was rarely seen on a world stage. Fortified by regular international appearances in cup competitions around the world, his ambitions would have been fulfilled and his skill given the international recognition it merited. Restricted by nationality, he remained an outsider, never able to reach the centre of top international footballing events. It was like an actor such as John Gielgud being denied the National Theatre stage and forced to appear on the fringe with a small workshop company. I am sure this tipped the balance in Best's personality, and finally drove him away.

True or false? Would playing for a better, more successful international team have kept George on an even keel for longer? His answer is both instantaneous and unequivocal. 'Yes.'

chapter eleven

Hindsight is always twenty-twenty and, given that benefit, Matt Busby should have taken his knighthood and retired at the end of the 1967–8 season, ambitions all handsomely fulfilled. He turned fifty-nine on 26 May 1968, which may not sound ancient, but very few managers are still in harness in their sixtieth year. For purposes of comparison, two of his great contemporaries, Bill Nicholson of Tottenham and Everton's Harry Catterick, exchanged tracksuits for the pipe and slippers at fifty-five and fifty-four respectively. And neither had suffered the horrors of Munich.

In the opinion of his players, Busby was never the same man after 1958 and the air crash which nearly cost him his life. Wilf McGuinness, his protégé, who played under him and succeeded him briefly as manager, says: 'After Munich we all wanted to believe that the old Matt was back, but he wasn't. It had taken so much out of him. We could hardly recognize him at first. His wife didn't recognize him in the hospital, that's how bad it was. When he did come back he seemed a much older man. Older, with scars and nightmares. I think there were times when he felt: I don't really need all this.'

Weakened both in body and spirit, Busby had had to be talked out of retiring after the European Cup disappointment of 1966, when Manchester United went out in the semi-finals. In 1968–9, as United went into steep decline, it became increasingly obvious that for various reasons – sentimental loyalty to players who had served him well, and diminishing desire among them – he had neglected to rejuvenate a team in need of it.

The popular belief that United's European Cup winners were an old side is a myth. The eleven players on duty at Wembley were aged as follows: Stepney 23, Brennan 31, Dunne 26, Crerand 29, Foulkes 36, Stiles 26, Best 22, Kidd 19, Charlton 30, Sadler 22, Aston 20. Seven members of the team were aged twenty-six or under, and only two – Foulkes and Brennan – were past their sell-by date. That said, there are other good reasons besides age for bringing fresh faces to a club. Players become blasé when there is no real competition for places, and a signing or two keeps everyone on their toes. Incoming transfers are also a positive statement of intent, of continued ambition.

At the start of 1968–9, United were badly in need of an injection of new blood. Busby had bought just one player, Alex Stepney, in four years. The team was too cosy and comfortable, dangerously close to staleness and stagnation. David Sadler says the obsessive pursuit of the European Cup was allowed to override all other considerations, including team development. 'Success in Europe had become a crusade which dominated everything, and because we were getting through the rounds, everything else got pushed to one side. Matt was getting on, he had never been quite the same, physically, after Munich, and for him it became all about the present, with insufficient thought given to the future. It was all about what the group of players we had was going to do. By the time we won the European Cup it was too late to rebuild because the supply of talent that had been coming through the junior teams wasn't there any more. The reservoir had dried up.'

George Best, who was friendly with both men, knew that Mike England and Alan Ball had hankered after moves to Old Trafford in 1966, but to his, and their disappointment, the best centre-half and most dynamic midfielder in the country were allowed to go instead to Tottenham and Everton respectively. A replacement for Bill Foulkes, who would be thirty-seven before the season was out, was clearly the most pressing requirement in the summer of 1968, but when Busby finally took the plunge, in September, it was to pay £100,000 for a winger, Burnley's Willie Morgan. Wingers were not what United needed, and Best was unimpressed. 'Not a championship player' his verdict.

The new season dawned brightly enough, United beating Everton 2–1 at home on the opening day, with Best and Charlton scoring the goals, but they were to win just two of their next eight League games, and the warning was writ large when on successive Saturdays in August they lost 4–0 at home to Chelsea and 5–4 at Sheffield Wednesday. A 3–1 victory over Newcastle, in which George scored twice, offered only temporary respite, one win in nine games between 5 October and 23 November plunging them deep into the wrong half of the table. Six months after winning the European Cup, Manchester United were on the greasy pole which was eventually to deposit them in the Second Division.

Foreign fields, and the defence of their European title, provided intermittent relief, but only after the ugliest of curtain-raisers. As Europe's finest, United had the dubious privilege of contesting the World Club Championship with Estudiantes, the South American champions, whose brutal approach to the games at home and away evoked memories of the Argentine team Sir Alf Ramsey had called 'animals' at the 1966 World Cup. In the first leg, played in Buenos Aires, Nobby Stiles was singled out for sustained provocation, and was sent off. The return saw Best go the same way for squaring up to an opponent, Hugo Medina, who was banished with him. For what it was worth (which was deemed by United to be very little) Estudiantes won 2–1 on aggregate.

The second game against the Argentinians was on 16 October 1968, sandwiched between League defeats away to Liverpool and at home to Southampton. United were losing as many games as they won now, and George Best, still young and eager, was not a happy man. The seeds of his dissatisfaction had taken root:

> I suppose I was spoilt. I'd had success right from day one, and now it was disappearing before my eyes, when I'd really hardly started. We had proved ourselves to be the best in Europe, and then the next season we were middle of the table and trying to put it down to the fact that because we were the European champions, everybody wanted to beat us. The fact is that they shouldn't have been able to. I think quite a few players thought we had done what we set out to do, and relaxed a bit. I certainly didn't see it that way. I was only twenty-two, I wanted to keep winning things, and I felt we had every chance of retaining the European Cup.

The defence of the trophy started with the routine drubbing of Waterford, part-timers from the Republic of Ireland, who were dispatched on a 10–2 aggregate. Denis Law filled his shooting boots with four goals at home and three away. Anderlecht, of Belgium, were more problematic in the next round, particularly with Best sitting out both legs, suspended for his sending-off against Estudiantes. It was a close-run thing, United winning 3–0 at home and losing the return 3–1, with Carlo Sartori's away goal proving decisive.

Meanwhile, back in the League, all was not well. Four losses in five games took United into 1969 in a state of mounting crisis, sixteenth in the table, nineteen points behind the leaders, Liverpool. The fourth of these defeats was against Leeds, the eventual champions, whose playmaker, Johnny Giles, was as noted before not as surprised as some by his old club's decline:

> Leeds didn't have the same individual ability as Manchester United, but we were better organized. Our manager, Don Revie, was more modern than Matt Busby in his approach.

He had our players organized, defensively, in a way that United weren't. In 1965 we were pipped for the League by United on goal average, and beat them in the semi-finals of the FA Cup, when we weren't in the same class as players. That was when United were at their best. I think they were a great team for three seasons, between 1964 and 1967. They were already on their way down when they won the European Cup in 1968.

In 1964–5, 1965–6 and 1966–7 they were outstanding. They had great individual talent in Best, Law and Charlton and a lot of good, unsung players in support, like Tony Dunne and Shay Brennan. But I had played with most of them, and there was never the same spirit at United that we had at Leeds. The dressing room camaraderie at Leeds was much greater. There were a lot of divisions in the Manchester United camp. When I was there, Bobby, Denis and George didn't get on. I think Denis got on with George very well, but George didn't get on with Bobby and Bobby didn't get on that well with Denis. When Leeds played Manchester United there was a much greater sense of togetherness about our team, and from 1968 onwards we became a much better side than United. We were coming to our peak while they were going the other way.

When United won the European Cup they should have rebuilt their side, but in those days they were never big spenders. If you look at that cup-winning team in 1968, Denis Law and David Herd didn't play, so only Alex Stepney and Pat Crerand had been bought. The rest cost them nothing. Nowadays, the policy is that if you're successful, you buy a couple of players with the proceeds. That's what United should have done.

Busby's sins of omission had caught up with him, and he knew it. After building three great teams he had neither the will nor the vigour to assemble a fourth, and on 14 January 1969, three days after the defeat at Leeds, it was announced that he would be stepping aside at the end of the season, or rather stepping up, as general manager. The chairman, Louis Edwards, said: 'Of course we knew that it had to come, but this does not mean that Sir Matt will be any less involved with Manchester United. In fact, the post of general manager carries even wider responsibilities, and my board are well content to think that in future they can call upon Sir Matt's unique football experience.'

If the directors had 'known that it had to come', the timing of Busby's decision, in mid-season and little more than a year after signing a ten-year contract, left them in a quandary. They spoke of advertising for a successor, but did nothing, preferring privately to try to persuade him to change his mind. Meanwhile, the team was allowed to drift, lacking firm direction. Pat Crerand, Busby's trusted lieutenant and golfing partner, says:

> Matt was going to quit, so why should he do anything radical? His attitude was: Let's bring in a younger man and let him sort it out. Matt had come a long way with the players in that team, and he wanted somebody else to make changes, rather than him be the bad guy. I know those were the thoughts going through his head because he told me so, much later. He had been ready to retire for a couple of years, from 1966, when he only allowed himself to be persuaded to stay because he was so desperate to win the European Cup. That was his fulfilment. He should really have gone after that.

Denis Law agrees that Busby had had his day by 1969. 'He was never what you would call a well man after Munich. Don't forget he nearly died in the crash and it left him with a bad back, not to mention the injuries you couldn't see. As a manager, you have your time, and then suddenly it's not yours any longer. That's what happened to Matt.' In George Best's opinion, his old mentor was 'tired out'. He says: 'It was as if the sheer size of the job had exhausted him. It had been hard, hard work, a long slog for him, but he had stuck to it, and now he had done it all. He had decided it was time to go, and the club had to replace him, but how can you replace a man like that? It's impossible.'

Busby soldiered on pending the appointment of a successor, his team firing in fits and starts. In their first match after his momentous decision they beat Sunderland 4–1, with a hat-trick from Law and the fourth from Best, but then five League games without a win included a derby defeat at home to Manchester City, and it was clear that if they were to salvage anything from a season of disintegration, it was going to have to be in one of the knockout competitions. In the FA Cup another hat-trick from the resurgent Law saw them safely past Birmingham in the fifth round, only to lose at home to Everton in the sixth, so it was all down to Europe.

After eliminating Waterford and Anderlecht, United were paired with Rapid Vienna in the last eight – no easy task, this, against a team that had just put out Real Madrid, but Best made it so. He ran the Austrians ragged, scoring twice in a 3–0 home win to render the away leg little more than a formality, a performance that moved the Rapid coach, Rudolf Vytacil, to describe George as 'the top player in all Europe'.

Coaches everywhere had identified him as United's most dangerous player and the key to their success. As such, he was invariably singled out for special attention, and never more so than in the semi-final against the bristling *catenaccio* defence of AC Milan. Well held, by fair means or foul, he could find no way through in the San Siro, where goals from Angelo Sermani and Kurt Hamrin gave the Italians a 2–0 advantage to take into the return.

The tie was nicely balanced, and the United players maintain to this day that they would have pulled it around at Old Trafford but for a decisive mistake by the match officials. Best had set up

United's 100th goal in European football, scored by Charlton, and with thirteen minutes left everyone in the ground, with the exception of the referee and his linesman, thought they had levelled the aggregate at 2–2. Crerand played the ball in to Law, whose shot appeared to have crossed the line before Anquiletti cleared it. 'It was two feet over,' Law says. 'That would have been the equalizing goal, and I'm sure we would have gone on to beat them. We should have been in the final again, and we would definitely have done better than Milan, who lost 4–1 to Ajax.' No one was more incensed than Crerand:

> The refereeing over the two games against Milan was diabolical. Out there, the referee was definitely 'at it'. When their centre-forward, Sermani, scored he brought the ball down with his hand. We all stopped playing, he put it in the back of the net and the referee gave a goal. Their other scorer was a little fella called Hamrin, who played for Sweden. He had a go at John Fitzpatrick, then went down screaming, and the referee sent John off. Some of the decisions were disgraceful. We were the better side, and we could have gone on to win the cup again.

Best is also of the 'we wuz robbed' school of thought – 'the goal Denis scored was a yard over the line' – but a more balanced view is provided by Brian Kidd, who says: 'I think we were the better team, but by that time Sir Matt had had enough, and wanted to get away from it all. I think that lack of intensity from the top was a key factor – with the older players, certainly.'

It was to be eight troubled years before United qualified for Europe again.

Every big name in the game was linked with the managerial vacancy, Don Revie, Brian Clough and Ron Greenwood among them, but no one of such calibre was ever going to agree to work under the control of a general manager, not even one as eminent as Matt Busby, and when the appointment came it was made from within. To the incredulity of the players, the thirty-one-year-old reserve coach, Wilf McGuinness, was promoted to take charge of the first team. The decision was made public in April in the following club statement: 'The board has given further consideration to the changes which will occur at the end of the season, and has decided to appoint a chief coach who will be responsible for team selection, coaching, training and tactics. Mr Wilf McGuinness has been selected for this position, and will take up his duties as from 1 June, and in these circumstances it is not necessary to advertise for applications, as was first intended. Sir Matt will be responsible for all other matters affecting the club and players, and will continue as club spokesman.'

The choice was greeted with scepticism all round. The players, always quick to grasp the significance of such things, noted that McGuinness had not been given the title of manager, nor was he to speak for the club. His authority was undermined from the start. As far as the first team was concerned, it was business as usual. Busby was still the man in charge.

The new coach was not quite the wet-behind-the-ears novice he has been portrayed. Manchester United to the core, Wilf McGuinness played in three FA Youth Cup-winning sides before making his debut as one of the original 'Busby Babes' in October 1955. His problem was that he played left-half, the position occupied by the peerless Duncan Edwards. But for a knee injury, which forced him to miss the trip, McGuinness might have perished with Edwards at Munich. Instead, his best season came after the tragedy, in 1958–9, when he made thirty-nine League appearances and was good enough to play twice for England, against Northern Ireland and Mexico. With a promising career before him, he broke his leg badly in December 1959, and after an abortive comeback his playing days were over at twenty-two. Taken on to the backroom staff, his reputation as a coach was such that Alf Ramsey invited him to assist in England's preparations for the 1966 World Cup, and in 1968 he became manager of the England youth team.

McGuinness, then, was no mug, and the suggestion that United put Best, Law, Charlton *et al* in the hands of an unqualified novice is a source of undiminished irritation. Approaching pensionable age, he still lives in the same road where he had his first club house as a player, and is a regular at Old Trafford, where he provides match analysis for a local radio station and acts as master of ceremonies for the well-heeled patrons of the Manchester United Luncheon Club. Like George Best, he has overcome innate shyness to earn good money on the after-dinner speaking circuit.

The team McGuinness inherited had finished eleventh in the First Division in 1968–9 – a catastrophe in Best's eyes. On a personal level, he had enjoyed another excellent season, top scorer again with nineteen goals in forty-one League games and named European Footballer of the Year, but the demons were gathering in the corners of his mind. Manchester United had hit their crisis, his was just around the corner. 'Coming eleventh was a disaster after winning the European Cup,' he says. 'Team spirit was falling apart. Cliques were forming, which we'd never had before, and there was a fair bit of backstabbing going on. I hated what was happening, it really got me down, and when I was down I turned to drink.' Phyllis's, the unlicensed all-night drinking den, was now a regular haunt, and Best was banned from driving for six months and fined twenty-five pounds in July 1968 after one of his nocturnal expeditions ended in an early-morning accident.

For the first time, George was relieved when the end of the season came and he could head for Spain and forget his footballing worries. The appointment of McGuinness had not filled him with great enthusiasm, but at least the club had recognized that change was necessary and, unlike some of the older players, he viewed the new regime with an open mind.

The odds were stacked against McGuinness from the start. Busby was always going to be a hard act to follow, for anyone, and his continued presence in an overlord's role did nothing for his successor's authority. Worse, having played alongside some of them, 'good old Wilf' was seen by the senior players as one of the lads, and it was not going to be easy to adjust to taking instructions from him as 'The Gaffer'. Some of them, Best says, never tried. Bobby Charlton was a fortnight older than his new boss and, as a much bigger name, it was widely felt that he might have had the job ahead of him. 'Wilf was given it too young,' he says. 'The best thing for him would have been to go somewhere else and prove himself in management, then maybe come back later. What the club did was to go from the absolute master, Matt Busby, to a schoolboy by comparison. Wilf was a bright lad and a good organizer, but Matt had personality and presence, and you can't learn that on a coaching course. Under Wilf we lost our way.' Denis Law says: 'Wilf had played with Bobby Charlton and Shay Brennan, who was his best mate. He was good pals with Nobby Stiles too, and what is it they say familiarity breeds? He was too young and inexperienced for the job.' Pat Crerand confirms that there was a definite lack of respect among the senior players. 'Wilf had mixed with all of us as a pal, and he just didn't have that aura that Matt Busby had. It didn't help that he inherited a lot of problems with the team. Some of us were getting on a bit and the young players coming through were really not good enough.'

McGuinness took charge of a team in need of modernizing, in every way. It was not just new blood but updated tactics that were required. He agrees unreservedly with Johnny Giles's assertion that Leeds, and others, were more 'with it' in their approach. 'I remember Maurice Setters and Noel Cantwell saying that if we could combine our flamboyance with Leeds's efficiency we would be unbeatable. I was on the coaching staff, but I was their age, and I would go for a pint with them and argue Matt Busby's corner. I thought it was my duty. But I always knew that if we paid a bit more attention to organization and the defensive side we would have won a lot more.'

Busby had been entirely responsible for tactics and strategy, McGuinness says. The widespread belief that his assistant, Jimmy Murphy, had a major influence on the way the team played was 'a myth'. So, too, was the notion, fuelled by Best and others, that Busby was an off the cuff man, with no time for specific game plans:

> Matt talked tactics all right. He had a blackboard with magnetized discs on it to represent players. He started all that. Every Friday he would have a tactics meeting. He would go through the opposition individually, telling everyone how they played, their strengths and weaknesses. He wouldn't over-elaborate, he kept it nice and simple. 'His left foot is weak, he turns this way, he does this in the air' – that sort of thing. Then he'd tell you how he wanted you to play, again keeping it simple. When I was playing he'd say to me: 'So and so is a good player so stay with him. When you get the freedom you can move up in support, but when it breaks down he's the one you look for.' So Matt did talk tactics, on a Friday. Denis Law used to say that it was a good thing that he gave the team talk on a Friday because come the game on Saturday everyone had forgotten the mumbo-jumbo. It was his little joke. Denis didn't dare forget.
>
> But players don't remember Matt for tactics. They remember the last thing he used to say before every match, which was 'Go out and enjoy yourselves, go and entertain.' At half-time, if things weren't going well, he'd say: 'You're not playing like you can. Just change the play.' He said nothing complicated, and he would only speak for a minute. He never

shouted and bawled and very rarely lost his temper. If there was a problem out there, he talked you through it, calmly.

He was thorough and his methods worked. But in the mid-sixties it was all changing. The modern game was getting more defensive-minded, with more emphasis on set plays – what the professionals call restarts. When I mentioned restarts, I remember Paddy Crerand saying: 'What the bloody hell is that?' They all know now.

I had coached for the Football Association, I was the England youth team manager and I had worked with the 1966 World Cup squad, so I had learned from Alf Ramsey. I was also trainer to the England Under-23 side for a time, working with Bill Nicholson, and I had played under Ron Greenwood in the England Under-23 team. I wasn't blinkered in my views, whereas some of the United players had been indoctrinated exclusively in Matt Busby's style. Under Matt, United were attack-orientated and relied on the players' intelligence, rather than coaching, when it came to defence. Teams like Leeds were more thorough on the defensive side.

Approaching his first season, 1969–70, McGuinness knew better than anyone that reinforcements were required, but he found himself baulked, rather than aided, by the *éminence grise* in the general manager's office. He had wanted to buy Mick Mills, Colin Todd and Malcolm Macdonald, three rising young stars who were destined to play for England, but in each case Busby withheld the backing he needed. During two seasons in which a flagging team cried out for invigoration, McGuinness was allowed to sign just one player, and then one not his own choice. 'We needed a replacement for Bill Foulkes,' he says, 'and I allowed Matt and Jimmy Murphy to talk me into taking Ian Ure. I had gone to watch Ure play for Arsenal, and I have to say I wasn't a great admirer, but we did need a centre-half because Big

Bill had had it by then. In the third match of the season, at home to Southampton, we lost 4–1 and Ron Davies, who Bill was marking, scored all four. I had wanted Colin Todd to play off the centre-half, with someone else doing the stopper's job, but rather than get no one I went Matt's way and we got Ure.' It was a bad buy. Ure, approaching his thirtieth birthday when he signed, was to make just forty-seven appearances for United before he was packed off to St Mirren in the old Scottish Second Division on a free transfer.

Relying on the same old faces, United started the new season with an ominous run of six games without a win, failing to score in four of them, and at once there was concern all round. If Busby did not have sufficient faith in his protégé to back his judgement in the transfer market, how could the players be expected to have confidence in him?

It was George Best who rescued McGuinness from the stickiest of starts. Sensing that a likeable, thoroughly decent man was not being given a fair chance by some of the older players, George decided to do something about it – and was good enough to deliver. He rattled in thirteen goals in fourteen games between 30 August and 20 October, by which time a run of six wins and three draws in ten League matches had hoisted United up to eighth place in the First Division. That was to be the extent of the revival. They had found their level. Best and Charlton were good enough to beat anyone when the fancy took them, but both were becoming increasingly frustrated and demoralized by the club's failure to improve a team which now, on occasions, featured individuals who were plainly not up to the standard expected of a Manchester United player. Paul Edwards, Steve James and Carlo Sartori, all of whom appeared in 1969–70, would have been lucky to get in the reserves five years earlier. Others were coming to the end of their natural span. Foulkes played three times that season before retiring, Shay Brennan was pensioned off on a free transfer after his last eight League games, and Stiles and Law, both increasingly injury prone, managed just eighteen First Division appearances between them.

On a good day United could still rise to the occasion, but their collective shortcomings prevented them from sustaining form long enough to make an impression in the League. Better suited to the one-off requirements of tournament football, they reached the semi-finals of both the FA and the League Cups, which saw George Best in classic Jekyll and Hyde mode. In the first leg of the League Cup semi-final against Manchester City, at Maine Road, he was booked for dissent when a free-kick was awarded against him, and knocked the ball out of the referee's hands at the final whistle. This petulant piece of nonsense was captured on television, causing a media-inspired furore, and when the referee, Jack Taylor, mentioned it in his report to the Football Association, it brought Best a four-week suspension and a £100 fine. Whether or not the gesture was serious enough to warrant the charge of bringing the game into disrepute is a moot point. What is certain is that the FA's punishment was draconian, and would be contested by m'learned friends in identical circumstances today.

Thirty years ago footballers and football clubs were less litigious, and George served his ban before returning in February, when his eagerness to make up for lost time was intensified by suggestions in the media, and elsewhere, that the team, unbeaten in his absence, was better off without him. Northampton Town, of the old Fourth Division, fancied themselves as giant-killers when they were drawn at home to Manchester United in the fifth round of the FA Cup, but the embarrassment was all theirs, George scoring six in an 8–2 rout which remains essential viewing every time television dips into the archive marked 'Best'. Even allowing for the standard of the opposition it was a remarkable, virtuoso performance, the maestro running through his full bamboozling repertoire of dribbles, swerves and feints, his mesmeric dexterity capped by finishing of the highest order.

Everyone was impressed, not least the Prime Minister, Harold Wilson, who had taken to writing George fan letters, and invited him to No. 10 Downing Street on 2 March. Unfortunately for United, and McGuinness in particular, 'The Genius', as the *Observer* called him at Northampton, almost immediately took on the prefix 'flawed'. The semi-finals of the FA Cup paired United with Leeds, and after a goalless bore at Hillsborough, the tie was replayed at Villa Park.

For George, cloistered away in the team's Birmingham hotel, anticipation soon gave way to boredom, from which he sought relief with a girl he had met and chatted up on the stairs. McGuinness, who had taken to patrolling the corridors to guard against such debilitating distractions, was apoplectic when he caught them *in flagrante delicto* and wanted to send Best home, but Matt Busby counselled against it and, as usual, the Great Man had his way. McGuinness says: 'George didn't have a girl in his room, he was in hers, but hers or not, I went into that room and I was blazing. I was really furious with him. It was the one time he really let me down badly. Matt persuaded me to let him play and he had an absolute nightmare. We drew 0–0 again and George had the chance to win it, but fell over the ball in front of goal.'

Nowhere does gossip travel faster than through football dressing rooms, and Leeds were aware that George had been caught 'at it' before the game. Johnny Giles did not approve, and made his point the way he knew best. Forcibly.

> We'd drawn at Hillsborough in a terrible match. Don Revie had Paul Reaney marking George and Paul Madeley on Bobby Charlton, and that distorted the shape of our team because George didn't stay on the left wing in those days, he used to go wandering all over the place, and Reaney wasn't sure whether to go with him or pass him on to the nearest man. So it is fair to say that George had us concerned before the

replay. We needn't have worried. He was caught in the afternoon with a bird, and was in no state to give of his best in the game.

I had a go at George that night, because we'd heard what had happened. It was to our advantage, but I must say that as a professional I was disgusted by it. I'm no angel, but that wasn't the way to behave before such an important game, and I gave George a bit of a kicking for it. He complained afterwards that I'd called him unprofessional about ten times during the match, and kicked him each time, which was true, but he didn't tell the whole story. He didn't give the reason. I remember on the night he had a good chance to score when he was clean through and stepped on the ball, which was totally out of character.

The feeling among the Leeds lads was that what he'd done wasn't on. It was a contradiction of professionalism. George said I was having a go at him for being unprofessional and at the same time I was kicking him, which was not very professional either, and that's true. But he was the one who let his mates down. For the third match, which was played at Bolton, Don Revie said: 'We're going to play the way we want to play. We can forget about man-marking Charlton and Best.' As it turned out, George played outside-left on the night, Paul Reaney took care of him as usual, and we won 1–0.

Losing two semi-finals – the other to Manchester City, of all clubs – was a colossal disappointment, but finishing eighth in the League was an improvement of three places on the previous season and, all things considered, McGuinness had not done badly in his first season in charge. George Best was the club's leading scorer for the third year in succession with fifteen goals in thirty-seven League games, and twenty-five in all competitions. Charlton and Kidd weighed in with a dozen apiece, and the new coach should have been reasonably pleased with his start. Instead, he knew he was in trouble:

> When I got the job, I'd left too many grey areas. Matt still had all the power. He'd said he was standing down, but he hadn't surrendered control. Matt had told me: 'We'll call you chief coach, but you're the team manager really. It's just to protect you from the boardroom side of things. I'll look after that, you don't have to worry about it.' It was an unusual set-up at that time, and I had only a general idea, not an A to Z picture, of my responsibilities. That's where I slipped up. I should have had the job properly defined.
>
> If I had been stronger, not just in terms of my position but in the way I expressed my views, perhaps I would have got the new players I wanted – not to take over from the senior ones, but to be ready to take over when the time came. To lift the older ones and carry them a bit sometimes, because Charlton and Law weren't turning it on game after game like they used to. We definitely needed new players, but I wasn't strong enough to stand up to Matt and force the issue.

At this stage, despite George Best's mounting dissatisfaction at the way the club was being run and his increasingly dissolute lifestyle, McGuinness did not see him as a major problem:

> George was just one of the lads in my first season in charge. He was a bit wayward, but he had not reached what I call his daft period. I was annoyed and I did feel let down when I found him with the girl before the semi-final, but as far as I know that was the only occasion in my first season when his behaviour off the field left him unable to produce on it. Basically, he was a nice lad who just had this weakness for the nightclub life. He got away with it so long because in

training he worked harder than anyone. Mind you, he had to, burning the candle at both ends like he did.

McGuinness prefers to gloss over Best's lack of discipline, and the club's failure to instil it, but by 1969 the rot had set in and he was starting to make headlines for the wrong reasons. He was still easily the best player in the country, but drinking on the nightshift was beginning to undermine his constitution, and therefore his performance, and too often he was operating well under optimum effectiveness. Worried by his late-night carousing, and some of the company he was keeping, Matt Busby suggested that he should 'find a nice girl' and 'settle down'. The girl he chose was not quite what old Matt had in mind.

On a pre-season trip with United to Copenhagen, George was asked for his autograph by a statuesque blonde and 'fell in love with a pair of knockers'. The girl was with her boyfriend, a rather large butcher, at the time, so all she got was a signature, but back home the great Lothario could not get the striking Viking out of his mind and made an appeal, via the Danish press, for his 'Danish dream girl' to get in touch. He received a sackful of replies, and identified twenty-one-year-old Eva Haraldsted from Aarhus by the photograph she sent. George invited her over, met her at Heathrow and took her to Mrs Fullaway's in Manchester where he proposed many things, including marriage. Busby was aghast, then relieved. The engagement was off by November, George Best not the marrying kind. 'I soon got fed up with her,' he said. The lovely Eva sued for breach of promise, prompting George to make an out-of-court settlement of £500 the following April – 'and I've never paid for it since'.

It was not the end of the story. Subsequently, on a night out, Best and Pat Crerand bumped into George's erstwhile fiancée in the company of two brothers in Blinkers nightclub, and an acrimonious exchange resulted in Crerand being accused of assaulting one of the men and causing grievous bodily harm to the other. He was cleared on both charges, but it would be a long time before Matt Busby suggested that George Best go looking for female companionship again.

There were other distractions. Having bought out Mike Summerbee's interest in his first boutique in Sale, George opened another, 'George Best Rogue', in September 1969. He also acquired a one-third share in a racehorse, Slim Gypsy, in company with Ian Walker, the Newmarket trainer, and Everton's Alan Ball. And then there was the drinking. Best horrified Busby and McGuinness, who had been trying to play down the problem, by giving an interview to the *Daily Sketch* in which he was quoted as saying: 'I've been playing badly for a couple of months now, due mostly to late nights and drink. I didn't think about it at the beginning. I just knew I was fed up with everyone and everything around me. So I went on going out every night and drinking.' Looking back, George says 1969 was the year when he started to lose control, and the desire to regain it. 'Whatever he tells people, poor Wilf had all sorts of problems with me because I was starting to miss training and generally screwing around.' Busby said: 'I'll sort him out if it's the last thing I do.'

Belatedly granted the title 'team manager' in the summer of 1970, McGuinness started the clear-out everyone knew was needed. Bill Foulkes retired, after eighteen years of First Division football, Denis Law was transfer listed at £60,000 and nine players were released, including Shay Brennan who, at thirty-three, might have expected it but still took the decision hard. Best friends, McGuinness had been best man at Brennan's wedding, and vice versa. Now they weren't to speak for years. 'I wanted to make changes because I knew they were needed,' McGuinness says. Again, however, he was hamstrung by Matt Busby's 'court of appeal', as the golf course came to be known. 'I left out Alex Stepney, Paddy Crerand and Willie Morgan. The next thing I knew, they were making up a four at golf with Sir Matt! I don't know if the players were going behind my back to see Matt in his office, but they definitely had contact away from the club, which didn't help.'

McGuinness knew he needed a good start to his second season. Instead, United lost their opening match, at home to the Giles-inspired Leeds, were held 0–0 by Chelsea at Old Trafford and were thumped 4–0 at Arsenal. After three games they had one point and no goals. A 2–0 win at Burnley, Law scoring both, held out the promise of better things, but another 4–0 drubbing, this time from Bobby Robson's Ipswich, was followed by defeat at home to Crystal Palace, fomenting unrest in a dressing room riven by factional infighting.

A terrible sequence of eight games without a win between 21 November and Boxing Day brought matters to a head. Again a good cup run had kept the willing Wilf hanging in there, but in the space of eleven days United were beaten 4–1 at home to Manchester City and lost in the semi-finals of the League Cup to a Third Division team, Aston Villa, and that was that. The older players, Law and Charlton included, had been to Busby to say that the new regime wasn't working. Now they had their way. On 28 December 1970, after just eighteen months in nominal charge, McGuinness was sacked as manager. One of his critics in the dressing room was reported, anonymously, in the *Sunday Times* as saying: 'The problem for Wilf was he had no personality. He did not understand that the team he was controlling needed handling in a special way. We had won the European Cup and were being told what to do by a man who had never been anywhere. People go on about us buying our way out of trouble, but I believe we would have been screwed even if Wilf had had a million quid to spend.'

Busby, who had been enjoying the best of both worlds – power without responsibility – stepped into the firing line again with the utmost reluctance. He said: 'I did not want to take charge of the team again, but the directors asked me to. At my age, I feel I have had enough of managerial worries. I feel very sorry for Wilf, who was appointed on my recommendation. He may have been a wee bit raw.' To say McGuinness was bitter is an understatement:

> I was shafted by some of the players, and by Matt Busby's willingness to listen to them all the time. They were going to him with this constant drip-drip of complaints. It was: 'Wilf's not up to it, boss,' or 'The lads aren't happy,' then 'He's lost it with the lads,' and 'It's not going to work.' I was entitled to more support. I expected Matt to tell them: 'Hold on a bit, he knows what he's doing, give him time and it will come right.' I thought he'd stand by me.
>
> When Matt called me in and told me it wasn't working, I wasn't going to make it easy for him. I argued with him for two hours. I made sure I put all my points across. I said: 'I thought we were in this together? I've done my part. If I'd got more help from you, if I'd been allowed to sign the players I wanted, I might have done better. If you give me time, it could still come right.' Oh, I battled all right, but it was no good. He just said: 'I'm sorry, but you're on your way,' and they announced it the next day. I felt so hurt – anyone would have been in that situation. They would have felt, like I did, that it wasn't their fault.

Adding insult to injury, Busby offered McGuinness his old job back, as coach to the reserves. Aware that he would be a laughing stock among the players if he accepted, his answer was brief – the second word was 'off'. 'I wouldn't say it was a cruel streak in Matt, but I didn't like it. I had been very hurt, and I wanted to hurt him. I told him I was going to tell the press everything. I didn't do it, but I let on that I would.'

McGuinness left the club that had been his whole life for seventeen years a few weeks later, after negotiating a pay-off on a contract which had eighteen months to run. His distress took him to the verge of a nervous breakdown, a good head of hair falling out within a matter of months. He enjoyed brief success in Greece, first with Aris Salonika, then with Panachaiki, whom he took into Europe for the first time, then came back to work in the backwoods of York and Hull City, where his coaching career petered out. 'The experience made me ill at the time,' he says, 'but now I remember only the good things about Manchester United.'

It is through those same rose-tinted spectacles that he chooses to remember George Best's matchwinning efforts on his behalf, forgetting the fact that by failing to turn up for training on Christmas Day 1970, to prepare for the match at Derby the following afternoon, he added to the impression of dereliction which brought about the change of management three days later.

> George was a good worker by inclination. Of course I would have liked more discipline from him, but it just wasn't in his make-up. Still, George had some great games for me. I was manager when he scored a fantastic goal against Chelsea, dribbling past 'Chopper' Harris, who kept trying to kick him, and Marvin Hinton before taking the ball round Peter Bonetti and sticking it in the net. And it was in my time that he beat Tottenham's Pat Jennings at the Stretford End with that famous chip. He produced so many great games and great goals for me. He was still turning it on and I was happy enough with that. He let me down a few times, by not turning up for training, or with girls in his room, but he was worse with other managers. In my time, the problems tended to be with birds rather than booze. He was a great lad, but he had this weakness. He followed his dick. But the drinking, and the absences, were always worse under Sir Matt.

As the Great Man was about to be reminded.

A week after Busby's reappointment as manager, Best travelled to London to appear before an FA disciplinary commission. He turned up ninety minutes late and was sick in the lift at Lancaster Gate, pleading that he was 'unwell'. Shades of Geoffrey Barnard.

chapter twelve

Alcoholism is a disease, and it is impossible to pinpoint exactly when George Best fell ill, when enjoying a good night out became the compulsive need for a drink or two before he could face the new day. His own best estimate is around 1972, but he was halfway down the slippery slope two years earlier.

George is not the first Irishman to seek the meaning of life, or refuge from it, in the bottom of a glass and, never short of an excuse, he calls it 'The Irish Problem'. Like another Ulsterman, Alex Higgins (the snooker player, with whom he does not get on well), the most celebrated British footballer of the modern era is a classic case. All the characteristic, paradoxical symptoms of the alcoholic are there: a huge ego but low self-esteem; the party animal who loves to be the centre of attention but who, back in the privacy of his hotel room or at home, does not think much of himself.

George first started drinking as a seventeen-year-old when, without celebrity to smooth his passage, he needed Dutch courage to chat up girls who would laugh at his heavy Irish accent. Later, he used vodka to turn him into the extrovert personality he thought his public expected him to be. 'Everybody, it seemed, was happy to drink with George Best, and who was I to disappoint them? It didn't take too many drinks to become the Georgie Best they wanted to drink with.' He began to drink heavily because he thought he was inadequate – not as a footballer, he always thought he was well named when it came to that, but as a person. His alcoholism was, and remains, a personality disorder. He used spirits as Popeye used spinach, to transform himself into George Best, superhero.

In mitigation, surely any young man would have had his head turned, and character changed, by the pressures George Best was subjected to in the Swinging Sixties, when he went from gauche, anonymous teenager to football's first pop star almost overnight. As the first of the breed, he had no precedents to learn from, no help from parents or employers who, taken by surprise, were nonplussed by the phenomenon. Jimmy Greaves, a recovering alcoholic and playing contemporary, who understands George better than most, says: 'When a pop star sees teenage girls screaming at him, it probably makes sense. He is their age, good-looking and spending a fortune on appearance and clothes to get exactly that sort of adulation. But when a seventeen-year-old, fresh from the youth team, sees men old enough to be his father go weak at the knees, it's a different emotion altogether. That is the pressure I played under, and the pressure George Best played under.'

George has never really liked the taste of alcohol, drinking because he enjoys the ambience, and the effect, to be found at the bar. In his early youth team days he discovered that beer or lager bloated him without producing the quick 'buzz' he could get from shorts. Vodka became his drink, but it had to be sweetened with lemonade.

From 1965, when he joined Manchester City, Mike Summerbee became George's running mate for regular nocturnal excursions. Summerbee insists normal training was sufficient to run off the effects of a late night in any of the nightclubs that were proliferating in Manchester at the time. It was the casinos, where another aspect of Best's addictive personality was surfacing, and Phyllis's, the all-night drinking den, that had him, and others, worried. Summerbee would go with George to Phyllis's for a last drink after a night out, but not often, and never on his own, as George would. There was enough booze, and birds, to be had in the clubs that were legit, he felt. Malcolm Wagner, a friend to both men for more than thirty years, agrees:

> I think the Phyllis's run was very, very bad for George. You'd had your fill by the time you'd done the nightclubs, and then to go on to Phyllis's until four o'clock in the morning, and come home with the birds singing, wasn't good for anyone. All you would do in Phyllis's is drink, there was nothing else happening. I went a few times, but it wasn't really my bag. I'd had enough to drink by two in the morning. But it became a habit for George, when the clubs had shut.
>
> That's when all the talk started about hangers-on who were a bad influence on him, but his mates – his real mates – never went to Phyllis's as a regular thing. People used to say to us: 'Why are you leading him astray? Can't you see it's affecting him?' So we all made a pact that we wouldn't go, and that we would try to discourage him from going, but it was a waste of time. George has always done just what he wants to do. Persuasion has no effect.

Summerbee says the extent of Best's celebrity had to be seen to be believed, and was enough to turn a saint to drink. 'George became an icon in the sixties, the fifth Beatle. He was as famous as them, renowned all over the world because of his ability as a footballer. He was also a good-looking lad, trendy and smart, and the girls loved him. All that made it very difficult to stay on the straight and narrow. I was in a position to see just how difficult. I've been in George's company when girls have been queuing up, swimming all over him, and it's very hard to cope with that sort of adulation so young. I think he used to drink to help him cope with all the attention.'

By 1967 George had the key to his favourite pub, the Brown Bull, and could get a drink at any time of day or night, but although this easy access to, and propensity for, alcohol was obviously a cause for concern, Matt Busby contented himself that his young star was training like a Trojan and playing like a god. At that stage, given proper guidance and the sort of counselling from which Paul Gascoigne, Tony Adams and Paul Merson benefited a generation on, it is just conceivable that George Best might have been dragged back from the abyss. Alcoholics Anonymous literature states: 'We believe that early in our drinking careers most of us could have stopped drinking, but the difficulty is that few alcoholics have enough desire to stop while there is yet time.' Unfortunately, counselling was not available thirty years ago, and between 1968 and 1970 a combination of circumstances saw to it that for George Best there would be no turning back.

George always says it was the sharp downturn in Manchester United's fortunes, more than anything, that pushed him into the clutches of the demon drink, but other factors were no less, and possibly more, influential. Mike Summerbee was a kindred spirit in terms of his sybaritic lifestyle but, three years Best's senior, he knew just how far a professional sportsman could go without endangering his fitness, and when that time came he went home, and usually prevailed upon George to do the same. In September 1968 Summerbee married his girlfriend, Tina, sold his interest in the first of George's boutiques, and a restraining influence was lost. There was another significant wedding that year, David Sadler's, which meant that in a matter of months George was deprived of the fellow pro who told him when to go home to his digs and the sensible team-mate who offered him nothing but good advice when he got there. Summerbee is certain that his disappearance from Best's social circle had a detrimental effect:

> Because I wasn't a hanger-on, I was a friend. Without me and Dave Sadler, he was at the mercy of non-footballing influences, and although George always denies it, I know there

> were a few people who never put their hand in their pocket when he was around, and who used him in more ways than that. When George Best was there, there was always more than one girl around, and once he'd had his pick, the others had their chance, made more attractive by their association with him.
>
> He didn't need those people, he needed a stabilizing influence. His father, Dickie, is a superb man, but although his mum was a lovely woman, she was too similar to George, and Dickie had his hands full there.

Here, Summerbee has touched on the one aspect of George Best's life that the man himself considers truly tragic. The abbreviation of a coruscating career pales into insignificance in comparison with his neglect of his mother, and the awful death she died in his absence. He has never forgiven himself, and a strong sense of guilt played a major part in his descent into dissipation.

By 1970 Ann Best was an alcoholic. She had not taken a drink until she was 40, when her firstborn was establishing himself in the Manchester United first team. Now, at 45, she was a slave to it. A shy, private woman, George says she hated the attention which came with her son's celebrity and, like him, sought solace in the opium of the masses. Her devoted husband, Dickie, who has never remarried, prefers to blame some 'bad company' she fell into at work. She died in 1978, more of which later, but Dickie says George first became aware of her 'problem' when he made a rare return to the family home for his parents' twenty-fifth wedding anniversary in June 1970. After that, his visits became even more infrequent, and another stabilizing influence had all but gone out of his life.

To summarize, at the end of 1970, when Sir Matt Busby reluctantly resumed the managership of Manchester United, the favourite he had indulged for so long was in danger of losing the plot. Suffering, almost certainly, from a clinical depression rooted in footballing problems and accentuated by his mother's illness, George Best was lurching towards full-blown alcoholism on two and three-day benders which sometimes left him incapable of getting out of bed in the morning to train. The problem hit Busby like a blitz, his half-hearted response leaving the rest of the team complaining about one law for Best, and another for others. On Christmas Day, three days before the demotion of Wilf McGuinness, George had failed to turn up to train in preparation for the Boxing Day match at Derby. McGuinness said the truant should be sent home when he reported for the game the following day, and Busby agreed, but then had second thoughts. Best was fined fifty pounds instead, and duly scored in a 4–4 draw. Decision justified? Hardly. The question posed by David Meek of the *Manchester Evening News* – 'Should expediency have come before discipline?' – seems even more apposite now than it did at the time. Too often, throughout Best's career, that was the way of it.

Less than a fortnight later, on 4 January 1971, George was to travel to London with Busby to appear before an FA disciplinary commission after accumulating three bookings, the third for a tackle which left Glyn Pardoe of Manchester City with a double fracture of his right leg. Due to meet his manager at Manchester's Piccadilly station, Best was hung-over and unable to get out of bed in time to catch the train, so Busby travelled alone. The hearing was put back ninety minutes, and when its subject finally arrived, pleading that he had been 'unwell', he was fined a record £250 and given a suspended six-week ban.

It was getting worse. Within four days George Best's crisis became public property when he missed training, and another train. By this time no one was too surprised when he opted out of the Friday session before United's match at Chelsea on 9 January, but Busby did expect to see him at the station, to travel to London with the team, the following day. Again the manager was left scouring the platform in vain, like a scene from *Brief Encounter*. Exasperated, he summoned John Aston as a replacement and left word that Best need not bother travelling later, he was not required. But wanted by United or not, George did journey to London that afternoon to see his new girlfriend, the Irish actress Sinead Cusack.

Forty-eight hours later, they were still holed up together in Miss Cusack's Islington flat, besieged by a phalanx of television crews, photographers, journalists and rubber-neckers, all beside themselves to know what was going on. TV news gave regular updates on events at the 'love nest', while on the pavement gangs of juveniles chanted 'We want George' and 'Georgie Best is on the nest.' What was going on behind the curtains, away from the prurient, prying lenses? 'Sinead was a classy lady and a good friend,' George says. 'I was in a bit of a state, and she was good to talk to. Mostly, that's what we did – just talk.'

Eventually, on the Monday, Malcolm Mooney charged in like the cavalry to lift the siege, but even now nothing went right for the fugitive. A car breakdown on the return journey meant George was six hours late for the dressing down at which Busby suspended him for two weeks, without pay. He imposed the punishment with a heavy heart. Much later he said: 'I don't think any other single thing that happened to the boy brought home to me his problem as much as that did. All right, he had been silly and irresponsible, but for three days and nights he was front page and back page news. Cameras watched all night for him. He was the top story on TV news. I sat there and wondered how he was to survive it all.'

For a weekend 'on the nest', it was all taken terribly seriously. On 12 January *The Times*, in a leader headed 'The Price of Indiscipline', thundered:

> To the outside observer, the suspension of a fortnight imposed by Manchester United on George Best may seem a

> remarkably lenient punishment for an episode which has so harmed the reputation of the game, the club and the player. Such leniency may be understandable, and it may be justified in individual cases by circumstances of which the outside observer is not aware. But in the long run, football will retain its present hold over the general public only if discipline can be restored, on and off the field. Nothing so damages any great sport over a period of time as for attention to be diverted consistently away from the game itself to the storms and tempests on the fringe.

The dear old *Guardian*, at least, could be relied upon to keep a sense of perspective. In a lovely, droll leader, it teased:

> Now that famed soccer idol George ('I was wrong') Best had made his peace with doyen manager ('We start from scratch again') Busby, what are we to make of Monday's Islington flat drama and business associate Malcolm Mooney's 11th hour M1 car dash? Before these incidents sink again into the obscurity from which they should never have emerged, let us wring what agony remains from stormy petrel Best's tiff with award-winning United's world-renowned Sir ('Mr Football') Matt.
>
> Enquirers at the 23-year-old player's £35,000 Bramhall, Cheshire dream house got a brusque 'no comment' late last night when they asked whether the Babes' ebullient outside-left had missed three London-bound expresses accidentally or on purpose. The boutique-owning soccer wizard was not available to reporters. Meanwhile, we can reveal that blonde Irish actor's daughter Sinead (say Shin-aid) Cusack was at dinner with successful Manchester businessman Best on Sunday night, prior to the practice session at Manchester United's The Cliff training ground, where Best's dramatic Monday morning non-appearance led stern-faced Sir Matt to invoke a two-week suspension of the star. Later, *Guardian*-

> reader Sinead took in milk from the crowd-thronged doorstep of her Noel Road, Islington flat. '(Bearded international) George (Best) is very upset,' confided Miss Cusack, 22. Best ('I've apologized') sat yesterday at the right of 61-year-old Freeman of Manchester Sir Matt and said: 'It was completely wrong and I know it.'
>
> Thus ended a seven-day saga culminating in the 'Pimpernel' Ulsterman's police-escorted departure from the flat of girlfriend Sinead in a white Jaguar. 'Indiscipline', reproved London's prestigious *Times* newspaper. 'Tedium' says the (former Manchester) *Guardian*.

United won 2–1 at Chelsea without their 'pimpernel', ending a run of eight games without a win and prompting suggestions in the press that they were now a better side in his absence. It was paper talk, patent nonsense. Even in a mental mess, Best was still Busby's most potent weapon, and he knew it. Despite his occasional absences from training, George missed only two League games in 1970–1, when he was United's leading scorer again, with eighteen goals in forty League appearances, twenty-one in all competitions. As soon as he had served his suspension, he was restored to the team and, with results improving, manager and errant genius joked together about the Cusack incident when they met over drinks at George's housewarming party in February.

After ten years at Mrs Fullaway's, and at the age of twenty-four, he had decided it was time he had a home of his own. His initial preference was for an old country cottage on the moors outside Manchester, but he has always found it hard to say 'No', and he allowed himself to be talked round by an architect he met, Fraser Crane, who wanted to build his 'dream house' and was looking for someone to commission it. Courtesy of Mr Crane, and at a cost of £35,000, George acquired an ultra-modern bachelor pad which, with its prominent white tiling, was likened to a public convenience by everyone who saw it. It had a lovely view of the Pennines but, with its open-plan design and panoramic windows, it provided an even better view of George Best, and within days of him moving in the local Arthur Daley was bussing day trippers out of Manchester to gawp. They stole fish out of the pond, which had to be replenished every week, and star-struck girls camped in his garden, some equipped with binoculars.

Inside, it was a futuristic nightmare. James Bond meets Frank Spencer. Every conceivable gadget was operated from a console in the chimney breast, but crossed wires turned the procedure into Whitehall farce. When George pressed the button marked 'Lights' the curtains opened with the occupant undraped. The sunken bath he had ordered filled automatically, often without bidding, but never with more than two inches of water. The *News of the World* ran a competition to name the property and, before the days of *Fawlty Towers*, a Miss E. Bardsley of Manchester scooped the prize for the imaginative 'Che Sera'. Another paper, the *Daily Express*, paid for the housewarming party in return for exclusive rights, and were left with pictures resembling the Royal Command Performance on a bad year – Tommy Trinder, Bob Monkhouse, Lionel Blair, etc. George kept the house for two years, but hardly lived in it, returning to Mrs Fullaway's in January 1972. It was sold to Pat O'Dwyer, a former trench digger, the following December for its original price, £35,000.

On the field, Manchester United perked up considerably under Busby's interim management, the players pleased to have 'The Old Man' back at the helm. Best's mood certainly brightened, and he celebrated his return to the side after the Cusack affair by scoring six goals in nine games, United winning six of them.

One of George's goals during this purple patch features in his all-time top ten. It came in a 2–1 home win against Tottenham – his favourite opposition – and was scored to the embarrassment of his great friend and Northern Ireland team-mate, Pat Jennings.

Playing at Old Trafford for the first time since his suspension, and with his father Dickie in attendance, George was determined to put on a show, and it was just like old times. He destroyed the team he had come to regard as his 'bunnies', opening the scoring after fifteen minutes with a marvellously deft piece of finishing. Hampered by his centre-half, Peter Collins, and by Alan Gowling's challenge, Jennings made an uncharacteristically weak punch at the ball in the air. It flew straight to Best, some ten yards out, but there were five Spurs players, including the retreating goalkeeper, blocking the path to goal. No problem to the Merlin of the eighteen-yard box. One wave of the magic wand that was his right leg and he spirited them all out of the game with a sumptuous chip, the trajectory of which utterly defeated Jennings and Phil Beal, who had scampered back to the goal-line to cover.

Of the nineteen matches played in Busby's second term United won eleven and lost six, again finishing eighth in the First Division. The second half of the season was an improvement on the way they had been heading under Wilf McGuinness, but not quite the return to the good old days that George had in mind. 'The players welcomed Matt back,' he says, 'but we knew he didn't want the job. And by this time changes of manager weren't needed so much as new players. It didn't matter who was in charge, the squad just wasn't good enough to win anything. As usual, there had been a lot of talk about new signings coming, but nobody did.' By 1971, United had bought three players – Alex Stepney, Willie Morgan and Ian Ure – in six years. There was a two-year gap after Ure, who was bad, but not that bad. In the circumstances, Best says, any improvement could only be temporary. 'Things picked up for a while, and I think some of us thought: The boss is back, now it's all going to change, but we were kidding ourselves. Sir Matt was getting older, and he'd been through such a lot. You don't like to say his heart wasn't in it, because Matt Busby's heart *was* Manchester United, but his time had passed.'

George thought he had hit on a way forward, for himself and for the team. He went to Busby and asked to be made captain, suggesting that the side should be rebuilt around him. He went away with a flea in his ear. 'The boss told me to leave the running of the team to him. He said that was his job and I should get on with mine. He said I was not responsible enough to be captain. I said: "Make me captain, and I will be responsible." I think he did toy with the idea afterwards, but it never happened. It might not have solved the whole problem, but I think the responsibility would have helped me.'

Busby was more interested in finding a new manager. When he stood down again, at the end of the season, he knew there could be no more pussyfooting, no more protégés. He had to go for the best, which is what he did. In the summer of 1971, when United went head-hunting again, Jock Stein was celebrating a sixth Scottish championship in a row with Celtic. During that sequence he had also beaten United, by a year, in the race to become the first British club to win the European Cup. A big man was needed, and they came no bigger than Jock Stein. Busby sounded out a mutual friend and confidant, Pat Crerand, about his availability. Crerand says:

> Jock nearly came. Everyone knew that Matt was standing down at the end of the season, and he had spoken to me about the job, and who could do it. I remember Celtic were playing Ajax in the quarter-finals of the European Cup in 1971 and I said to Matt: 'You know, Jock Stein has not got a contract at Celtic Park. No Celtic manager has ever had one.' Matt said he hadn't realized that, and I told him I was going up to Glasgow on the Wednesday for the match against Ajax, and that I'd see if Jock would speak to me. Celtic won 1–0 at

Hampden Park [Celtic Park was being refurbished at the time], and after the game I walked over to Jock's house, which was just behind Hampden. When I got there, Jock said his son, George, was up in bed, and would I go and see him. George was only a young kid at the time, and he was unhappy because Celtic had been knocked out on aggregate. He was a big United fan, and I said: 'The reason I'm here is that Matt wants your old man to become manager.' He loved that. 'Fantastic,' he said.

Then Jock came up, and I told him the main reason I'd come to the house. He was totally stunned. Jock's daughter, Ray, came in and thought it was marvellous, but then his wife, Jean, marched up the stairs and gave us all a right bollocking. 'I've got guests downstairs, and you lot have been up here for three-quarters of an hour,' she said. 'It's the height of bad manners.' I said: 'Jean, Matt wants to speak to Jock about the manager's job at Old Trafford.' She didn't like that. 'Pat,' she said, 'I'm a Celtic supporter, I don't want to leave Glasgow.'

Anyway, we fixed it up. Jock travelled down to meet Matt and the chairman, Louis Edwards. He met Matt again, in a petrol station near Haydock racecourse after Liverpool had played Leeds in the semi-finals of the UEFA Cup, and Jock shook hands on it and said he was coming. Then two days later he changed his mind, and said he wasn't. We were playing Chelsea in London and on the train to London Matt came up to me and said: 'Your pal has let me down. He's not coming.' Matt thought Jock had played along to get more money out of Celtic, but I know he wasn't doing that. He wanted to come to Old Trafford, but his wife talked him out of it. They both lived to regret it, and I know the club did. He would have been the perfect manager for Manchester United at that time.

Don Revie, whose pragmatic, no-holds-barred management had seen Leeds replace United as the dominant force in English football, was Busby's second choice, but 'The Don' could not be prised from Elland Road. After him, the usual suspects were rounded up, but talk of Brian Clough, Ron Greenwood and Don Howe came to nothing, and when the appointment was made it was comparatively low-key.

Frank O'Farrell, of Leicester City, was not the household name the players had been expecting. He had taken his first League club, Torquay, from the Fourth Division to the Third and had restored Leicester to the First Division, after suffering relegation in his first season in charge. He had also guided Leicester to the 1969 FA Cup Final, where they lost 1–0 to Manchester City. It was not a bad record, but Manchester United was a different world for this soft-spoken son of an Irish train driver who had started his own working life shovelling coal on the footplate before moving from his native Cork to play for West Ham. To succeed he needed a fair wind, and at least he had no general manager to report to. Stung by suggestions that his interference had denied McGuinness a fair chance, Matt Busby swapped his overseer's job for a seat on the board.

Big name or not, O'Farrell, who was forty-two, made a supercharged start. A 2–0 victory at home to the early pacemakers, Sheffield United, and a 3–0 win at Huddersfield put United on top of the League in October 1971 for the first time for three years. Best scored in both games, a spectacular shot on the run against the Blades of Sheffield followed by a soaring header at Leeds Road, and on 16 October, before Derby County played at Old Trafford, an appreciative O'Farrell was presented with the Manager of the Month award for September. United celebrated with a 1–0 win, George scoring for the third match in a row. He made it four in four with another winner at Newcastle, and after fourteen games United had lost just once. By the middle of

December, after rattling in seventeen goals in five matches, they were five points clear at the top. Required to play two home fixtures at neutral venues because of a knife-throwing incident at Old Trafford the previous February, they won them both, beating Arsenal at Anfield and West Bromwich Albion at the Victoria Ground, Stoke.

George Best had perked up dramatically, and was scoring freely again, with hat-tricks against West Ham and Southampton. One of the many components of his discontent had been the iniquity of the wage structure at Old Trafford, which had Denis Law and Bobby Charlton both paid considerably more than him. George had raised the subject with Matt Busby, and was assured that the anomaly would be rectified, but it never was. Now O'Farrell put it right, raising Best's wages from £170 a week to £230, the same as Law and Charlton. All three were earning less than Alan Ball, whose new contract with Arsenal was worth £250 a week.

George, however, was happy with his lot – briefly. It was never all sweetness and light, and in O'Farrell's second match, at Chelsea, he had been sent off. Norman Burtenshaw banished him for 'foul and abusive language', but he was cleared by the FA, who accepted his plea that he had been swearing at a team-mate, Willie Morgan, not the referee. This was entirely plausible, as the two players had never got on, their antipathy dating from Morgan's Burnley days when, after a match at Turf Moor, Best was collared by Morgan's mother. 'She grabbed hold of me,' George says, 'and shouted that her son was a better player than me, and not only that, he had long hair before I did! What was I supposed to make of that? Morgan always seemed a bit jealous.' So who had he been swearing at? 'The referee – but I didn't mind people thinking it was Willie!' Morgan says of Best: 'He thought he was the James Bond of football. He had everything he wanted, and he pleased himself. He had money, girls and tremendous publicity. He lived from day to day. Until right at the end, he always got away with it when he missed training or ran away. So he didn't care. People always made excuses for him. He didn't even have to bother to make them himself.'

George was not sure what to make of his new boss. 'He was OK, but he was very quiet. A little too quiet. Denis Law always says that he came as a stranger and left the same way, and I'd go along with that. It sums him up. I've seen Frank recently, and he's still a shy one. Manchester United is a big, big club, and running it is no job for an introvert. Dave Sexton was another manager who discovered that.'

O'Farrell had brought his own first-team coach, Malcolm Musgrove, who had played with him at West Ham, and together they improved a mercurial, inconsistent team by working on collective organization. The new manager said: 'A number of players are operating in slightly different roles, and have had to make adjustments to their game, but they have shown a willingness to play for each other and combine teamwork with individuality. This gives me great confidence – a feeling that I am sure is shared by the players. Looking at our progress so far, I think we have done enough to suggest that we are worth our position in the League. In fact, I would say that we have no cause to worry about anyone else, provided that we keep working hard.'

Rousing stuff, but justifiable pride in a restorative start was followed by a nasty tumble. The new year brought a new crisis, seven successive defeats, including a 5–1 drubbing from the old enemy Leeds, plunging the leaders into freefall. George's form, and mind, had unravelled a little earlier. In the run-up to the Newcastle game on 23 October, he had received death threats from a man purporting to represent the IRA which, with the Ulster Troubles escalating, the police took seriously, and his house was placed under surveillance. Rumours had been circulating in Belfast that he had donated £3,000 to Ian Paisley's

Democratic Unionist Party. George's family are of that persuasion, but having moved to England so young, he has no political affiliations, and insists the stories were 'rubbish'.

For the trip to Newcastle, George was accompanied on the team coach by two Special Branch 'minders', who told him that under no circumstances was he to go near the window. His meals were taken in his room, in the presence of the detectives, who never left his side. Best's peace of mind, or that of the local police, was hardly helped when the coach was broken into in the hotel car park during the players' overnight stop, and by the time the game was played he was in such a state that he dared not stand still. Forty policemen were positioned in the crowd. 'Whatever happened, I kept moving,' he says. Agitated or not, he moved well enough to score the winning goal. After the match, two police cars escorted the United coach all the way back to Manchester.

A week later, a woman who lived near George was approached by two sinister-looking men who asked her if she knew his address. She told police that when she looked out of her window as the men left, one of them appeared to be carrying a gun. After that, the police paid him a visit every two hours, to check that he was all right. Left in a state of high anxiety by all the terrorist talk, Best 'flipped' when the local paper, the *Manchester Evening News*, received a letter, saying that he could expect 'a knife in the back', and would 'never return to England' if he played for Northern Ireland against Spain in Belfast in November.

For George Best, the damage was incalculable. He had been inching along the precipice between sobriety and drunkenness, and fear for his life pushed him over the edge. He hit the bottle like there was no tomorrow (in case there wasn't), and was dropped from the team to play Wolves on 8 January after missing training for a week, much of which was spent in London with his latest girlfriend, the reigning Miss Great Britain, Carolyn Moore. No one knew it at the time, but the run of form which had brought him thirteen goals in sixteen League games between 23 August and 27 November was to be the last of its kind. He was just twenty-five, but Manchester United, and the world in general, had seen the Best. Only the rest – the worst – remained.

Determined to make a stand where he felt Matt Busby had been over-indulgent, O'Farrell fined him two weeks' wages and ordered him to train mornings and afternoons until further notice, with no day off for five weeks. He also ordered him to move out of his goldfish bowl at Bramhall and back into digs with Mrs Fullaway. 'He has had some problems, and problems tend to get on top of George,' the exasperated manager said. With Best on a bender, Eamonn Andrews's back-up staff had a terrible time pinning him down for *This is Your Life* in November 1971. The following month he was runner-up in the BBC's Sports Personality of the Year poll, behind Princess Anne, and was named *Daily Telegraph* Sportsman of the Year for the second time, having been honoured previously in 1969.

As was his wont when returning after suspension, George was determined to make a point when he was restored to the team for the third-round FA Cup replay at home to Southampton, and scored twice. He was immediately in trouble again, however, for signalling his two goals, in the direction of the press box, with the appropriate number of fingers.

O'Farrell responded to his team's nosedive down the First Division by doing what someone should have done years earlier. In March 1972 he signed the top-quality central defender United had been crying out for since Anno Domini caught up with Bill Foulkes, paying Aberdeen £125,000 for the Scottish Footballer of the Year, Martin Buchan. With an eye, no doubt, on Best's unreliability, he invested another £200,000 in Ian Storey-Moore, snatching Nottingham Forest's much-admired winger from under the noses of Derby County, who were so certain of getting their man that they paraded him around the Baseball Ground.

The rewards were instantaneous. Organized by Buchan, who

was not only a poised, classy player but a born leader, United's previously porous defence kept three successive clean sheets, and with Storey-Moore scoring on each of his first three appearances, a sequence of three wins and a draw in four matches quickly reversed the slide. With Buchan in the team, United lost four of their last twelve League games, and Storey-Moore finished with a very respectable return of five goals from his first eleven starts. For the third season in succession, United finished eighth in the First Division, which was disappointing after their runaway start, but certainly no disgrace. There was much promise, O'Farrell felt, in the success of his two new recruits and in the team's improvement after their introduction.

George Best, however, was not a happy man. He had been top scorer for the fifth year in a row, but two thirds of his goals had come in the first half of the season and well before the end he had 'had enough of football'. The game he loved had become a chore:

> In our good years, as soon as I finished training I was looking forward to coming in the next day, or playing the next match. We were playing three games every eight days then, because we were always involved in one competition or other, and there was always something to look forward to. From 1970 onwards it was very different. Instead of revolving around me, the team depended on me, and I couldn't handle that pressure. I had always played for fun, because I loved entertaining people. Now that there was responsibility, it was just a job.
>
> I got on OK with Frank O'Farrell, but I started going missing because I didn't want to train. I didn't think the effort was worth it. I was going out and getting drunk two or three nights in a row. After a match I'd go straight to the Brown Bull, have a few drinks and think: It's not worth going home now. I'd go on to a club, then somewhere else and so on.

> Saturday night would turn into Sunday morning at Phyllis's, then I'd crawl into bed for a couple of hours and go straight out again. I'd miss training on Monday. It was a cycle that became a vicious circle. I'd lost all my enthusiasm for football. I wasn't looking forward to the games any more because I didn't want to go out and get stuffed 4–0 by teams who wouldn't have held a candle to Manchester United two or three years earlier.
>
> Frank tried to improve the side by individual coaching, but the good ones among us didn't need to be taught, and resented it, and some of the others were just not good enough to be taught anything.

George signed off with a goal in the last game of the season, at home to Stoke, then headed for Marbella, instead of joining up with the Northern Ireland squad for the home internationals. By a sun-soaked Spanish pool, he announced his retirement. It was the day before his twenty-sixth birthday. O'Farrell, not as surprised as some, said:

> I know he has been drinking a lot, going out with a lot of girlfriends and keeping late hours. These things, and pressures from outside the game, have wrecked him. He is, like all other geniuses, difficult to understand. I don't think he can cope with his own problems, and there is nobody he can really lean on for help. He is like a boy lost. He needs someone to help him. We at Old Trafford have done everything possible to help him. He acknowledges this, but the plain fact is he finds it extremely difficult to communicate his problems to other people, and I feel we have not really reached him.

At Matt Busby's suggestion, Best had been sent to see a psychiatrist. He sat and laughed at his questions. George's friends were appalled by his downward spiral. David Sadler says:

Bestie should have been the linchpin of the next great Manchester United side. In his mid-twenties, we still had the best to come from him as a player. I was married with a family by this time and he was still doing his bachelor bit, but we still roomed together on away trips and got on great, doing all the things we'd been doing for years. We loved a game of cards, or crib, and we'd go to our room and talk for hours about what was going on. The team was struggling a bit, so it was 'What's he doing in the team?' or 'Why aren't we doing this?' – that sort of talk.

He was a different lad now, changed by the drinking, but he was still great company, and I was saddened by what was happening to him. He was doing a lot of boozing and I would sit him down and say: 'Christ, what are you doing to yourself? Think of your health, if nothing else.' To be honest, my reasons were partly selfish. If I could get George out of the bar, there was an even chance that I'd pick up a win bonus, because even when he was hitting the bottle he was still capable of producing phenomenal things on the pitch. Most of us liked George so much and were so unhappy about the things that were happening to him. Every time he went missing and came back we'd grab him back into the family and hope. Hope against hope that this time we could keep him there.

Not everyone was so sympathetic.

chapter thirteen

Bobby Charlton and George Best are chalk and cheese, the saint and the sinner. They have mellowed, and struck a truce in late middle age, but for nearly thirty years there was a mutual disapproval which bordered on open hostility. When George started playing up and missing training it was anathema to the man universally regarded as the consummate professional, and Charlton made a point of registering his objection.

As Johnny Giles has revealed elsewhere in these pages, Manchester United's 'Holy Trinity', Best, Law and Charlton, were not exactly the Three Amigos. They are on better terms now, and Law and Best holiday together nearly every year, but in their playing days they were colleagues, rather than friends. Law and Charlton resented Best's monopoly of the ball and his tendency to pass it only *in extremis*. Law blames George's selfish obsession with beating opponents on the dribble, instead of crossing the ball early, for his own diminishing goals return, and Charlton speaks earlier in this book of his annoyance at Best's failure to recognize and make use of his runs in support. Law was closer to Best than to Charlton, but objected just as strongly to George's antics, absences and preferential treatment.

At the start of his career, George Best had nothing but admiration for the most celebrated of all England's World Cup winners, and it was Bobby Charlton he used as his example when he put in those extra hours on the training ground to become equally proficient with either foot. He wanted to be 'like

Bobby'. But on getting into the first team and becoming accepted as 'one of the lads', George soon found that Charlton was not a lad, and they were on divergent paths almost from the outset. According to his erstwhile team-mates, Charlton was standoffish and tended to socialize more with the board than with them. On away trips, when United stayed overnight, he would often be seen in the company of the management and the directors – usually, it has to be said, at their invitation. George, of course, preferred younger company. Preferably female.

While the errant genius trained, and played, to the best of his matchwinning ability, Charlton reluctantly put up with his peccadillos off the pitch, and his frustrating greediness on it. But when Best's form and behaviour deteriorated he was quick, in his role as captain, to make representations to the manager:

> A few of the players were complaining that we were going in training and George wasn't bothering. I was the captain, and they kept coming to me and saying: 'Hey, this isn't right.' It was then my job to speak to the manager about it, which I did on several occasions. I was always told: 'We'll handle it, management will handle it.' They never did, of course. Basically, we were more worried than angry. Anybody who had any feelings for the club, and enjoyed being successful, wanted George to be there – wanted him to be playing. You'd be mad to say you didn't want George Best in your team. But the players were resentful that he wasn't doing as much as he could. They weren't bothered that he was paid more money, or that he got more favours than anybody else, as long as he turned up and did his job. That was all they asked.

Law was among those complaining: 'Yeah, I objected to Bestie messing everyone around, but Bobby was the one who told him what he, and the rest of us, felt. He thought it was his duty to do something, and he had a right go at George, more than once. Of course it made no difference at all. George was George. No one was going to change him. No one ever will.

George would not argue with that. Of his relationship with Charlton, he says:

> I have nothing but respect for Bobby now, but we were totally different characters, and for a long time we didn't get on. There was one similarity. Like me, he was his own man. He spoke his mind and did exactly what he wanted to do. He didn't socialize much with the rest of the lads, but then he'd probably say they didn't see too much of me, either.
>
> He called me greedy on the ball, but I thought he was, too, in a different way. A lot of the time he'd go for the spectacular long pass crossfield, which looked good, but was very irritating when a shorter, simpler one was on.
>
> For a long time I didn't want anything to do with him and avoided talking to him, or even passing the ball to him. I thought: If he wants to go for that crossfield stuff instead of giving it to me, why should I give it to him? It was soon spotted, of course. It was the talk of Manchester, people saying: 'Have you noticed how Bestie and Bobby aren't passing to each other? They don't even speak.' They were right. I can remember him looking up and deliberately not passing to me when I was open, and I know I did the same. It was all very childish, and it only got like that when the team started going downhill. If you look at the videos of the good years, they're full of goals he set up for me and vice versa, and when we scored, we were the first to congratulate each other.
>
> It is hard to say where it went wrong. I suppose there was a clash of egos. There was certainly a clash of personalities. I thought he was too good to be true. I was dying for him to say 'fuck', just once. I knew he didn't like me swearing, so I probably did it all the more. Really, we should both have

been interested in only one thing, Manchester United's results, but as the team got worse, so our relationship did, too.

Wilf McGuinness tried mediation, to no avail, and under Frank O'Farrell the situation went from bad to worse when Charlton made a formal protest, on behalf of the team, about Best's 'selfish' behaviour and lenient treatment. The nadir came on 18 September 1972 when George failed to turn up for Charlton's testimonial match, preferring to spend the evening in the Brown Bull, where eggs were thrown at a portrait of the beneficiary hanging on the bar room wall.

Pat Crerand says:

> Everyone got on well with George, apart from Bobby. They fell out, and I can understand why. Bobby is a good, clean-living person who thinks everyone else should be perfect too. He didn't think the way George behaved was right, and George would be the first to admit that a lot of what he did was wrong. I told him that a million times, but it was water off a duck's back. George couldn't take criticism. He didn't like it, and always ignored it. Bobby was a bit more vehement about it than me, so they fell out, big time.
>
> It's true that they didn't get on, but the thing has become exaggerated over the years. There was no hatred, or anything like that. I think the reason George didn't play in Bobby's testimonial was that he was in the pub beforehand, and couldn't drag himself out. Don't forget, George went missing for big First Division games, never mind testimonials. When I had mine, he turned up just before the kick-off, laughing his head off. I could have killed him!

David Sadler, who runs the Manchester United ex-players' association, was credited with bringing about a rapprochement at the celebrations to mark the twenty-fifth anniversary of the 1968 European Cup Final. He says:

> When George started doing his disappearing act it was totally alien to Bobby's code of conduct. I know he felt George was showing disrespect to the rest of us. The results were not good, we were getting a bit of stick, but we all had to turn up and take it on the chin. We were expected to work hard, train hard and put ourselves in the best possible condition to pull things round. That was Bobby's reasoning. But by this time Bestie was more interested in boozing, and Bobby thought, and said to his face, that he didn't think George was behaving in a professional manner.
>
> I didn't see it as a major problem at the time. The simple fact of the matter was that they were very different characters. You get that in football. Once you've done your training, or played your match, you don't always want to spend your leisure time with the same people. I know I didn't. It happens in all walks of life. You can work with someone, even if you can't stand the person.
>
> There were periods towards the end when Bobby was a senior figure and he was constantly having people say to him: 'How can you allow George to upset the dressing room with his carrying on?' That was a difficult one for him to answer, because he was more pissed off by it than anyone.

Best and Charlton tended to polarize opinion among their team-mates, and Sadler is something of a rarity as a good friend to both men:

> Bobby wasn't easy to get to know. I'd been at Old Trafford a good few years before I felt he'd accepted me. But that's just Bob's nature. I know him well now, and he can be a very warm man, a humorous, funny guy, but there are few people

who get to see that side of him. There are very few occasions when he's relaxed, and not protecting who and what he is. Don't get me wrong, I don't think he built this Bobby Charlton persona deliberately, I think it evolved naturally. He is the biggest name in British football, and still will be when he's pushing up daisies. There is really nothing you can have a go at Bobby about. He sits up there comfortably on this pedestal people have put him on and doesn't disappoint anyone.

As time has passed, there has been a softening of Bobby's attitude to George, and vice versa. They now have a lot more respect for each other. I think Bobby could have helped George more when he was playing and things started to go wrong, but that's speaking with the benefit of twenty years of everyone mulling it over.

chapter fourteen

Appropriately enough for someone who, like another celebrated Irish roué, found work to be the curse of the drinking classes, George Best announced the first of several retirements at the Skol Hotel in Marbella. In an 'exclusive', for which he was paid £4,000, readers of the *Sunday Mirror* were told on 20 May 1972: 'I am no longer a footballer – and that is final.' He wanted to 'rest, write my autobiography and go into business as a clothes designer'.

Within a fortnight, the *Mirror* should have been asking for their money back (they didn't). On 2 June, in a change of heart which surprised no one, George met Frank O'Farrell in Manchester and it was agreed that he would play again in the coming season. The man who 'couldn't face kicking another ball' on 20 May reported for pre-season training three days early, on 10 July. As the club's latest attempt to curb his behavioural excesses, he was to live with Pat Crerand and his wife, Noreen. George was told to lodge there for four months. On the first night Noreen Crerand asked him what he liked for breakfast, and the next morning the eggs and bacon were laid out in the kitchen, to cook for himself. George went home.

Frank O'Farrell's first season had got off to a flier, the second could scarcely have been more different. The optimism engendered by a decent finish to 1971–2 was blown away by a truly awful start. On the opening day, United lost 2–1 at home to Ipswich – a match memorable only for producing Denis Law's last League goal for the club. They lost their next two, to Liverpool and Everton, and were into their tenth League game by the time they managed their first win.

O'Farrell responded to his second major crisis the same way he had dealt with the first, by reaching for the cheque-book. This time, however, he was rather less successful than he had been with the classy Martin Buchan and Ian Storey-Moore, whose career was to be cruelly curtailed by injury after a promising start. The first of the new intake was Wyn Davies, a tall, somewhat ungainly striker who cost £60,000 from Manchester City. The Welshman was hardly one for the future at thirty years of age, nor was he prolific with eight goals in his forty-five appearances for City, but a goal on his debut at home to Derby helped United to their much-needed first win in the League. It was not enough to improve their parlous position in the table, where they had hit rock bottom. O'Farrell dipped into the transfer market again, paying £200,000 for Bournemouth's Ted MacDougall, and again he did not have to wait long for the first return on his investment, MacDougall scoring the winner on his second appearance at home to Birmingham. But these sporadic successes were oases in a desert of defeats, and a 4–1 drubbing in the next home game against Spurs, then a 3–0 loss in the Manchester derby, had supporters and directors in twitchy mode. The *Manchester Evening News* was the voice of reason, urging the club to be fair to O'Farrell and to give him time. The writer, David Meek, was banned from the team coach for his presumption.

By this stage, with United anchored in the bottom three and playing like relegation material, George Best had had enough. Adversity brought out the worst in him, and he was drinking more than ever. He was fined on 22 November for missing training, and fined and dropped a week later after going AWOL again.

The whole situation was a nightmare. The team was disintegrating, and with dressing room cliques all pulling in different directions there was no way it was going to get better. O'Farrell and Musgrove were strangers – not people I felt I could talk to. And it was not just me. All the other players were saying the same.

We were getting stuffed by ordinary sides and I was coming off the pitch totally devastated, thinking: We've lost 4–1 to that load of crap. For years we'd been invincible at home and now teams who weren't particularly good were coming to Old Trafford and taking the mickey out of us. We'd had so many great wins against great sides. We'd beaten Real Madrid and Benfica, and now the Coventrys and Stokes were stuffing us at home. It was painful. What did I do? I went straight out and got pissed. All right, if the results had been good I would still have gone out for a good drink, but I would have been happy drunk. When we lost badly, I went out to get absolutely slaughtered, to try to forget. That's a big difference.

I felt helpless, with no one to take my troubles to. There has been a lot of talk over the years about Sir Matt being like a second father, and of course he was good to me, but I never went to the boss with my problems. You couldn't go and talk to Matt. He was such a great man, you didn't feel you should bother him. I remember doing it once, and it took some doing. I mean, you didn't go and see the boss unless you were told to. But just once I went in and told him I wasn't happy with the situation, and the ability of some of the players who were coming into the team. He just sat there, smiling. It was as if I wasn't there. I tried to put my point of view across, but it didn't register, and I walked out feeling such a prat. Generally, if I went to anyone, it was Jimmy Murphy. He was the perfect number two. He would call me in sometimes, or phone me, and say: 'George, what's up?' and we'd talk things through. He was a lovely, lovely man. If there was something wrong, he'd be the one I'd go to and say: 'I'm not happy about this.' He was always fair to me. Towards the end, when we talked about the way the club was going, he'd say: 'Yeah, you're right, it's not the same, but we'll get it back. We'll put it right.' He was Manchester United through and through.

Murphy, who died in 1989 aged seventy-nine, was pensioned off in 1971 and given a scouting role. Like Wilf McGuinness before him, he felt betrayed by Busby, to whom he had always been intensely loyal, and expected more in return. 'All of a sudden, with Jimmy gone, there was no one for me to go to,' Best says. By November 1972 he had lost the plot completely. In the space of a fortnight he was fined and dropped for twice missing training, suspended for three World Cup matches for kicking an opponent in Bulgaria and charged with causing actual bodily harm to a twenty-year-old waitress in Reuben's nightclub. As if he had anything to celebrate, he took delivery of a white Rolls-Royce on 1 December, at a cost of £11,000.

Another bender, in London, finally exhausted O'Farrell's patience, and on 5 December, after an emergency board meeting, Best was suspended for two weeks and transfer-listed at £300,000. Making the announcement, the manager said: 'We had to consider so many things, including the future and morale of the club and the discipline of the players. I have tried all the time I have been here to support George Best. It is very disappointing he did not respond to advice. He is a great player, but he has not behaved like a top-class professional should.' Joe Mercer's reaction to Best's appearance on the transfer market was fairly typical. 'It's bad enough inheriting that problem,' he said. 'Who wants to pay £300,000 for it?'

The end was coming. Stylo, the football boot manufacturer, announced that Kevin Keegan was to replace George Best as its star name for 1973, and a clothing company that had bought the rights to George's name painted it out at their Manchester shop. But still Manchester United could not bring themselves to grasp the nettle. Spellbound by the memory of Best's genius, they turned the other cheek yet again, and on 14 December, just nine days after suspending and putting him up for sale, Busby and the United chairman, Louis Edwards, met him at Old Trafford and he was taken off the transfer list. Edwards said: 'I have seen Best and discussed recent happenings. He says he only wants to play for Manchester United. I have spoken to the directors and to the manager, Frank O'Farrell, and Best will start training again as soon as possible.'

George called the chairman 'Champagne' Louis Edwards, because of his extravagant lifestyle. In that respect, they might have been kindred spirits, but they weren't:

> He was a big, fat guy who liked a drink and a bird. Obviously I had nothing against him there, but when it came to football he was too weak. Matt Busby made his decisions for him. Whatever Matt said, Edwards did. There was no doubt who had the real power, and it wasn't Louis Edwards. With a stronger chairman, we would have had better managers after Matt.
>
> When I went to see them I told them I didn't really want to leave, but nor did I want to stay if the situation didn't improve. I tried to explain to them what I thought was wrong with the team and what needed to be done, but it was the same old thing. They agreed, but did nothing. Looking back, I would have been better off moving on, but I'd been with United a long time and just couldn't imagine playing for anyone else. We agreed that I'd give it one last go. Frank

> O'Farrell was furious. He said I'd gone behind his back, which I suppose I had, but only because I couldn't communicate with him.

O'Farrell said nothing, but privately he was seething. His authority had been undermined, but short of resigning, there was nothing he could do about it. His own position was in extreme jeopardy after the latest defeat, at home to Stoke. He had spent £585,000 – a considerable sum in those days – on five players (Buchan, Storey-Moore, MacDougall, Davies and Trevor Anderson, from Portadown), and Manchester United, the world's most famous football club, were rooted to the bottom of the First Division.

The last straw came on 16 December when, without Best, United were thrashed 5–0 at Crystal Palace. Tommy Docherty, manager of Scotland at the time, attended the match and was asked by Busby afterwards if he was interested in coming to Old Trafford. 'The Doc' replied that managing Manchester United was a lifelong ambition, and O'Farrell's fate was sealed. The eighteenth of December became known as 'the night of the long knives'. That evening, the coaching staff – O'Farrell, Musgrove and John Aston senior – attended a dinner dance which marked the end of Bobby Charlton's testimonial year. It was their last supper. The directors bade them 'good night', knowing they were going to sack all three the next morning.

They were not alone. Docherty wanted a fresh start, free from troublesome influences. A statement issued by the board said: 'George Best will remain on the transfer list, and will not be selected again for Manchester United as it is felt it is in the best interests of the club, and the player, that he leaves Old Trafford.' Best had scored just four goals in his nineteen appearances in 1972–3 and, no longer a potential matchwinner, his minuses, as an indisciplined drunk, now outweighed the pluses in terms of his value to the team. Elaborating on the club's decision, Busby added: 'We want to get him out of our hair. We are at the end of our tether with him.'

George had seen it coming and, in his cups after a week's heavy drinking, sought to beat the directors to the punch with a rambling, maudlin letter. He wrote:

> I had thought seriously of coming personally and asking for a chance to speak at the board meeting, but once again I am afraid when it comes to saying things face to face, and I might not have been completely honest. I am afraid through my somewhat unorthodox ways of trying to sort my own problems out I have caused Manchester United even bigger problems.
>
> I wanted you to read this letter before the board meeting commenced, so as to let you know my feelings before any decision or statements are issued following the meeting. When I said last summer I was going to quit football, contrary to what many people said or thought, I seriously meant it, because I had lost interest in the game for various reasons. While in Spain I received a lot of letters from both friends and well-wishers, quite a few asking me to reconsider. I did so, and after weeks of thinking it over, I decided to give it another try. I came back hoping my appetite for the game would return, and even though I like to think I gave 100 per cent in every game, there was something missing. Even now, I am not quite sure what. Therefore, I have decided not to play football again, and this time no one will change my mind.
>
> In conclusion, I would like to wish the club the best of luck for the remainder of the season, and for the future. Because even though I personally have tarnished the club's name in recent times, to me, and thousands of others, Manchester United still means something special.

The apologia was no more than a postscript. The board took their decision before reading it.

O'Farrell, who had three and a half years of his contract to run, had it honoured in full, receiving £40,000 in severance pay. He left a bitter man and, a generation on, still refuses to talk about Manchester United. Alone among all those who have known George Best, he refused to be interviewed for this book. Through an intermediary, he said he had no complaints about George's efforts on his behalf when he was fit enough to play, but that he felt that some of the other players he inherited had never given him their all. David Meek, of the *Manchester Evening News*, knew O'Farrell well. In his definitive book *The Illustrated History of Manchester United*, he writes: 'Frank left the club with great bitterness, a feeling which persisted for many years, and perhaps will for the rest of his life. His departure certainly ended his career as a top manager, though he did return in an advisory capacity with Torquay for a while. From where Frank stood, other teams had left United behind in terms of effort and teamwork. He considered that players who had enjoyed success under the old regime resented his new methods. He likened Old Trafford to Sleepy Valley. The old stars were going out.'

For the 'old stars', it was a case of good riddance. Denis Law says: 'Frank came as a stranger and left the same way. I have nothing against the guy, but he wasn't one of us. Manchester United was like a family, and he was an outsider.' Pat Crerand added: 'Frank was a nice man, and I got on well enough with him, but I know he blamed a lot of people for what was basically his fault. I just don't think he was up to the job. He wasn't strong enough.' David Sadler believes it was 'player power' that did for O'Farrell in the end:

> History has shown how difficult it was to follow Matt Busby, but I don't think Frank gave himself a chance. It seemed he didn't want to get to know the senior players, he wanted to

get us out and get his own men in. He became very remote. We'd literally go from week to week and only see him just before a game. By the end, there were definitely a few people not giving him 100 per cent.

I always thought player power was totally out of order, a very unprofessional thing, but he was certainly a victim of it. Even if I had been so inclined, I never felt I was in a strong enough position personally to go to Matt and say: 'You've got to do something about this guy.' It was people like Willie Morgan who were involved in that. I didn't think it was right. I was always at odds with that.

Busby confirmed that the players had influenced the board's decision when he said, much later: 'The Second Division was staring us in the face. The team had lost all fight. There were observations by a number of senior players that there did not seem to be a close enough relationship between manager and players. Eventually, after the 5–0 defeat at Crystal Palace, the board decided, unanimously, that Frank O'Farrell must go.'

The team bottom of the table, the manager subverted by a dressing room coup, the star player sacked as a hopeless drunk – just four years after winning the European Cup, Manchester United were at their lowest ebb. Arthur Hopcraft, author of probably the finest book on the sport ever written, *The Football Man*, observed:

> The events at Old Trafford between the summer of '69 and the close of '72 had a distressing shabbiness. Wilf McGuinness, a product of the famous Busby nursery of the 1950s, was callously given the responsibility of managing the players while denied convincing authority because Sir Matt stayed in his old office, an intimidating grey eminence called 'general manager'. When McGuinness failed, inevitably, he was humiliated by being returned to the reserve team (he left

the club later) and Sir Matt took the reins again. A new manager, Frank O'Farrell, lasted 18 months before the cumulative hindrances of acrimony in the dressing room, disfavour in the newspapers and the defection of George Best to Never-Never Land unfitted him for the job in the eyes of the directors, of whom Sir Matt was now one. It was a sorry tale of equivocation and disavowal.

Out of work, and more often than not out of his head, George staggered from one scrape to another. Vandals did so much damage to his Rolls-Royce that he sold it in January 1973 after less than two months of high-profile motoring. On 11 January he was found guilty of causing actual bodily harm to Stevie Sloniecka, the unemployed waitress he had assaulted in Reuben's nightclub, and was ordered to pay twenty-five pounds damages, costs of seventy-five pounds and given a conditional discharge for twelve months. How had The Great Lover of Women come to strike one?

I was in Reuben's early one night with a pal of mine called Doug Welsby, who ran the Queen's Club in Manchester. At first we thought we were the only two people in there, but in a corner, where we couldn't see them, were a group of girls starting out on a hen night. One of them spotted me and came over. She was really drunk, and although she could see we were talking business, she kept asking me to dance. I said to her: 'Look, I'm sorry, I don't dance, and we're trying to have a conversation here.' She just wouldn't leave us alone, and after she'd come up a couple more times Dougie said to her: 'Please, we're trying to have a business meeting, and he's told you he doesn't want to dance.' With that, she started mouthing off, calling me names, and smacked my face. She went off, had a giggle with her pals, and then came back and tried to hit me again. I wasn't having that, and I gave her a

> slap. She ended up with a hairline fracture in her nose, and took me to court. I shouldn't have done it, but even the magistrate said there had been provocation. I was getting that sort of thing nearly every day, with all sorts of people trying to wind me up.

The stipendiary magistrate who heard the case, Mr John Bamber, said: 'I think there was a great deal of provocation here. The person who was injured did an awful lot to provoke Mr Best.' The complainant was two thirds to blame, he found. In another incident, Carl Boyce, a student, took out a private summons against Best, alleging assault and battery in Bridge Street, Manchester. The magistrate refused to serve the summons.

Keen to get away from a hothouse environment, where the next punter was as likely to throw a punch as ask for his autograph, George flew to Toronto on 16 January, to discuss playing in the World Indoor Soccer League. He had no intention of doing it, but the Canadians were happy enough with the attendant publicity, and it got him out of the country, all expenses paid. He was much more interested when New York Cosmos, star-spangled standard bearers of the North American Soccer League, approached Manchester United for permission to negotiate terms. 'The Cosmos were owned by Warner Brothers, who called me and said: "Would you like to come and play for us?" So I went over there for a week or so to have a look. I spoke to them, and it all sounded good. The problem was, they wanted me to live there permanently. Their league ran for only five months of the year, and I didn't want to move to New York lock, stock and barrel. The place is OK for a visit, but that's all, as far as I'm concerned, so the thing fell through. They didn't do so badly. They signed Pele instead!'

After holidaying with Malcolm Wagner in Los Angeles, Palm Springs and Acapulco, Best returned to Manchester in mid-February and sold his boutiques. Now he had nothing to do but drink 'and feel sorry for myself'. His friends, and United managers, always said they could judge the severity of one of his benders by his shaving habits. When he grew a beard, he was in bad shape, and the pictures taken at the time make him look like one of The Dubliners. With no football to detain him, and his house sold, George left early for the summer revels in Spain that year. He planned to stay for a couple of months, but was back in little more than a week after the biggest scare of a life not short on hair-raising moments.

Sitting in the International Bar in Marbella, he noticed a numbness and a slight swelling in his right leg. The swelling got worse, and when the numbness gave way to real discomfort, Best consulted a local doctor, who prescribed pills and a pain-killing spray, and said the condition would clear up within forty-eight hours. It was some diagnosis. By five a.m. the leg, like the dodgy doctor's wallet, was twice its normal size, and George could not stand it – or stand on it – any longer:

> My girlfriend at the time, who is now Mrs Frank Stapleton, was with me, and I told her: 'This isn't good. I've got to get home.' She managed to get me a flight the next day. Meantime, I called my GP in Manchester, and he said if it was that bad, he'd meet me off the plane. So I've got on this charter flight, chock-a-block with holidaymakers, and I'm in agony. The pain was indescribable, I really thought I was dying. The sweat was pouring off me, and the leg seemed to be getting larger by the second. I was carrying my shoe, I couldn't get it on. So there I am, clenching my teeth and praying, and half the plane is queuing up for autographs and wanting me to pose for photographs with them.
>
> Somehow I made it. When I got back to Manchester airport I didn't even bother to pick up my luggage, I made straight for the exit where Geoff, my doctor, was waiting. He took one

> look at me and said 'Drop your trousers.' His next words were 'Oh, fucking hell,' and he drove me straight to hospital. A thrombosis had started on the inside of my leg and luckily it had moved down, into the calf. Had it moved up, I could easily have died. The man up there looked after me!

The Old Trafford deity was about to, too. Best's first visitor in hospital was Sir Matt Busby. 'The boss popped his head round the corner to surprise me, stayed for a little while, and when he left he said: "Isn't it about time you were playing again?"'

Between Frank O'Farrell's dismissal and Tommy Docherty's arrival, United played twice under the caretaker management of Pat Crerand, drawing 1–1 at home to Leeds and losing 3–1 at Derby. Anyone looking for an instant transformation when Docherty took charge was disappointed. His first match, away to Arsenal on 6 January 1973, was lost 3–1, his second saw United knocked out of the FA Cup in the third round, by Wolves.

Too much needed to be done for there to be any quick and easy solutions, but at last Busby had got the right man. Manchester United and Tommy Docherty were made for each other, the size of the club matched only by the new manager's personality. Docherty's reputation has been devalued by a string of failures, but in the early seventies he was at the peak of his powers, and exactly what United needed. He had done well at Chelsea, as the youngest manager in the League, and after less successful spells with Rotherham, Queen's Park Rangers, Aston Villa and Porto of Portugal, was in the process of proving his worth all over again with Scotland when the chance came to fulfil his greatest ambition. There was no danger of 'The Doc' kowtowing to Matt Busby, and the supreme wheeler-dealer was too streetwise to fall victim to the dressing room conspirators who had undermined Wilf McGuinness and Frank O'Farrell. He would do it his way, and anyone who didn't like it would be out quicker than you could say 'sold'. The breath of fresh air which blew away the stench of stagnation felt more like a whirlwind, although some might say 'twister' was more apt.

Docherty took one look at the squad he had inherited and declared: 'There are players here who are not up to Manchester United standard.' It might have been George Best talking. Typically, he wasted no time when it came to changing them. George Graham was his first buy, from Arsenal on 27 December, and another Scot, Alex Forsyth, arrived within days. Two more, Jim Holton and Lou Macari, followed after the Cup defeat at Wolves, and with Mick Martin joining from Bohemians of Dublin, there were five new signings in the team on 24 January when, with United still bottom of the table, a full-house 59,000 packed Old Trafford for a goalless draw with Everton.

The new broom had brought in more players in five weeks than previous regimes had in five years, and interest in the changing team was at fever pitch, even if results remained modest. Docherty had to wait six games for his first win, at home to Wolves, and that came courtesy of two goals from the oldest of the old hands, Bobby Charlton. But by 17 March, when Newcastle were beaten 2–1, 'The Doc' and his transfusions of new blood had effected a cure, and an unbeaten run of eight matches, five of which were won, saw United finish eighteenth, clear of the relegation places.

At the end of the season Bobby Charlton retired, aged thirty-five and more than 600 League games after his first appearance in October 1956. Denis Law and Tony Dunne both went with him, on free transfers, Law indicating that he was not best pleased by his release at the age of thirty-three.

Against the grain, for he was determined to cut the old sentimental ties with the past, Docherty now weighed up the odds and decided that a gamble was in order. On a nothing ventured, nothing gained basis, and in the face of advice to the contrary, he re-signed George Best. Matt Busby (who else?) had suggested it, in the belief (he would never learn) that George was ready to buckle down after his scare with the thrombosis. Pat Crerand, who was now Docherty's assistant, made the necessary arrangements as intermediary.

Best and Docherty had met in a Spanish bar in the sixties, and had got on well. Now, the speed with which the new manager was making the sort of changes George had been advocating for years impressed him, and he was ready to play again:

> I was at a loose end. I had no idea what I was going to do with my life, none at all, and when United invited me to go back, it had real appeal. After a bit of to-ing and fro-ing, with Paddy [Crerand] as the go-between, I met 'The Doc' and we decided to give it another go. The problem was, I wasn't fit. I was seriously overweight after the best part of a year on the booze, and the thrombosis had hardly helped. I said I'd need time – two or three months – to get in shape, and that I didn't want to be rushed. I'd work hard, morning and afternoon, and play in the reserves, and let's see how it went. 'The Doc' agreed, and I thought that with a good motivator like him in charge, working with my old mate Paddy Crerand, it could be the start of something good.

George resumed training on 10 September 1973. As promised, he worked like a zealot, twice a day, supplementing the morning sessions with the rest of the players with afternoon work-outs under the direction of Crerand and the reserve coach, Bill Foulkes. The weight was coming off, the fitness coming back. He played in Eusebio's testimonial match in Lisbon, and in a friendly against Shamrock Rovers. 'I could feel myself getting back into shape, and I loved it. I was still only twenty-seven, after all.'

Docherty kept asking how he felt, George kept saying 'Don't rush me', but results were not on their side. United won just three of their first twelve games in 1973–4, and were eighteenth in the table. It was a case of needs must. On 20 October, having trained for just six weeks after his nine-month lay-off, George Best was given a hero's welcome when he ran out at Old Trafford to play against Birmingham City. Lifted by the emotion of the occasion, United halted a run of three successive defeats with a 1–0 win. The matchwinner was not Best, but Alex Stepney, of all people. It was a sign of the times that the goalkeeper's second penalty of the season made him joint top scorer. 'I wasn't happy with my fitness,' George says. 'I'd definitely been brought back too soon, and I had to be taken off at half-time. But gradually it was coming back. In my fourth game I scored against Spurs, as I always seemed to down the years, and then I felt right. I was starting to go past people again. I scored again against Coventry on 15 December, and thought I was getting better all the time.'

George Best may have been, Manchester United certainly weren't. After the victory over Birmingham on his comeback, they went nine League games without a win, and on 1 January 1974, when they were beaten 3–0 away to Queen's Park Rangers, they were twentieth in the First Division. As is his wont, George prefers to blame it on the 'downer' of playing in a poor team, but the new year festivities had more to do with it when he failed to turn up for training on 3 January. He had been to a party, 'to lift my spirits', and had lifted one spirit too many.

In the old days, he would have got away with it; under Docherty, no chance. He trained as normal on the Friday, with nothing said, and was totally unprepared for the fateful events of Saturday, 5 January, which remain at issue to this day. United were playing Plymouth Argyle at home in the third round of the FA Cup. George Best's version of what happened runs as follows:

> I missed training on the Thursday morning, because I'd been out with a couple of mates the night before, but I went in in

the afternoon to make up for it with Paddy [Crerand]. When I trained on the Friday 'The Doc' never said anything to me, and on the Saturday there was nothing until an hour or so before the kick-off. I was just starting to get changed when I received word that Docherty and Paddy wanted to see me in the referee's room. 'The Doc' just said: 'I'm leaving you out today because you missed training on Thursday,' and walked out. I turned to Paddy, astonished, and said: 'If I don't play today, I won't play again. That's me finished.'

Docherty has said since that I turned up in no fit state to play, with a bird in tow, but that's total rubbish. Even in those days, I never went out on a Friday night before a game, and I was perfectly fit to play. If there was a girl with me, which I can't remember, she would have been a normal matchday guest. When I was told I wasn't playing, I was devastated. I couldn't wait to play. I felt I was almost there, in terms of getting it all back, and I thought this was a good chance to see what I could do – to turn it on. We were at home to Plymouth in the Cup, and I thought: If I can't get in the side against them, what chance is there against Liverpool or Arsenal? I might as well pack it in.

After Docherty had left us in the referee's dressing room, Paddy said: 'Don't do anything silly. Sleep on it and come in for training as normal on Monday. You'll be OK.' I said: 'Paddy, I can't.' He kept on at me: 'Come on, son, come on. It'll be all right.' I told him: 'No, that's definitely it,' and he said: 'Well, I've got to go back into the dressing room now, I'll see you later.' It was about a quarter to two, I suppose, and I just sat down and cried my eyes out. I knew I wouldn't be coming back. I didn't even watch the game. I went into the players' lounge and sat drinking tea. Sammy McIlroy and a couple of the other lads came up to me, asking: 'What's the problem?' and I just said: 'I'm not playing. He's left me out.'

If I'd been in no fit state, as Docherty said, I would have stayed there and got pissed. Instead, I had a couple of cups of tea and a sandwich and then the game finished. We won 1–0, the boys came in and I had a few beers with them, and stayed a couple of hours. Then I went up into the stand and sat there on my own for a while, thinking of all the great times. I shed a few more tears up there, and then walked straight out. I knew I wouldn't be going back and I never did, not as a player.

Docherty, like George Best, never scaled the heights again after his sacking by Manchester United in 1977 for setting up home with the wife of the club's physiotherapist, Laurie Brown. He arrived in the elephant's graveyard that is the after-dinner speaking circuit on a downward spiral which took him to Derby, QPR, Sydney (twice), Preston, Wolves and Altrincham. Not far short of his seventieth birthday, he had just offered to help Manchester City out of their 1997 managerial crisis (Francis Lee choked on his cornflakes over that one) when we met to discuss his part in George Best's demise. A witty charmer, with a fund of hilarious stories, 'The Doc' is marvellous company, and it is easy to fall under his spell and take everything he says at face value. Much the same is true of George Best, but when interpreting their very different versions of events it is worth bearing in mind that Docherty was the one who, in aborting a libel action against Willie Morgan in 1978, admitted he had told 'a pack of lies' in court. His story of Best's final departure from Old Trafford runs as follows:

I first met George when I was manager of Chelsea. I was on holiday in Majorca, and we bumped into each other there. He seemed a really nice lad, and I still had that impression after meeting him whenever Chelsea played Manchester United.

He had that fantastic game against us in 1964, when he was absolutely brilliant.

I took over at Old Trafford in December 1972, at the same time that George had been sacked, and about nine months later, in the September, Matt Busby and Pat Crerand said to me: 'D'you think George could do us a turn?' I said: 'If he's up to it, we could certainly do with him.' He'd been out a long while, but Pat Crerand had a chat with him and we decided to bring him back and give him another crack.

He came back and he worked at it, but not as hard as he should have done. Maybe the leg was still bothering him after the thrombosis, I don't know. You couldn't really sit him down and talk to him, he wasn't much of a talker. He always wanted to be on the move, doing something. I knew he wouldn't train every morning, because he was always going to have a few nights out, but I decided to give him a bit of leeway.

I just wanted him to go out there and play – we'd get the ball, give it to him, and he could knock it about – but it didn't work out. The best thing he did was to put 5,000 or more on the gate, which the club loved. He always brought money through the turnstiles, but football-wise, it was a failure. He came back and played, and he could still beat people. His passing and vision were always great, too, but he had lost his zip. In the old days, when he beat people he used to leave them for dead, but now when he got past them they could catch him up and dispossess him. After two or three games I thought he looked a bit frightened. For the first time I saw fear in his eyes. Fear that he couldn't do it any more. The other players weren't happy when they were training every morning and George came in when he felt like it. It wasn't a good situation.

But the story that I dropped George for the Plymouth cup

tie for missing training in the week is just not true. It's a myth. He had been down to play, he was going to play. The players had to be at Old Trafford for their pre-match meal at 11.30 for twelve o'clock and he wasn't there. At half past two I had to go to the referee to hand in our teamsheet, and he still hadn't turned up. I was just starting to gee-up the lads – 'C'mon son, do this, do that' – and there was a knock on the door. Tommy Cavanagh, my right-hand man, went to the dressing room door and came back to me and said 'It's Bestie.' I walked over and he was standing there, pissed out of his mind, and with a young lady. I wouldn't say she was drunk, but she had a good drink in her. He was totally gone. I just said: 'George, I'll see you on Monday.' He said: 'But I want to play.' I told him: 'There's no way you can play, I will see you on Monday.' I was told later that he stormed off, without watching the game.

George blames me for kicking him out, but it was his choice. Personally, I still have a lot of time for him. He was a genius, he really was. When he came back, I was hoping that he'd be an outstanding success, because if he had been, I would have had all the credit for his rebirth. But it was never going to work. He was too fond of the good life really. That was his problem. That, and the company he kept. He's a good lad, but he lets everyone down – always has. He's the same on the after-dinner circuit, where he doesn't turn up half the time.

The way he finished was sad. At twenty-seven, he should just have been coming into his prime when he left.

According to George Best, the only witness to what occurred before the Plymouth game was Pat Crerand, and he corroborates Best's side of the story. It should be borne in mind, however, that his testimony is not free from bias. Crerand has been one of George's best friends for thirty years, and has fought all comers more than once on his behalf. Docherty and Crerand, on the other hand, have been at daggers drawn since Docherty went to the board and had his fellow Scot sacked as assistant manager, then gave him a negative reference when he applied for the manager's job at Northampton. Crerand says:

> George had missed training on the Thursday, but he was expecting to play against Plymouth. All that stuff about him turning up half an hour before the kick-off with a girl with him and being dropped for that reason is bullshit. The teamsheet was ready before that, and his name wasn't on it. The problem was that he'd missed training, and he couldn't afford to. To be fair, I could see George was cracking up. I was his biggest admirer, but I couldn't see him getting back to the standard of fitness required to play in the First Division. He needed extra training, and he would do a little bit, but it was never going to be enough.
>
> We always had a meal before the game at twelve o'clock, and George turned up around then. All that half past two stuff is garbage. He was there for the pre-match meal, and then Docherty called him into the referee's room before the game and told him he wasn't playing. I was there with Tommy Doc when George came in and Docherty told him. I took one look at George and knew that was it. He was devastated. He could hardly say a word. I said: 'Give it a day or two, don't do anything rash,' but you could see that he had made his mind up, and that was it.
>
> You have to remember that some of the players who were playing for United then weren't fit to clean George's boots. I mean that. They had no right to be in the same dressing room as him. George knew his standard of fitness wasn't what it should have been, but he probably thought: Well, if I'm not worth a place in this team, I'd better forget it. After that, I never expected to see him back. I knew that was it. I never

thought I'd see him play again because he loved playing for Manchester United so much that I couldn't imagine him playing for anyone else.

The players' memories have been blurred by the passage of time, but most of them say Best was present that Saturday for the pre-match meal. Brian Kidd's evidence is fairly typical: 'I wouldn't want to call anybody a liar but I'm pretty sure that Bestie was there for the meal. I can definitely remember him telling me he wasn't playing, and that would have been well before half past two. These things are difficult for managers. At the end of the day, it's human nature to cover your own arse.' There is common agreement with Docherty on one thing: that George's last, twelve-match comeback was doomed to fail from the start. Kidd says:

> I can remember 'The Doc' saying he could control him, and to be fair, he tried his best. But we'd be going off for a match tomorrow and George would go to Haydock races, and be late for the coach. That was the way he was. He always made me laugh. I shared rooms with him once when United went to Majorca, and I'll never forget it. We were in Palma, which Bestie helped to make the in place, and when we got to the hotel we walked into our room, George put his case on the bed and without opening it he was straight off out, on the piss. We were supposed to be on a golfing trip, but he didn't play golf. We would see him now and again in the hotel, his beard getting fuller all the time. That was Bestie. How could anyone control him? It was too late for 'The Doc' to try.

Pat Crerand says: 'I think George had lost it by Frank O'Farrell's time. He was not living the way a professional footballer should, and couldn't get back to the level of fitness required. The odd bit of extra training was never going to be enough.' Denis Law agrees that the O'Farrell era was when Best really 'lost it':

> George was an extremely good trainer, but then he started not turning up. No one can get away with that. You've got to do what you're paid for. You've got to train and you've got to play the matches. That's your life, isn't it? You can mess about away from the game, but within it you've got to do your bit. He knew that as well as anyone. I don't think it was wise for him to go back under Docherty. It was the wrong decision. He wanted to come back and perform like the George Best of old, but he was going through problems, within himself, that made that impossible.

David Sadler was not surprised, and certainly had no objections, when his old room-mate was given one last chance:

> He had good friends in the dressing room, we all knew that he was an exceptional talent and we all knew that he was better than us. George Best coming back could only improve what was a pretty poor side. Even well under 100 per cent, he was still better than anything we'd got. But he wasn't the old George. The pace had gone, and he was taking a bit of hammer, physically. By the early seventies we were really just hoping. His friends had been through a lot with him, and we hoped that the penny, finally, had dropped. Your head told you that it was not going to be, but your heart kept hoping. After the Plymouth game, I knew it was the finish. Even before then, I just couldn't see it working.

Despite his protestations that it was 'all starting to come back', the man himself knew it wasn't going to work too, and was always planning a career change. In November 1973 George had become part owner of a Manchester nightclub, and in one of our more candid interviews he told me: 'I was working on the club, Slack Alice, from about the October onwards, so I think you could say the comeback wasn't too serious!'

After he had gone, the unthinkable happened: Manchester United were relegated on 29 April 1974. George Best was on the way down, too.

chapter fifteen

Matt Busby went to his grave wondering whether he had been too lenient with George Best, whether it was sparing the rod that spoiled the child. On balance, he thought not. History may disagree.

There are those, well placed to judge, who are adamant that George would have had a better chance of enjoying a fuller, more normal career given firmer handling and guidance in his formative years. It is impossible to be certain, and there is no rush here to be too judgemental. We are talking about an alcoholic, and such people are predictable only in their unreliability, notoriously difficult to control. Best would have been a handful for any manager in any era, even without the unprecedented problems which came with his mega-celebrity as the first footballer to straddle the divide between sport and showbusiness.

That said, the great imponderable is what might have happened had there been a greater degree of supervision before drink and an addictive personality took hold.

Busby had assembled his first three championship-winning teams in the days of the maximum wage, when Best's fifties equivalent, Duncan Edwards, travelled to Old Trafford for matches not in a Rolls-Royce but on the bus, chatting to the fans. The most successful manager of his generation was used to dealing with uncomplicated lads with modest incomes and aspirations to match. Suddenly, just as he was beginning to contemplate retirement, Busby had the 'Fifth Beatle' on his hands. George Best, with his good looks and brooding, James Dean attitude, was as popular with teenage girls as he was with their dads – probably more so – and he had the money, the time and the inclination to take full advantage. Footballers had never appeared on the pop, fashion and pin-up pages before, and with no precedent to go by, a new code of conduct had to be made up on the hoof. Or rather it should have been.

Best started to stray because there were so few rules. From that first, brief visit to Old Trafford with Eric McMordie, there was too little supervision. Too often, and for too long, George was left to his own devices, and throughout his life boredom, more than innate perversity, has turned idle hands to deviant work. From the age of seventeen, he had more money and free time than he knew what to do with and, given no proper advice on how to spend either, it was a dangerous combination.

By the time he was nineteen his circle of friends included bookmakers and nightclub owners, he had the key to his local pub, and he thought nothing of staying out until breakfast time at Phyllis's, the unlicensed, all-night drinking den where just about everything was available bar a good night's sleep. Matt Busby, who had informants everywhere, was aware of all this but, apart from a few unheeded homilies, he chose to indulge his budding genius and in so doing he established a pattern it became impossible to break. By the time the cosy chats became 'bollockings' and suspensions, it was too late. Best was in cruise control on the road to ruin, and sat staring into space or counting photographs during the managerial strictures, the venom of which always came with the antidote of a forgiving wink at the end.

When George went AWOL, the man he still calls 'the boss' welcomed the prodigal 'home' time and again. When Wilf McGuinness wanted to drop him for sexual misconduct before an important cup semi-final, Busby would not allow it. When

Frank O'Farrell put him on the transfer list after another bender, Busby took him off it. When the directors sacked him, good old Matt invited him back. Michael Parkinson, the television celebrity and journalist, is a friend of Best's who wrote a lurid seventies biography which did neither man great credit. He was spot on, however, when he said at the time that too many 'hard-line statements' were followed by 'soft-soap retractions', and that for too long the club opted for 'appeasement and reconciliation' when the best thing for both parties might have been 'a parting of the ways'. Seeking to justify his forbearance, Busby said later:

> What were we to do, shoot him? I always looked for a cure with George. It would have been easy to have transferred him, but that wasn't the answer. Special rules for George? I suppose so, but only in the sense that he was a special player. I mean, you make it different once you say someone is a good player and the man next to him is a genius. George is a genius.
>
> People often say: 'You're well rid of him, Matt. He must have given you some headaches,' but I don't think about that. I think about the unforgettable moments he gave me, when he lifted me from my seat with excitement and joy. That's what I remember. I don't know what went wrong. I've tried to search my heart, honestly, and I don't think I could have done any more. I even offered him a place in my home, asked him to come and live with me and my family, but I don't think that would have changed things.
>
> I think there was a basic flaw in George's make-up. It might be this self-destruction thing that people talk about. But there is something there I didn't see in other people. Something that I sensed would ultimately destroy his career, no matter what we did to help him. It worries me that I failed with George, because although I couldn't have done any more, I still get a sense of failure when I think about him. He

was one of the nicest boys I've ever had, good as gold at the club. Always polite, always charming, a pleasure to be with. And look what happened. Still, I wouldn't have changed a minute of it. People say: 'You must rue the day you set eyes on him.' What nonsense. Every manager goes through his life looking for one great player, praying he'll find one. Just one. I was more lucky than most, I found two. Big Duncan Edwards and George. I suppose, in their own ways, they both died, didn't they?

It was his tolerance, as much as his nurturing of Best's talent in adolescence and admiration of it in full flower, that had Matt Busby spoken of as George's second father, but while there undoubtedly was a mutual affection between manager and favourite player, the parental analogy is an excessively romantic one, with obvious weaknesses. In charge of a first-team squad that was twenty-strong, Busby had too many players to concern him to be in a position to devote his full attention to one. And, regardless of his avuncular public persona, he was not the type to play nursemaid to anyone. Wilf McGuinness and Jimmy Murphy, trusty lieutenants and loyal servants, were both dumped and hurt by his ruthless streak, and there is a feeling among the players present at the time that, favourite or not, George Best would have suffered the same fate as Johnny Giles, transferred out, had he been playing a few years earlier. Instead, by the late sixties, Busby was coasting towards retirement, and the fire in his belly had been dowsed. He was looking for a quiet life rather than confrontation. Bobby Charlton says:

The second father thing was a bit overdone. Matt was a father figure to everybody, he didn't have favourites. I know he was very disappointed in George, but he probably thought to himself: When you're dealing with somebody of this quality, you have to make allowances and handle him a little bit

> differently. If he had his time all over again, I'm sure he would lean the other way. If he had been younger, maybe he would have kicked George out earlier. He tried his best to sort him out, but it just didn't work – solely because of the sort of person George was. The habit he had.

Denis Law agrees: 'Matt wasn't well, and could have done without all the aggro George gave him. Five years earlier, he would have been much firmer. Then, we all got a hammering for doing something or other. But towards the end Matt was getting mellow, and wanted a quieter life.'

Johnny Giles offers an alternative view. Giles, sold in 1963 after daring to dispute his omission from the team, insists Busby was never a great disciplinarian:

> In the fifties Dennis Violett was the forerunner of George Best – a great player with a drink problem. Even when it was common knowledge that he was living it up and letting it affect his performance on the field, Matt did nothing. Dennis had broken the club scoring record in 1959–60 with thirty-two League goals [the record still stands], and just like George, he could do much as he pleased off the field. There was no sense of discipline in that respect. In the age Matt came from – the old days – if the players drank it was so what?, as long as they did their stuff on a Saturday afternoon. Matt played with Hughie Gallacher [the prolific Scottish international centre-forward who committed suicide, an alcoholic, at the age of fifty-four], and saw players drinking before they went out to play, and I always had the impression that if George was turning it on on a Saturday, that was all that Matt wanted to know about.
>
> I've heard George say Matt was a second father to him, and he probably believes it, but I don't see any evidence that he was getting proper protection from him. I think it's a myth,

I really do. One of George's big problems was that with his dad, Dickie, back in Belfast, he *didn't* have a father figure, from the age of seventeen, to take him under his wing and look after his interests. Bestie was a phenomenon, the first player to hit it that big in the history of the game. Sure, we'd had superstars before, like Tom Finney and Stan Matthews, but they didn't get the level of publicity that George attracted. This was the sixties, he was the 'Fifth Beatle', and he had more exposure on television and in the media than any footballer had experienced before.

When it began, George was a young, innocent boy suddenly exposed to film star attention, and totally unprepared for it. People have condemned him since, and said he could have handled himself better, but very few lads could have handled what George went through. These days they have agents, solicitors and accountants to advise them, and some still can't cope. He had none of that help when he needed it. Matt had seen nothing like it before – nobody had – and he wasn't prepared for it. If anything, he was absent as the father figure. He wasn't conscious that George needed one and left him stranded. I certainly think he could have done more for George when it first became apparent that things were getting out of hand, but it was always a case of: If he's doing the business out on the field, that's good enough for me.

The danger was there from the start because Manchester United didn't keep a proper check on young players. I remember going to Old Trafford from Ireland at fifteen, just like George, and being left to my own devices. If the digs they gave you were no good, it was up to you to find your own. There was no real supervision. If I had wanted to go out drinking every night, I could have done it. There was so much talent there then that if someone misbehaved, and didn't make it, so what? Somebody else would come through.

The club wasn't set up to handle George Best, and when

he became showbiz they made it up as they went along. He got in with the wrong crowd, and I don't believe Matt did anything to stop it. From what I remember, George was left, the same as everybody else, to look after himself. I think he was cut adrift, and I don't think anybody at seventeen, eighteen or nineteen years of age could have handled the pressures he had.

By the end, they let him become bigger than the club. He was drawing the crowds, of course, but in the long run they paid a high price for accommodating him, regardless. He cleared off and came back, behaving worse than ever, and you can't run a team properly with players messing about like he did. Manchester United was the biggest club in the country, and they were leaning over backwards to keep a playboy when they might have been better off kicking him out.

David Sadler is prepared to defend Busby's treatment of Best – up to a point:

Matt was never the total angel everyone paints him. He could be strong and he could be weak. He said some things that he contradicted later. He had scallywags and all sorts of people to deal with in my time, and he put most of them in their place with a fine here and a ban there. Whenever I stepped out of line, he quickly brought me to my senses. He had such an aura about him that with me it just needed a word or two. But Bestie took Matt into areas he didn't know. He didn't have a clue about the discos, the nightclubs and the fashion world, none of that. Why should he? It wasn't his lifestyle. He liked a drink, along with the rest of us, but not to excess. Not like George.

I don't think Matt knew quite how to handle Bestie. There were great players before him, of course, and there have been

> since – some of whom have certainly benefited from what happened to George. But he was the first pop star footballer. He wasn't what you'd call a regular guy. He wasn't normal in anything he did – least of all in what he did on a football pitch – and because he was such a bundle of talent, Matt was reluctant to do anything that might disturb that. On a personal level they were pretty close, and had a tremendous admiration and respect for one another. But when George's career started falling apart Matt wasn't a young man, and I don't think he had the heart to fight what was happening.
>
> In fairness, I was close to Bestie then, and I still am now, and from where I sit it would have needed someone with the strength and modern attributes of Alex Ferguson to have had any chance of controlling him, and even then I doubt whether he could have done it.

Best agrees. He would have nothing said against the manager he regarded as his mentor when Busby was alive, and is not about to start speaking ill of the dead:

> The boss tried all he knew to help, but he never really understood. He thought my problem was hangers-on, keeping me out all hours, but it was just the opposite. The people I was with – and they were mostly real friends, not hangers-on – wanted to go home because they had to go to work in the morning, and I was the one trying to keep them out a bit longer. As for being more strict, the way I was, it would probably have made me worse.
>
> They kept trying to come up with a solution, but really there wasn't one. I wouldn't accept it then, but I was an alcoholic.

chapter sixteen

George Best has always fancied himself as Humphrey Bogart in *Casablanca*, and on 18 December 1973, just over a fortnight before he walked out on Manchester United for the last time, he opened his first nightclub. It was a logical step, really. Having spent a fortune on the expensive side of bars the world over, the idea of making money while he drank had irresistible appeal.

In October, George and two entrepreneurial friends – Malcolm Wagner, the hairdresser, and Colin Burne, who had a stake in Reuben's and ran another nightclub called the Sandpiper – paid £10,000 for the lease of the Club del Sol in Bootle Street in the centre of Manchester. Equal partners, they put in just over £3,000 each, and spent as much again on refurbishing the run-down premises before reopening as Slack Alice, the name taken from Larry Grayson's comedy character. George says: 'Colin, who was already in the business, came to me and said: "I've found this place I think may be a goer, do you want to have a look at it?" So the three of us went to see it, and it was disgusting, a pigsty. The layout broke all the rules. Most successful nightclubs are in basements, this was two flights up. It was in the same street as a police station, which was hardly an attraction, and there was no parking. It was nuts, but we thought: What the hell, let's have a go.'

The three of them knew immediately who they wanted to run the bar and restaurant. On their summer jaunts they had become regulars at the Gomilla Grill in Majorca, where mine host was Felix Izquierdo-Moreno, a football-daft Spaniard with a mind-boggling capacity for hard graft. George says: 'We'd met Felix over there, where he was doing absolutely everything in this little bar-restaurant which was owned, I think, by a wealthy guy from Manchester. Felix was such a bubbly character, he didn't rest for a minute. He cooked, he waited on tables, he served drinks, he washed up – the place was on two levels and he was up and down like a yo-yo. Anyway, his wife was from Manchester and wanted to come home, so when we bought Slack Alice I said there was only one person to run it. It had to be him.'

Twenty-five years on, Felix is still in Manchester, where he has his own smart restaurant, Harper's, in the city centre. When he invited me to lunch to reminisce, he was exactly how George had described him, singing 'Everything is Beautiful' in a heavy Spanish accent as he scurried from table to table, like a mother hen on speed. He was not so much happy as eager to yarn about old times, gesturing to signed portraits of Best and Atlético Madrid (his other love) on the wall.

> When I met George Best I was working at the Gomilla Grill. The Manchester United players used to call it the Gorilla Grill. It was a few weeks after the European Cup Final in 1968 that we first met. The game was live on Spanish radio, and I remember the commentator talking about Georgie Best and translating the name into Spanish as Gorge el Mejor. Loving football as I did, it stuck in my mind that he was 'The Best'. I thought: I'd love to meet that gentleman, The Best, and then, not long after, it happened. He appeared in my bar. It was one of those amazing things that happen in life. George walked in one afternoon, all on his own. I will never forget it, it was about half past five. I was so excited, I recognized him at once and went to tell the other boys: 'Gorge el Mejor is downstairs.' They all came running from upstairs, where the restaurant

was. For us, it was such an honour that he came in the place. He was very famous, a hero. I had seen him on television. I remember he had a Heineken beer. I said: 'Have it on the house – anything you want.' After that, he kept coming back. To me, he was like somebody sent from heaven. He started bringing all the other players. Alex Stepney, Paddy Crerand and Martin Buchan all came. Later there was George Graham, Lou Macari and many more.

As long as I was there, George kept coming back, and then in December 1973 he said: 'I'm going to open a nightclub in Manchester, do you want to work for me?' I wasn't sure, so he said: 'Just come over for two or three weeks and give it a try.' He wanted me to come for the opening, at Christmas, but I had my own place to look after, so he said: 'OK, just come when you are ready.' Early in January I came for two weeks to see what was happening, and I'm still here. Slack Alice, as a place, was nothing special, but the people who came made it *the* club. Anybody who was anybody used to go to Slack Alice, to see George.

Malcolm Wagner remembers a night when Jimmy Tarbuck, Dave Allen, Bruce Forsyth and Mike and Bernie Winters were in. 'After closing time, we sat round a table, open mouthed, and listened to them rap. That sort of thing happened quite often. We used to get all the stars from Granada TV in.' George recalls another occasion when Mick Jagger and a black African dance troupe took the club over and 'bombed the place'. Regular visitors included Leo Sayer, Gilbert O'Sullivan, Bryan Ferry, David Essex and Phyllis's son from Thin Lizzy, Phil Lynott.

One Sunday night, not long after the club had opened, there was a call from the organizers of the Miss World contest, who were looking to show off the latest incumbent in the company of George Best. The man himself takes up the story: 'We were the only decent place open in Manchester on a Sunday night, and the people who run Miss World wanted to bring her in for a meal and a drink. They said: "There will be a fee involved, but it will be good publicity for you." They wanted £150. I said: "Yeah, I need publicity. You're welcome, but we're not paying anyone to come here." They didn't like that, but they called back and said: "OK, we'll come anyway."' George was to wish they hadn't. The lady in question was Marjorie Wallace, the curvaceous, flirtatious, but disputatious American who was to have him charged with a serious theft.

To the surprise of no one present that Sunday night, the pin-up ex-footballer and the girl said to be the most beautiful in the world hit it off instantly, and a relationship started at once. Miss Wallace already had a boyfriend, the racing driver Peter Revson, but she was seeing Tom Jones and Jimmy Connors too, and clearly felt that one more wouldn't hurt. George, however, has never been the sharing type. A stranger to the concept of fidelity himself, he nonetheless demands unswerving devotion from all his partners, and the discovery that he was just one among several this time brought the affair to a swift and stormy conclusion.

He was in Wallace's mews flat in Marylebone, west London, when she took a phone call in which she spoke of her love for Revson, who was to die shortly afterwards during practice for the South African Grand Prix. Best, predictably, hit the roof, and a furious row ensued. He says:

> One of Revson's family called and she said how much she loved him and missed him. This was in front of me, which I thought was slightly out of order. We had a disagreement over it, and she went off with one of her girlfriends. I was packing up to go, making myself a cup of coffee, when the phone rang. I picked it up but said nothing, and whoever was on the other end didn't speak and put the phone down. Then, about ten minutes later, the doorbell went. I looked out and

> there was a chauffeur in a Rolls-Royce outside. I left about half an hour later and got a train back to Manchester. That was on the Saturday.

The following Wednesday, on 21 February 1974, George Best was arrested in the bar at Slack Alice, taken to London and charged at Marylebone Magistrates Court with stealing from Marjorie Wallace, between 18 February and 20 February, a fur coat, passport, cheque-book and jewellery. George says:

> They sent two detectives up from London to pick me up and take me back for questioning. I called my solicitor, Geoff Miller, and told him to get down to London as quickly as possible, and in front of him they started going through my movements. They knew which cinema I'd been to with Marji, which film we'd seen, where we'd been for dinner and that we'd been at Tramp nightclub until three in the morning. They had it all there, but the days were wrong. When I was supposed to have nicked the coat I was in Slack Alice, with about 600 witnesses. Then they started saying that after going back to Manchester on the Sunday I sneaked back to London and got into the flat, took the stuff and got back to Manchester, all without anybody seeing me. For a start I didn't have a key, and there was no sign of a forced entry.

With the police in some confusion, George was released on bail in the sum of £6,000, pending further inquiries.

Strangely – and there has never been an adequate explanation – Marjorie Wallace's passport and an item of jewellery were sent to the *Sunday People* newspaper on 2 March. After a tip-off, various other possessions, including a tiara, were found in a London telephone kiosk a week later. George was further remanded on bail on 27 March, when Wallace did not appear in court, as scheduled, to testify against him, and the case was dropped on 24 April, when she failed to turn up for the second time. Stripped of her Miss World title as a result of the bad publicity her various affairs had attracted, she flew back to America for Peter Revson's funeral and never returned. And the famous mink coat? 'No idea what happened to it,' George says, 'but if I had been the police I'd have been more interested in the guy who got out of that chauffeur-driven Rolls.' Malcolm Wagner begs to differ: 'George told me he threw it [the coat] in a waste bin. He used to do things like that in a fit of pique – if a girl wouldn't go out with him, or whatever. Once, when we were in Spain, he threw a girl's handbag over a balcony, with all her bits and pieces in it, because she wouldn't cooperate. He'd do that sort of thing. I think he used the coat like that, and threw it away, when he found out that Wallace had been phoning Tom Jones and Peter Revson.' All's well that ends well, and George made £12,000 out of the affair by selling his side of the story to the *Sunday People*.

Court appearances apart, he was enjoying life in his new role as nightclub proprietor. For Dickie Best, however, it was a desperate time. As if his wife's degenerative alcoholism was not enough, he was dismayed when his son turned his back on football to wallow in drink, and there were other, terrible blows raining in, testing his spirit. With the Troubles in Northern Ireland going from bad to worse, George's sister, Barbara, was shot in the leg one night as she left a Belfast dance hall. And on 25 February 1974 his seventeen-year-old cousin, Gary Reid, was caught in crossfire and killed by an Army bullet. Dickie had had to give up the fish and chip restaurant George had bought him because of Ann Best's incapacity. Now he agonized over what was becoming of his son. Ever the doting father, he could think of blaming only one person. Himself. 'To this day,' he says, 'I keep asking myself if I could have done more to make it different.' The poor man's ill-founded guilt complex was destined to get much worse.

Unlike his angst-ridden father, George found myriad ways of taking his mind off such matters. In May, just after Manchester United had been relegated, he jetted off to South Africa with Malcolm Wagner to play for a team called the Jewish Guild. Wagner, who helped to set up the deal, says:

> It was a terrific contract but, as usual, George didn't want to go without a mate with him. I said: 'George, I can't, it's for eight weeks. I can't leave my business that long.' The hairdresser's was going really well at the time, and I didn't want to leave it. Anyway, he kept on and on, saying: 'What are you worried about? You've got the staff to handle it while you're away.' So eventually I asked them. I had two guys working with me, Dean Crossley and David Thorpe, and truth be told, they really could run the place. They were terrific. I said to them: 'Look, George wants me to go to South Africa for eight weeks, what do you think?' They said: 'Go on, it's the chance of a lifetime,' so off we went.
>
> Jewish Guild was a league team playing in Johannesburg, where we got the full five-star treatment. We had a huge hotel suite each, with parties to go to nearly every night. The contract was for £11,000, which was a fortune then. They wanted to pay it in krugerrands, which I was all for, but when I told George what they could be worth as an investment he said: 'Nah, Waggy, just get the readies.' Short term – it was always short term with George.

The money was still rolling in, but there was a new problem brewing. Gambling. As if his addiction to alcohol was not bad enough, George now developed another potentially ruinous habit.

> I got hooked. I was at it every night. After I left United, I had nothing to do but hang around, trying to enjoy myself, and

not get bored. Slack Alice closed at two a.m., and after a few bottles of wine in there I still wouldn't be ready for bed, so I got into the routine of going on to the casino. Malcolm Wagner never came, he didn't gamble, but Colin Burne and I did. Heavily. We'd take £500 each out of the till at Slack's every night and go straight to a casino off Deansgate. I can't remember what it was called, but the owner was a guy named Emile Semprese, and he loved us. He used to invite us for a bottle of champagne at closing time. If we'd done our money, we'd need it. We always kept a tenner in our top pockets to get us home.

On one memorable occasion, in September 1974, Best and Burne found themselves £17,000 down with no way of raising the money, short of pledging their shares in Slack Alice. George was panicking, but enjoying every trembling moment, the flush of excitement providing a buzz he had not experienced since the halcyon days at Old Trafford. The place came to a standstill as Lady Luck changed sides, and in a turnabout they still talk about in Manchester today, Best and Burne came out with a £26,000 profit. From £17,000 down they played dice from 2.20 until four a.m. without a losing roll, a run worth £43,000. 'Emile was great about it,' George says. 'He bought us a bottle of champagne and congratulated us like he really meant it.' The following day George went out and bought a new E-type Jaguar. For cash. 'The experience of being £17,000 down, with no way to pay, should have scared us off for life,' he says. 'Instead, we were taking more and more out of the business to finance our gambling.' Felix was George's driver on his nocturnal expeditions:

He used to gamble a lot of money, but George was a winner, and usually came out ahead. I used to bet on him, and I usually made money doing it. On one occasion we were in the Playboy casino in Manchester and he was playing dice. He preferred dice then [now it is roulette]. Seven and eleven were his numbers. Always seven and eleven. Anyway, this time he had a fantastic run, and he was giving me £25 chips every time he won. When I went to cash them, I had £1,850. He'd given me nearly £2,000, so imagine how much he must have won! After that win we went to Majorca, supposedly for George to buy a villa. The villa was beautiful, but he was never going to buy it. We were there for a holiday.

By now, Best was the archetypal night owl, sleeping all day and drinking and gambling all night. Describing his daily routine, he says he would get up late in the afternoon, meet his drinking mates in the Brown Bull between six and seven o'clock, and move on to Slack Alice at about ten. There, he would drink perhaps four bottles of wine before adjourning to the casino some time after two a.m. When that closed he would have a couple of drinks with the proprietor, 'to relax', and go home to bed just as 'normal' people were going to work. This hedonistic lifestyle did not come cheap, and he overstretched himself when, the day after his remarkable reversal of fortune rolling dice, he bought into a second nightclub, acquiring the lease of Manchester's Waldorf Hotel with the same partners, Malcolm Wagner and Colin Burne. Wagner says: 'We bought the hotel from a company called Cannon Inns for £65,000. Again it was equal shares and again we had to pay a lot more to refurbish it completely before we reopened under the name Oscar's. We had very little capital, and we threw a lot of money at it – borrowed money.'

The second club was up and running in November, virtually doubling the workload for the much put-upon Felix. The starstruck Spaniard loved it; the alcoholic and the workaholic were a good combination:

> It was a fantastic operation. When we finished at Oscar's, we used to walk across to Slack Alice. I used to work all day in Oscar's, which was on four floors. There was a wine bar on the ground floor, for night-time drinking only, called Bucks Fizz. That was open from 8.30 to eleven. It was packed every night. Then there was Oscar's, the pub-restaurant with good, à la carte food; Saville's, which was a disco; and on the top floor there was a banqueting suite called Dorian Gray. The whole place was known as Oscar's. It was going for twelve years. It was when it finished that I opened my own place.

Buying and renovating the second club, at a time when his gambling was threatening to get out of hand, had given George 'cashflow problems', and he was forced to supplement his income by renting himself out as a football mercenary. In August 1974 he had played a couple of games for Dunstable Town in the Southern League, who were managed by an old friend, Barry Fry. In George's first season at Old Trafford, Fry, who was a year older and a winger of some promise, had kept him out of the Manchester United youth side. Now they teamed up against their old club, Best helping Dunstable beat a United XI 3–2 in a pre-season friendly. After that, he needed a police escort for his second game.

At this stage, George's appearances were still controlled by United, who had retained his registration as a player. 'Every time I wanted to play,' he says, 'I had to ask their permission, and that really got to me, because it was Tommy bloody Docherty who had to give the OK.' That problem was solved in November 1975 when the expiry of his contract finally severed all legal ties (the emotional ones remain binding to this day) between Manchester United and George Best. A free agent, he 'celebrated' by signing for Stockport County, who paid him £300 per game and allowed him to make his own training arrangements. They were never out of pocket. George's first appearance for a club then twentieth in the old Fourth Division attracted a crowd of 8,000 for a friendly match against Stoke City. He scored, in a 1–1 draw, then scored two more in his first League game when 9,220 – three times Stockport's average gate – turned out to witness a 3–2 victory over Swansea.

George Best's comeback made waves way beyond the backwaters of the Fourth Division, and he was much in demand again. Keen to sell himself to the highest bidder, he cloistered himself away in a Surrey health farm to shed a stone in weight, and when he scored twice in Peter Osgood's testimonial match at Stamford Bridge in November 1975, his performance was impressive enough to attract an approach from the Chelsea manager, Eddie McCreadie. Wary of George's record of absenteeism, McCreadie's proposal was that he should play on a match fee basis, his wages linked to attendances. Queen's Park Rangers and Southampton also declared an interest, but Chelsea came closest to putting George back among the best. He would have joined them had their chairman, Brian Mears, acceded to his wage demands, which were for an unheard-of £1,000 per game. 'I had a lot of offers, but Chelsea were the only side I would have signed for then. I was getting to be a London person by that stage, travelling down regularly for a couple of days at a time, and I had always been pally with people like "Ossie" [Osgood], Alan Hudson and "Chopper" Harris. Well, nearly in "Chopper's" case! Even today when I see them they say "You should have come," and maybe I should have done. They were a good club, a glamorous side, and I always admired Charlie Cooke.'

Money was the deciding factor. Chelsea were in financial difficulties, unable to pay his £1,000 per game, and George said at the time: 'I'll go to America after Christmas and negotiate to play there. There's so much money involved, I'd be a fool not to.' In December 1975 he signed for Los Angeles Aztecs of the North American Soccer League, joining the get-rich-quick influx which took some of the best players in the world to a country with next to no interest in the sport, where football meant only one thing. Gridiron.

Unable to spread the gospel further than the schools, where the global game was (and still is) enthusiastically embraced by those not blessed with the physique for the American version, the founding fathers of the NASL decided on a novel approach. The American public were only ever interested in the best, so that is what they would be given. Stalled when it came to building on their solid foundations, the League's commissioners would put the roof on and look to extend downwards. For a short time, it seemed this constructional unorthodoxy might pay off. Briefly, in the late seventies, the NASL was the place to be, crowds of 70,000-plus watching the New York Cosmos – featuring Pele, Beckenbauer, Carlos Alberto and Chinaglia – see off all comers. But with no native Americans to speak of coming through, support waned, financial backing went with it, and the League became an elephant's graveyard populated by ageing mercenaries looking for one last payday and failed pros who were not quite good enough to build a decent career in their own countries. Terry Mancini, for example, was nearly thirty-five, and on his last legs at Leyton Orient when the call came in 1977. With the Aztecs, he was voted one of the best defenders in the NASL. And Derek Smethurst was hardly a household name in Britain after nine goals in seventy appearances for Millwall, yet in America, with Tampa Bay Rowdies, he was a major star, outscoring Pele, Best and Chinaglia in 1977.

As 1975 turned to 1976, however, the bubble was still inflating, its bursting still a long way off. George had been invited to join the Cosmos, but preferred the more laid-back milieu of the West Coast. The Aztecs' general manager, John Chaffetz, fed his ego by telling him that he wanted a superstar to rival Pele in New York, and asked him to recommend any other players who might be of use. The response raised a few eyebrows back home. Bobby McAlinden was born on the same day as George Best, 22

May 1946, but there the similarity ends. McAlinden had played against George when the two Manchester clubs met in the semi-finals of the FA Youth Cup in 1964, but from that day on their careers had followed sharply divergent paths. The little midfield scrapper from Salford played just one League game for Manchester City before moving on to Port Vale and Stockport, where he never made the first team. Eight years after his release by Stockport, he was working for a bookmaker and playing his football for fun when he received an offer he couldn't refuse. George says:

> Bobby had been over to Ireland, and played a few games for Glentoran, the team I used to watch as a kid. Then, when I opened Slack Alice he used to come in quite a lot, and we started training together, with another couple of pals of mine, at the local YMCA. We played indoor football twice a week, just to keep in shape. When I decided to go to the States, I said to him: 'D'you fancy coming?' Of course he jumped at it, so I took him with me. He did well. He was a good little grafter, only small, but he worked his balls off and the crowd loved him for it. He's still out there, with his wife. They moved on to Portland, I think.

Between signing for the Aztecs in December and travelling to Los Angeles for the new season in February, George had a couple of months to kill, and agreed to play for Cork Celtic in the League of Ireland for £600 per match. As was usually the case by now, he had been signed as much for his pulling power at the turnstiles as anything he might accomplish on the field, and once the novelty had worn off he was dumped, after just three games.

In Los Angeles, Best and McAlinden shared an apartment in Hermosa Beach, where the Californian climate worked wonders. The sunshine state could scarcely have been more different to the dissolute, Prince of Darkness environment George had left behind, and free from temporal distractions his body became a temple again. Augmenting the Aztecs' training sessions with daily work-outs on the beach, he soon trimmed down to his optimum playing weight. At first, carrying the excess poundage of four years' hard drinking, it had been impossible to run even half a mile without collapsing in a heap, but McAlinden made him stick at it, and as the fitness returned so did much of the old enthusiasm.

Best's new team was not one of the NASL's strongest, but the lack of expectation, like his anonymity on the streets of LA, suited him during the initial period of detoxification and rehabilitation. And while the Aztecs were not the Cosmos, neither was he surrounded by mugs. In midfield the energetic McAlinden serviced two of the highest quality performers to be found anywhere in the world, Best and Charlie Cooke, and the centre-forward was Ron Davies, capped by Wales twenty-nine times in a career which took him, briefly, to Manchester United after distinguished spells at Norwich and Southampton. Davies was rising thirty-four, Cooke thirty-three. It was not a young team, but it was one capable of rising to the occasion.

In that first season, playing before curious crowds of 10,000 at El Camino College, they rose to it often enough to qualify for the NASL play-offs, the convoluted structure which eventually determined the League champions. To get into the play-offs, the Aztecs needed to win their last divisional game against Dallas Tornados, accruing nine points. A win was worth six points, goals one apiece, up to a maximum of three. The Aztecs had not scored more than two in a match all season, and a goalless first half did not bode well, but George was in the mood and, catching his second wind, struck twice in a 4–1 win. In the play-offs, coincidentally, the Aztecs played the Tornados again and lost 1–0, but it had been an encouraging start. In twenty-three appearances, Best had scored fifteen goals.

It had been a fun season, stimulating and restorative. George Best was in good condition for the first time in years, and enjoyed the feeling. It would be disingenuous to suggest that the problem with alcohol had gone away, or that he was playing as well as ever, but where four bottles of wine had been merely an aperitif, a drink now meant a few beers in comparatively innocent company, and he was fit enough, and performing well enough, to be a major player in a none-too-demanding League. Crucially, the alcoholic had regained his self-respect. He had also fallen under the salutary influence of the woman who was to be his first wife. Angela Macdonald Janes, from Southend, was a blonde go-getter who had lived in New York, where she had done some modelling, before moving to the West Coast to work as personal assistant to the singer-actress Cher, with whom she lived in Beverly Hills. After dumping his date to chat her up at a party, George had Angie move in to the house he and McAlinden had just bought in Hermosa Beach. It was to be another eighteen months before they wed.

Fit and happy, George was determined to stay that way, and not to let it all slip away in an off season of drunken debauchery back in Manchester, so when Fulham offered him a contract in August 1976, he accepted with alacrity. As usual, his new employers wanted George Best as a drawing card as much as a matchwinner. Surrounded by more glamorous competition, it has never been easy for Fulham to pull a crowd, and their latest attempt was to bring together some of the great entertainers, in the autumn of their careers, in a team more Barnum and Bailey than Mullery and Haynes. Bobby Moore, who was already there, was joined by Best and Rodney Marsh, who had also jumped on the transatlantic gravy train, moving from Manchester City to Tampa Bay Rowdies in 1975. George, as usual, was on 'top dollar': a £10,000 signing-on fee, wages of £500 a week, a rent-free London flat and a club car. A bureaucratic delay in the transfer of his registration from the Aztecs kept him waiting until 4 September for his debut, but he soon made up for lost time, his goal after just seventy-one seconds enough for a 1–0 victory over Bristol Rovers. Fulham were doubly delighted. The crowd at Craven Cottage was 21,127, twice the previous season's average.

Three days later, Best scored again in a 2–1 League Cup win at Peterborough where the attendance was 16,467 – three times their average gate. The George Best Show was on the road. For his second home game, against Wolves, the crowd was 25,794 – this in the old Second Division. George was happy and Fulham were ecstatic, their gamble on glamour paying handsome dividends. Graham Hortop, the club secretary, said: 'The interest is unbelievable. If we had signed two current England internationals I doubt if they would have made the same impact as George Best. It is up to us to sustain it.'

Rodney Marsh had been a friend since 1972, when Malcolm Allison signed him for Manchester City to be the George Best of Maine Road. Marsh became known as Malcolm's Folly when his introduction into a winning team caused such disruption that it cost City the championship that year, but he was a highly skilled showman, good enough to be capped by Alf Ramsey in an era when England were well blessed with forwards. With their shared penchant for the good life, he and George hit it off at once. Marsh says of their time together at Craven Cottage:

> For half a season the football that Fulham team played was fantastic. We were getting home gates of 25,000, the away crowds were massive, and we weren't kidding ourselves, they had all come to see George. He didn't let them down, nor did the rest of us. We were well up in the table for the first three months of the season, playing some great stuff. I always got on well with George, and we roomed together on away trips and socialized together. On the field we had a great relationship, too. We were on 'telly' a lot in those days, and when

they show the old footage you can see us laughing, really enjoying our football. In one sequence we're tackling each other. That was a case of: If you won't give me the ball, I'll take it off you, you greedy bugger!

To their mutual regret, it didn't last. A 4–1 win at home to Hereford on 25 September, in which Marsh scored twice, took Fulham to fourth place in the Second Division, but after that, it was downhill all the way. During a 4–1 defeat at Southampton the following week, Best was sent off for using 'foul and abusive language' in disputing a free-kick, and Marsh sustained an ankle ligament injury which kept him out of action for two months. 'The honeymoon period was over,' Marsh says. 'It all went pear-shaped after that.' It was the start of a run in which Fulham won one match in nine.

As usual when his team careered off the rails, so did George. All the good intentions, and all the good work in California, were drowned in a torrent of wine and vodka. 'At the start, it was good fun,' he says. 'It was like a Showbiz XI, with Rodney and me setting out to entertain and bringing laughter back into the game. The crowds loved it, and even the referees joined in the spirit, and laughed along with us. But it started to go sour when promises the club had made me were broken. It took them months to come up with my signing-on fee, the flat I was given was a dump which needed fumigating, and the car was never delivered, so I was taking taxis everywhere.' Angie, who had joined him from Beverly Hills, was not impressed. There were endless rows, and eventually she moved out, went to work at the Playboy Club in Park Lane, and rented a flat of her own. In a typical reaction to adversity, George went from bad to worse and took to drinking himself into a stupor and either making a scene or sleeping on her doorstep.

Fulham's attitude appeared to be: If you can't beat them, join them. The club chairman, Sir Eric Miller, who was to commit suicide when his business affairs came under investigation, took to drinking with Best, Marsh and Moore in the Duke of Wellington, a pub off the King's Road, and the manager, Bobby Campbell, kept his wayward star on the longest of reins. George says:

> Bobby was different class as far as I was concerned. He knew it was no good trying to keep me at home. If Manchester United couldn't do it, Fulham weren't going to, were they? Bobby caught me out time and again, but he was always sensible about it. As long as I turned up and played well, that was OK by him. I remember he took us away to a hotel before one cup tie and I decided to do a runner. I was sat in the Duke of Wellington, in Chelsea, just before closing time, chatting to two girls, and Bobby walked in. He came over and said: 'Hello Bestie, son. Introduce me to the girls then.' I said: 'I can't boss, I don't know their names.' He said: 'OK, well go and get the drinks in.' Now Bobby didn't drink, so I got him a Coke or something, and at about 11.30 he said: 'Are you ready to go, then?' We went, but not back to the team's hotel. Bobby said: 'We're going to stop off on the way,' and he pulled up at a Greek restaurant where Eric Miller was having a party. He kept me there until five a.m., and when we eventually got back to the hotel he said: 'You'd better play well today. If you don't, I'll have your bollocks.' I played well, and that was the end of the matter. Bobby was great.

Campbell may have been, his Fulham team weren't. They were without a win from 27 December to 19 March, losing nine out of twelve matches to plunge from ninth in the table to twentieth. The freefall started with a 2–0 defeat away to Chelsea, a west London derby which drew 55,000 to Stamford Bridge and saw George Best charged with bringing the game into disrepute. At the end of the game he had made a trembling wrist gesture at the referee, the same universal insult that had seen him sent off at Southampton in October. The FA found the disrepute charge proven, and fined Best seventy-five pounds. By now he was out of control, drinking as much as ever, and, driving home after yet another bender, at Tramp nightclub, he crashed a Fiat which belonged to the chairman's daughter, into a lamp-post outside Harrods. His head went through the windscreen, lacerating his face, and he fractured a shoulder blade. George needed fifty-seven stitches around his eyes and forehead, and some of the scars are still visible today. Told that he would be out of football for four months, he was back within five weeks, playing against medical advice with one side of his face totally numb.

The Best clouds often have a silver lining, and the accident brought Angie running back to look after him. Part of his signing-on fee having been paid, at last, they leased their own flat in Putney within walking distance of Craven Cottage. It was now that Rodney Marsh decided it was time for a few well chosen words:

> We were out one night at Tramp. I was on my own and Bestie was with Angela. I was sitting with George and she was a few feet away with the rest of the party, which included Bobby Moore. George was getting very drunk, not in good shape at all, and I pulled him to one side and said: 'You've got to eat something, pal.' He turned on me and said: 'Don't you ever fucking tell me what to do.' And we were close, good friends. I said: 'OK,' and held my hands up. I learned the hard way that there was no point in trying. I did what I thought was right, as a pal, and it was: 'Marshy, mind your own fucking business.'

Drinking or not, Best's modest return of six goals from thirty-two League games was enough to see him voted the supporters' Player of the Year for 1976–7. But long before the end of a disappointing season (Fulham trailed in seventeenth in the

Second Division) he was yearning to get back to LA. By the time he did so, in mid-May, the NASL season was a month old, and the Aztecs were in good shape. That was more than could be said for George Best, who had fallen off the wagon in a big way, but again, despite the apologists like Rodney Marsh who insist that American 'soccer' was highly competitive, George on the booze was not merely good enough to hold his own, he was one of the best players in the League.

For 1977, the Aztecs had moved from El Camino College to the Los Angeles Coliseum, and trained at the Hollywood Racetrack instead of on the beach. They were moving upmarket, becoming more professional. They had signed Mancini and Phil Beal, another experienced defender who had played nearly 400 times for Tottenham, but the most significant change was the recruitment of the fastest forward in the NASL, a Trinidadian by the name of Steve David. The Caribbean flyer was exactly what was needed – a pacy partner for the big man, Ron Davies, in attack. The West Coast's finest had the look of title aspirants.

George insists he had nothing but football on his mind, but the facts tell a different story. As soon as he got back to LA there were ominous echoes of Slack Alice when, in partnership with Bobby McAlinden and an American by the name of John Young, he bought the lease of a run-down bar called 'Hard Times' which had fallen on them. The two footballers sold the house they shared to raise the $30,000 needed, reopening under the name 'Bestie's'. Heavily into the wrong culture again, George would spend most days, and every night, in the bar. It is powerful testimony to his constitution, as well as his ability, that he could drink like the devil and play like a god. He had missed the first five games of the season, but still finished third under the unique points scoring system which ranked players according to goals scored and 'assists'. A goal was worth two points, an assist, or scoring pass, one, and George finished with eleven and eighteen respectively. Top scorer in the whole of the NASL was the Aztecs' Steve David, with twenty-six goals and six assists. A notable 4–1 win at home to Pele's New York Cosmos in July was not enough to prevent Dallas Tornados from taking the Southern Division title, but the Aztecs qualified for the play-offs again, and beat San José Earthquakes 2–1. That brought them up against Dallas in the two-leg Divisional Championship, which they won 5–1, but the Pacific Conference Championship was a bridge too far, Seattle Sounders squeezing them out on a 3–2 aggregate with Mike England and Mel Machin, at thirty-five and thirty-two, dominant in defence.

Best found life on America's West Coast much more laid back, and therefore more agreeable, than west London, and he was 'not keen' on fulfilling the second year of his contract with Fulham. The wrong end of the Second Division and venues like Mansfield, Oldham and Hull held few attractions after New York, Tampa and Fort Lauderdale, and Rodney Marsh opted not to return. George's reluctance was compounded by the Aztecs' dissatisfaction with the agreement under which the two clubs shared his services. The British and American seasons overlapped, and John Chaffetz, the general manager in LA, had negotiated compensation of $2,000 for every NASL match Best missed. By playing right up to the end of the 1976–7 season for Fulham, he had missed five, and Chaffetz wanted his money. When it was not forthcoming, despite several demands, the Football League and the Football Association became involved in what was seen as a test case. These disputes were occurring all the time as players criss-crossed the Atlantic, and eventually the lend-lease arrangements, which were open to all sorts of financial shenanigans, were outlawed. Transfers had to be conducted on a formal, permanent basis, or not at all.

On 1 September 1977 it took the intervention of FIFA to break the impasse and clear George Best to play for Fulham at home to Blackburn Rovers two days later. It was not the most auspicious of starts. A goalless draw was followed by a 1–0 defeat at

Tottenham, and after five games Fulham were without a win and nineteenth in the table. It hardly helped George's mood that one of his team-mates was now Peter Storey, the former Arsenal and England hatchet man for whom he had nothing but contempt. He need not have worried on that score. Storey was released 'by mutual consent' in November, and subsequently jailed for three years for conspiring, with others, to counterfeit half-sovereign gold coins between June and September 1978.

After that first match against Blackburn, George flew back to LA with Chaffetz while the vexed issue of who owned his registration was sorted out. He rejoined Fulham in time for a 3–1 defeat at Cardiff on 24 September, but did not linger long. He scored against Burnley and Sunderland, but with a poor team languishing in sixteenth place he did yet another of his 'runners' to rejoin the Aztecs in mid-November. His second season with Fulham had lasted just ten games. Brief though it was, it produced a fancy-that record which may never be equalled. When he turned out for Fulham at Crystal Palace on 1 October, he had played in all four home countries in the space of ten days, after club matches against Cardiff (in the League) and St Mirren (in the quarter-finals of the Anglo-Scottish Cup), and an international for Northern Ireland against Iceland in Belfast. Best has another reason to remember the Palace game. In it, his tackle fractured Ian Evans's leg in two places, ending his career. George says: 'I broke two players' legs – Glyn Pardoe was the other – and the incidents were almost identical. In both cases I went in with a sliding tackle, and the lads' momentum caused the damage. There was no real weight or vicious intent behind either challenge. I've nothing to feel guilty about.'

Back in LA, he was behaving increasingly like an alcoholic out of control. Short periods of comparative sobriety and lucidity would be followed by binges lasting three and four days which drove Angie, not to mention the Aztecs' management, to distraction. Once, having been missing for four days, in the company of a waitress he had picked up somewhere along the way, he walked through the front door and said he wanted something to eat. At the end of her tether, Angie stabbed him in the backside with a carving knife. They made up, but a couple of weeks later the wild rover was off on his travels again. This time, Angie decided to do some disappearing of her own, and a boozed Best ended up dossing outside Cher's home in Malibu, seeking forgiveness.

Not that it was all bad, far from it. There were weeks when they were a 'normal' couple, going out for meals, visiting friends, with George charm personified, but then Angie would come home from work one afternoon and he would be gone. Worried, she would go out to look for him, trawling all his known haunts. Sometimes she would find him, but when he was at his worst he would hitchhike to another town, and make sure she couldn't. Cher, and all her friends, told her to ditch this hopeless drunk who was making her life a misery, but like so many women who are drawn to incorrigible rogues, she thought she could succeed where all the others had failed, and change him.

Fear of losing her prompted George to propose in January 1978. Angie had been pictured in one of the newspapers with Dean Martin's hunkily handsome son Ricci and, always the jealous type, George was having no more of that. If marriage was what it took to put an end to it, so be it. 'I wasn't thinking straight at the time,' he says. 'I asked her, she said yes, and we flew off to Las Vegas to get it done. It was a disaster from start to finish.'

chapter seventeen

George Best comes a close second behind Bernard Manning on a list of speakers unlikely to be heard at your local WI. Some of his stories, delivered in front of his cringing second wife Alex, would have any self-respecting feminist reaching for the gelding gear.

To say he is unreconstructed is like suggesting Hugh Hefner may have had eyes for more than one woman. Well past fifty, he is the archetypal ageing roué. In his local pub, the Phene Arms in Chelsea, he habitually bets his drinking mates five pounds that he can get the phone number of any girl within five minutes of her walking through the door. It is a sad reflection on the distaff side that he always collects.

For a 'wind-up', I have seen him use the phone booth in the Phene to ring the pub's Spanish barmaid pretending to be her English boyfriend, fool her completely, and make her a laughing stock by conducting a whispered tête-à-tête, interspersed with 'I love yous'. Yet when Tim Graveney, the yuppie son of Tom the former England cricketer, struck up an entirely innocent conversation with Alex, he went ballistic, warning her publicly, in no uncertain terms, not to 'make a fool of him' again. This do-as-I-say-not-as-I-do attitude can be embarrassing to behold. It is dangerous for anyone to mention Alex's old boyfriends – especially John Scales, the Tottenham footballer – but she has to feign amusement at endless tales about her spouse's legendary love life. She stopped smiling long ago when he tells his audience: 'My problem was that I was always missing. Miss World,

Miss England, Miss UK...' 'I don't want to know about the girls he's had,' Alex says. 'He likes to provoke me like that. He likes to pick a fight. All that's bad enough now. I wouldn't have wanted to marry him when he was younger.'

That was the misfortune that befell Angela Janes (the Macdonald was an affectation, appended to the family name when she emigrated to New York) on 24 January 1978. George had proposed to her before, and had been turned down twice, first in December 1976 and again in August the following year. On the second occasion she said he 'took her for granted' and that she would not be 'treated like a doormat', but then softened the blow by adding: 'There is still an awful lot of feeling there. He knows it and I know it. Now, we're just being tough with each other.' When George popped the question a third time, it forced her to choose between him and Ricci Martin, son of Dean, who had also asked her to marry him. 'I've been seeing the two of them,' she said, 'and it's awful to have to decide. Poor Ricci is absolutely heartbroken. He can't believe that I don't want him.' Her two suitors had egos in common, too, it seems.

Angie's mother Marion, a civil servant with Customs and Excise, was not exactly ecstatic at the prospect of having George Best as a son-in law. 'Frankly,' she said, 'I just don't know whether Angela and George will be able to make a go of it. I have nothing against him. That's not to say that I approve of his past, but don't let us condemn him for life because of it. My daughter may be able to give him the stability he needs so much. If Angela really loves him as much as she thinks she does, then perhaps, just perhaps, it might work out.'

Fortunately, Marion missed the wedding, otherwise she would have given them no chance. It was a mockery from start to finish. Bride and groom seemed to sense that they were making a mistake, and both arrived late for the short flight from LA to Las Vegas, very much the worse for wear from the night before. George was still drunk. Angie had sold the 'exclusive' to the *Sun*, necessitating a two-hour chase around Vegas while they tried to lose the opposition who had formed up in convoy behind. Originally, the happy couple had chosen the 'We've Only Just Begun Wedding Chapel', but the re-routing, to shake off their media pursuers, took them to the 'Candlelight Chapel' where the twenty-dollar three-minute special was conducted against a background of cassette music (the organist would have cost an extra ten-dollars) and giggles from Angie, who could not contain herself at the sight and sound of a camp, gay minister decked out in lime green three-piece suit with braid trim. George had forgotten that a ring was required and had to borrow one from his best man, Bobby McAlinden.

The deed done, the first thing the bridegroom wanted was a drink, so the party adjourned to Caesar's Palace casino where a maladroit waiter spilled champagne over everyone while George lost all his money on the tables. There was no honeymoon. It was straight back to LA, where Angie's new husband started as he meant to go on, by going to the local with his mates and returning home 'stinking drunk' at four a.m., by which time his bride was fast asleep.

The responsibility of marriage was supposed to have a stabilizing effect, instead it had just the opposite. At thirty-one, George was nowhere near ready for domesticity, and the playboy in him rebelled against the very concept of 'settling down'. He was drinking all day, at Bestie's, and most nights, wherever they were not too particular about the sobriety of their clientele. The prospects for the coming season did nothing to improve his mood, or conduct. John Chaffetz and his associates had sold the Aztecs' franchise to a consortium of businessmen from Beverly Hills, who sought George's advice as to who they should sign to strengthen the team, then ignored all his recommendations. Mancini and Beal were out, replaced by a Leeds United reserve, Bobby Sibald, and an obscure, overweight Mexican by the name of Hector Pulido. Best was not impressed. 'I was wasting my time,' he says. 'I went back to the beach – and the booze.'

The defeats piled up, and after incurring a suspension for missing training, George said simply: 'I don't want to play for you any more,' and was offloaded in June 1978 to the Fort Lauderdale Strikers. 'I got lucky,' he says. 'It was a nice set-up, with some useful players.' The Strikers had an English coach, Ron Newman, and the bulk of his team was drawn from the Football League, with John Hickton, who had been a prolific centre-forward with Middlesbrough, partnered in attack by David Irving, an energetic bustler formerly with Everton and Oldham. The biggest name, Ian Callaghan, was to be found in midfield, where he left most of the running to the younger legs of Ray Hudson, a grafter from Newcastle, and Norman Piper, who had been capped by England at Under-23 level while making well over 500 appearances for Plymouth and Portsmouth. George recognized another familiar face, Tony Whelan, a forward who had been a reserve at Manchester United from 1969 to 1972.

There were some decent players, but they were underachieving. When George joined, the Strikers were something of a misnomer in the football sense having won eight games and lost eleven, and hopes were not exactly sky-high for his debut match against New York Cosmos, the NASL champions. The last time the two sides met the Cosmos had won 8–0, and Fort Lauderdale was bracing itself for another drubbing. But they were reckoning without George Best. The man's pride was such that he always tried everything he knew to make a favourable impression on new team-mates and supporters, and the impact was to be instantaneous this time. George scored with his first touch and added a second goal later, inspiring the Strikers to an improbable 5–3 win. He says: 'I flew in from LA in the afternoon, and my first game was that same night. They had never beaten the Cosmos, and we put five past them. It was some start.' It was the spark a slow-burning team had needed. That one, uplifting result ignited a hot streak that carried them into the play-offs and through to the Conference Championship, where they lost, on a shoot-out, to Tampa Bay Rowdies. Events during that defeat started a feud between Best and Newman which had lasting repercussions. George objected to being substituted in extra-time, and said so, with some venom. Newman would bide his time before having the last word.

Trouble came after promising beginnings, as sure as night follows day. With the intention of staying out of the local bars for a while, and making some worthwhile money at the same time, George readily agreed when Ken Adam, who had taken over from Ken Stanley as his agent when he joined Fulham, arranged for him to guest for another American team, Detroit Express, on a European tour in September 1978. He played two games in Austria, and the roof fell in. Fulham, still in dispute with LA Aztecs over his transfer, although he no longer played for either club, pointed out that the terms of his registration allowed him to play outside America only for them. George ditched Ken Adam, whose responsibilities included being aware of such things. 'I hadn't been happy with him anyway. When I went back to the States from Fulham, he was supposed to settle up for me. Fulham had paid the deposit on a flat, by way of a signing-on fee, and I told Adam to sell it and send on whatever profit there was. By the time I got to America, he said there was nothing left. I found out that he had given players at Fulham some of my belongings from the flat.' George made Angie his agent, saying: 'At least I know she's not in it just for the money,' but the damage was done. Fulham asked FIFA, world football's governing body, to suspend him from playing until the dispute was resolved, and on 11 October a global ban was imposed, preventing him from earning his living anywhere.

It was a hammer blow, but one which paled into insignificance the very next day. On 12 October 1978 Ann Best died in her bed in Belfast. In his absence, George's mother had lost the will to live and had drunk herself to death. Time and again, knowing that the two of them shared an illness the rest of the family could not understand, George's sisters had asked him to come home and help her to come to terms with the problem, but there had always been a reason why it was too inconvenient. Now it was too late, and he was devastated. It would take a long time to assuage his sense of guilt.

Twenty years on he is still trying.

chapter eighteen

Dickie Best is a lovely leprechaun of a man, the genial, story-telling grandad every kid would love to have. He is chirpier than anyone might reasonably expect after a life of hard toil and harder luck.

Dickie welcomes visitors to his neat and tidy shrine of a home in troubled Belfast with excuses for the lavatorial habits of the local mutts, who have made a mess of his garden again, and for the debris left from a morning of do-it-yourself on his old banger. Disappearing into the kitchen, he quickly produces the cup that cheers. Tea, yes, but he will have no sympathy. Like his prodigal son, he is too proud for any of that.

God knows, the poor soul deserves it. Perched on the edge of his armchair in the front room of the modest council house that his been his home for fifty years, surrounded by pictures from the past, he cuts a lonely figure, left only with his memories. Retirement was not meant to be like this, not for a man who worked hard until he was seventy-one years of age, first in the shipyards and then wherever they would have him. There should have been a wife with whom to share a contented old age; there should have been a wealthy son to lean on. Two of his extended family have been shot during the Troubles, one fatally, and his younger son, Ian, has to keep a profile bordering on the subterranean, in constant danger as an NCO in the British Army.

Dickie Best is not bitter about the handful of deuces fate dealt him, but sometimes the emotions spill over, betraying the hurt.

One such occasion was in September 1990 when George was drunk and foul-mouthed on television on the *Wogan* programme. Dickie, who was in the audience, looked on aghast. Mortified, then angry, he muttered: 'Bloody hell, George, why are you doing this to us? When are you going to stop it?' The answer, sadly, was even more depressing than his son's behaviour.

Twice during our conversation the tears well in his eyes, and he makes needless apologies as he pauses to wipe them away. The first time is when he recalls George's scintillating performance for Manchester United at Chelsea in 1964, when he first caught the eye of the national media. 'They said in one of the papers that the two teams stood and applauded him off the field, and that the little Irishman walked off with bowed head, embarrassed. I still get awfully emotional, thinking about that.' The second occasion is when he speaks of the terrible moment when he found his wife dead in bed:

> I'm seventy-seven, and people often say to me: 'You look young for your age, you must have had an easy life.' I think to myself: Christ, if you only knew the truth, mate. You have to live with alcoholism to realize what it is like, and what it does to people. Somehow, you have to carry on with your daily life, as if there's nothing wrong, but it's impossible, of course.
>
> George's mum was a lovely person, and for a long time we had a great life together. It was a hard life at times, bringing up six children with not too much money coming in, but we had a lovely life, until her drink problem started. People ask why it happened. There's no answer to that. As you might imagine, I've taken quite an interest in the subject. I used to go to open meetings of Alcoholics Anonymous with a recovering alcoholic. He'd been off the drink for five years after ending up in a mental hospital for four months. The way he described it to me, your head is like a ball of wool, and you've

got to get all the tangled strands separated into orderly, straight lines.

When my wife started drinking heavily we tried to hide it but we couldn't. Because of who we were – George Best's parents – we were well known in Belfast, and it seemed everyone knew our business, and what was happening. As her alcoholism took hold, I had to take over the running of the house, as well as doing my job. I tried to hide it from the children, to protect them from it, but there was no chance. George was away, in Manchester, but the others were there with us, they could see it. I had to keep money from my wife to stop her spending it all on drink. I did all the things I thought were right, but maybe they weren't. Maybe I was just antagonizing her to no purpose. That's the trouble when you're dealing with an alcoholic, you're forever banging your head against a brick wall and getting nowhere.

My biggest worry was the kids. What would they find when they came home from school, with me at work and not able to shield them from the worst? What state would their mum be in? At first, they used to think she was sick. They told me in later years that they would say to each other: 'I wonder if mummy is sick again today?' She wasn't physically sick, but that was the way they saw her. They didn't realize she had a drink problem, they were too young to understand.

We had never had rows in this house. My wife and I never had arguments, and there was no boss, we were equal partners in everything. Our relationship was great until the drink came along. Then the rows started. Alcoholics turn on their nearest and dearest, and it was difficult for me not to hit back. I don't mean physically abuse her, but she made it impossible for me not to have to curb her. I never hit my wife, but I did have to restrain her.

It was a terrible situation, one that was breaking my heart.

> Coming home from work at night, the nearer I got to my home the less I wanted to get there. My feet slowed down and my stomach churned over and over. I didn't know what I was coming in to see. When she was her normal self, she was a lovely person, and a good-looking woman, too. I'd have given her the world. But when I came in and saw her drunk and dirty it became revolting to me. She stopped eating, and from being a lovely woman she became an old hag to look at.
>
> People say to me: 'Why did you take your wife out, if you knew she was going to get drunk?' They couldn't understand. It was the lesser of two evils. Either I took her out with me, and tried to control her drinking, or I left her at home, under no control. But I couldn't win. I would say to George's mum: 'We're going to a function tonight. Don't have too much to drink, wait until afterwards.' That would have the opposite effect. She'd set out to get drunk. I was hurt, I was angry, I was disgusted – I went through all the emotions. I was livid, actually. There was no peace. I thought: I've got to face everybody, in the street, in the clubs, wherever. Most of them wouldn't say anything to me directly, but I knew what they were thinking. Even my son-in-law, Carol's husband, would ask my daughter: 'Why did your dad take your mum out, to get in that state?' Carol tells her husband: 'If you're not there all the time, you can't understand. You never really knew my mum – not my real mum. You only saw her with the devil in her.' It's hard to believe that a person can change, like Jekyll and Hyde, but my wife did.
>
> The end came more suddenly than I expected. I took her a cup of tea in bed one morning and she was dead.

Distressed by the memory, Dickie breaks down and sobs at this point. After a couple of minutes to recover his composure, he is determined to finish his heart-rending tale.

How long did the process take? It's hard to tell. My wife was forty-three when Ian was born, and it started a couple of years after that. She died when she was fifty-four, and she was really bad for six or seven years. But you can't put a finger on when it started, only when it ended. She died on 12 October 1978. My wife [it seems too painful for Dickie to mention Ann's name] didn't take a drink until she was past forty. Then she started in one of the jobs she had. There was drink being taken into the place, and she got involved with the wrong crowd. She worked in an ice-cream factory during the day, and I think a fair bit of drinking went on in there. It was such a shame, such a terrible, crying shame.

There is no doubt that Ann Best missed her firstborn, and favourite, when he settled in Manchester and his visits became ever more infrequent. George wishes he had gone home to see her more often, and wonders if things might have been different if he had. Typically, Dickie absolves his son from blame:

He used to come home whenever he could at first, then it tailed off, but that's the way it goes with most kids. They grow up and grow away, with new friends and families of their own. George was either training or playing every day except Sunday, and we understood. I have friends who've got family living in England and they haven't seen them for years and years.

I don't think there was much George could have done to help his mum. I tend to look at the reverse. If we had gone to live in Manchester and tried to change George, might it have been different for him? Matt Busby wanted to bring us across. He sent Frank O'Farrell over here to see me. Frank came to Belfast on the pretext of watching an international match. In fact, he came to this house and put it to me that it would be good for George to have us over there with him. He said

Playing in the USA for the Aztecs, 1976. Colorsport

The red card, 1976. Even Bobby Moore looks incredulous.
Times Newspapers

And again, at Southampton, the same year.
Ed Lacey

Returning to Britain with his wife, Angie, in 1979 after a season in Florida.
Press Association

Bestie enjoys a drink.
Tommy Hindley

The high life. George with his girlfriend Mary Stavin, Miss World, meets Prince Philip in 1983. Barratts

The low life. George Best was arrested and charged with drink-driving in 1984 but failed to appear in court. PA

Sentenced to prison, Best lodged an appeal. PA

Bestie and Bobby Charlton took different sides when they met at Wembley for a charity match in 1985. Sport & General

Best plays in a charity match at Wembley on his fortieth birthday, May 1986. PA

Out of the money. Leaving the bankruptcy courts with his long-term companion, Mary Shatila. Photo News Service

Good friends. With Rodney Marsh in 1993 . . .

. . . and Denis Law, at Sir Matt Busby's funeral in 1994. UPP/Times Newspapers

George and Alex Best celebrate the opening of an Italian restaurant in Fulham which bears his name.
Times Newspapers

Manchester United would get me a job, on a better wage than I was getting here, and they'd get us a house, fully furnished, at a nominal rent. Everything was ideal for us to go, but my wife's illness prevented it. How could I take her problem to Manchester, and have him and her at it in the same area? I had to tell Frank that because my wife was an alcoholic, I couldn't undertake what they had in mind. I had to think of my other kids as well, of course. It would have meant asking them to move away from their friends and go to a new school. And anyway, I couldn't be sure that us moving to Manchester would be like a magic wand, and that waving it would solve George's problem overnight. By this time he had a serious problem, and an obvious one. Everyone knew all about that by the time he was twenty-four or twenty-five.

Twenty years on, George still finds it difficult to talk about his mother's decline and death. A sadness that is visible – almost tangible – engulfs him at the mention of her name. His voice drops to a murmur as he says: 'I was in Los Angeles when it happened. I don't remember exactly what I was doing when I heard the news because I keep trying to blank it out of my mind. My dad told me all about it. It was the booze. I'd flown home a couple of times to talk to her, trying . . .' The sentence trails off, interrupted by awful memories, and is left unfinished. Swallowing the lump in his throat, he continues:

My dad told me that they went to bed one night and she just said: 'Dickie, I don't want to live any more.' He told her not to be so stupid, but when he took her a cup of tea the next morning she was gone. She died in bed. She just made up her mind to do it and died. When he told me that, when he called me and said I had to come home for the funeral and all that stuff, I was physically sick. My poor parents. They had been

> such a loving couple. My dad never looked at another woman. When he told me that, when he said she'd told him she didn't want to live any more . . .

Again the sentence is left hanging in the air, George unable to continue.

Eventually, like his father, he forces himself to go on, as if purging his grief:

> I felt guilty. Very, very guilty. I thought: I could have done more, I could have called more often, written more times. I could have been there for her. I wasn't there for years, and I felt it was my fault. In the early days I used to insist on flying home on a Saturday night, after a game, just to spend a couple of days with the family, but once the fixture list got heavier, and I was playing three times a week, I couldn't do it, and I drifted away. There's no real excuse, though. I could have gone in the summer, and spent a bit less time in Spain.

He could not remember his mother drinking when he was growing up. If she had been an alcoholic then, it might have deterred him:

> I think she started when I became famous. She found that difficult to handle – people coming up to her, saying: 'Aren't you George Best's mum?' and sometimes slagging me off. In a club once, when a woman walked up and told her I was a disgrace to Ireland, she thumped her in the face and my dad had to break them up. Normally, she wasn't like that at all, but fame, notoriety, whatever you want to call it, got to her. We'd been a working class family from a council house in Belfast, and all of a sudden there was a superstar there and she found that very hard to handle because she was very quiet, very shy. My dad was the outgoing one, mum was the

retiring type. I think she started drinking for Dutch courage, to cope with people bothering her.

In the mid-seventies, on one of the few occasions when George did go home, his mother drank incessantly, and became maudlin drunk. She showed no interest in what he said to her, but sat beside him, holding his arm and weeping. Profoundly distressed, George went back to Manchester and sought refuge in the self-same anaesthetic, opening a bottle of wine and drinking it on his own. It was the most destructive of vicious circles. Ann Best was drinking because of her son, who was drinking even more to blot out her alcoholism. There is a serious chicken and egg question here. Even Dickie Best is not sure whether it was his wife or son who became an alcoholic first, but he fears that the condition may be hereditary, in which case his grandson – George's son Calum – is clearly at risk:

> I've spoken to the leading authority on the subject in Northern Ireland, a Dr Moorhead, who told me that everyone is a potential alcoholic. Everyone is that first drink away from being one, there's no way of knowing. It's like a cancer, it's there before you know it, and then it's a deadly battle. Dr Moorhead's theory is that you have to let the alcoholic go all the way down into the gutter, to experience the very depths. Only then will they realize how low they've sunk, and from there, there's only one way they can go. George has been pretty close at times, but he's never sunk into the gutter. He's not been there yet. I'm waiting.

Today, Dickie Best still sees very little of his pride and joy, who has caused him occasional embarrassment, but of whom he will not entertain a single word of criticism. George visits only when he is working in Ireland, and then meets his father at the venue, or at his hotel, rather than in the family home. When I travelled with George to one gig in Belfast, Dickie arrived independently and had to wait until the general public had been satisfied before snatching a few precious moments with his son, and having him autograph some old posters. On another occasion, when I lunched with George in Belfast's Europa Hotel, Dickie was due to join us, but failed to turn up. The biter bit.

Father and son are close, but would like to be closer. George has spoken of buying a home in Belfast, 'to be near my dad', but it is no more than talk. He is unlikely to leave Chelsea where he has lived since 1984. Dickie, not as sprightly as he once was, would love to have his son around to cushion old age and creeping infirmity, but accepts that it is not going to happen. In times of trouble, they are always there for one another, but to his father's clear, if unspoken, regret, George has never been one to confide in him, reluctant to burden a man who has had more than his share of heartache with yet more problems:

> George has never really confided in people. Whenever I say this, nobody believes it, but he has never told me the story of why he left Manchester United. I only know what he has said in television programmes, books or whatever. He has never discussed it with me at all. I don't probe. If the time comes when he wants to talk about it, he will. It's a shame, but I don't see much of George nowadays, only when he comes here to work, and then I hardly get to speak to him. Everyone else wants to see and talk to him. I suppose that's one of the crosses I have to bear for having a famous son.

A modest man with modest needs, Dickie Best lives his pensioner's life pretty much on a shoestring, even to the extent of wearing second-hand clothes:

> George has said to me many times: 'Dad, if you need anything you just have to pick up the phone,' but I don't go around

with a begging bowl. That's not to say I'm too proud to take something if I'm given it. When a friend's husband died, she gave me two nice jackets of his. They both needed the sleeves shortening, and sitting here one night I thought: I'll have a go at that, and I altered one myself. Cut and shortened it as good as new. People say to me: 'You don't need a wife,' and I know what they mean. I couldn't knit, I couldn't bake and I couldn't sew, but I've done the lot.

The sums involved are nobody's business but their own, but George does help out financially. He always has done. Dickie says: 'I didn't have a car until George was nineteen, then he gave me the first one he had, an Austin 1100. He had it shipped over, on the boat. The car I've got now is a 1985 Nissan. It was five years old when George bought it for me. He wanted me to have a new one, but I had my eye on this Nissan. They wanted £4,000 for it, but I knocked them down to £3,500, and then got another £100 off when they heard it was George Best buying it. It still looks good, and so it should. I don't do 3,000 miles a year in it, just to the supermarket or the betting shop.'

In his late seventies, dapper Dickie has a lady friend, Viollet (George calls her his 'bird'), with whom he goes out dancing twice a week, but there is no question of him ever remarrying. No one could ever replace the late, lamented Ann.

chapter nineteen

Losing your livelihood and your mother in the space of two days would be enough to drive most people to strong drink, and George Best never needed any excuse to venture down that dark tunnel.

Fort Lauderdale took up the cudgels on his behalf, fighting FIFA's worldwide suspension all the way, which meant an expensive High Court hearing in London at which Fulham contested the lifting of his ban and the judge found in their favour. It could not last for ever, of course. A counter action, claiming restraint of trade, would have blown the two Fs out of the water, but George was no expert in such legalities, and it was a worrying time. Assured by Fort Lauderdale that all would be well sooner rather than later, he flew Angie, and their furniture, over from the West Coast to their new rented home in Florida, and together they sat back under the palm trees, drinks in hand, and waited.

George was ineligible for all Fort Lauderdale's pre-season games while FIFA procrastinated, and when the ban was finally rescinded, on 28 March 1979, he had not played for five months and was nowhere near match fit. He had been at odds with the club's English coach, Ron Newman, almost from the start, publicly deriding his unorthodox methods and idiosyncratic tactics, and now their strained relationship reached breaking point. Having missed the warm-up matches (through no fault of his own, for once), George asked Newman to keep him on for the full ninety minutes whenever possible while he built up his fitness. When, in the first match of the season against New England Teamen, he was substituted after an hour, he lost his temper and made the most public of protests. Stalking off, he threw his shirt at Newman and called him every name an extensive vocabulary could muster. After that there was no way back, which was a pity. Newman may not have been the best coach in the world (or even in America) but, with plenty of money to play with, he had assembled a good team with two World Cup stars, West Germany's Gerd Muller and Cubillas of Peru, supported in attack by Clive Walker, the Chelsea winger. With George Best, too, they would have turned any NASL defence to jelly, but Newman was unforgiving. George did more hanging from the bench than Judge Jeffreys and, increasingly frustrated, he sought solace in the usual company. The bottle.

He was suspended in July, for missing training and failing to turn up for a match, and by now even the long-suffering Angie had had enough. After yet another jag, George staggered home to an empty house, a terse note explaining that his wife had returned to Los Angeles to take up her old job with Cher. 'You're wasting your life, George,' she said. 'You're not going to waste mine as well.' Eventually, after months of persuasion, she went back, but it was a mistake. The worst was still to come.

The dispute with Newman was terminal, but July was too late for a transfer, so George went back to LA and a bachelor (or rather estranged husband's) life of birds and booze. The second half of 1979 was, he says, a 'desperate' time. Without Angie, and with no football to curb his excesses, he lurched into alcoholism's deepest abysses, drinking himself into oblivion every night and dossing wherever he finished up, sometimes on the beach. In September 1979, when he was at his wits' end, his life 'horribly empty' and going downhill fast, Angie suddenly walked into 'Bestie's' one night, like a ministering angel. But there was no sympathy, no reunion this time. She had an ultimatum. She was no longer prepared to be a punchbag for his emotions, and would only go back to him given hard evidence that he was prepared to get help and sort himself out. George would try anything, he said. He loved her and needed her. He would go back to England, get work, and prove that he had it in him to reform. She liked the sound of that. He was on. The good intentions would all come to naught, as usual, but when he signed to play for Hibernian, in the Scottish Premier Division, Angie was sufficiently impressed to try again.

There was another hard knock first. In October 1979, the month before his latest new start took him to Edinburgh, he suffered a snub that cut him to the quick, and which still pains him today. Manchester United, in whose colours he had run the full gamut in 464 appearances (scoring 178 goals), refused George Best a testimonial. He had played for them from September 1963, when he made his debut, until 1 January 1974, and players are normally eligible for a testimonial after ten years' service, but the genius who in the good years did so much to embellish United's name was told he had not played long enough. In another sense, most of us would agree, but given that Pat Crerand played fewer games (304) over a shorter period (1962–70), and was granted a testimonial, the decision seems not just petty, but indefensible. George is still bitter about it:

> I don't know who it was on the board that said no, but somebody blocked the idea. To this day I'm still annoyed because I played for the club for eleven years, and I've turned out in countless testimonial games for others. I don't know how many players from that 1968 side did get testimonials, but I like to think that I had a bit more to do with winning the European Cup than most. It annoyed me at the time, and still does, because I can't see what the problem was, but I wasn't going to go to them and beg. I never asked for a testimonial in the first place, my pals in Manchester asked for me. They came up with another idea, to hire Old Trafford and

put a game on, but United wouldn't let them do that either. It's disappointing, to say the least, considering what I've done for the club.

George joined Hibernian on 16 November 1979 at the invitation of their chairman, Tom Hart. The signing was instigated by the board rather than the club's manager, Willie Ormond, and the directors made no bones about the motivation behind paying Fulham £50,000 for Best's registration and the man himself £2,500 per game. They wanted bums on seats. George says: 'The chairman called me and said: "You can come up every Thursday night, stay in a hotel, train with the boys on Friday, stay over to play on Saturday, then you can be back in London on Saturday night. How about it?" I said: "It sounds fine, but I'm nowhere near fit." He told me not to worry about that, just to give it a go. They were offering a lot of money, so I had a crack.'

As usual, George Best's name on the programme meant overtime at the turnstiles. His debut for Hibs was away to St Mirren on 24 November. George scored in a 2–1 defeat, but the most significant statistic was the 13,670 crowd – double St Mirren's average. The Best effect was even more marked the following week when 20,622 packed Easter Road for the visit of Partick Thistle. For purposes of comparison, Hibs played them again at home towards the end of the season, by which time George had returned to America. The attendance was 1,191.

Best, a stone overweight, had joined an inadequate team destined for relegation, and he was not fit enough to make much difference. Staying alone in an Edinburgh hotel was no help. He was not one to sit in his room reading or watching television, and if he was ever 'on the wagon', as he had promised Angie he would be, he soon tumbled off it. When he was in London, where he was now spending most of his time, or Manchester, he didn't bother to train, and two days a week with Hibs was nowhere near enough to restore him to a decent level of fitness. 'It was useless, really,' he says. 'They were a poor side, with no decent players to speak of. The team was struggling and I was there just to put a few on the gate, which I did for the first few games. From that point of view the club was happy, and thought it worked.'

George was less happy, and it showed. On 15 December, just four weeks after signing for Hibs, he failed to turn up for their match away to Morton. On 12 January he atoned with a goal which was enough to prise a draw out of the League leaders, Celtic, but on 11 February 1980 he went AWOL again, and was suspended for missing the home game against Morton. 'It was hard for me to take it seriously,' he says. 'Too hard. I had no friends up there, and I didn't really mix with the players because I wasn't with them often enough to get to know them. After training, we would go and have a couple of drinks, but then they would go home to their families, and I was stuck on my own at night in the hotel. There were times when I'd disappear down to London for some company, but old Tom, the chairman, understood. He was a lovely man.'

Lovely man he may have been, but Tom Hart's patience was not inexhaustible, and on 17 February George Best was sacked by Hibernian for being in no condition to play in a Scottish Cup tie against Ayr United. The game was played on a Sunday, and the previous night George had fallen into the company of some formidable drinking partners. The French rugby team. France had lost 22–14 to Scotland at Murrayfield and were in the process of drowning their sorrows when George volunteered to help:

> I was having a drink on my own when the French team arrived in the hotel. They were all ordering drinks when Jean-Pierre Rives spotted me and invited me to join them. That was it. The next thing I know, it's Sunday and Hibernian have come to pick me up to take me to the game. The trainer took one look at me and said: 'You can't play today, can you?' I told him I couldn't and that was that. I can't remember much

> about the night before, not even if I got to bed, but I know Rives could drink as well as he played. They all could. And they could hold it, as well.

George laughs about the episode now, and Hibs, remembering that they had agreed to take him 'warts and all', relented and welcomed him back the following week, but 'going on the missing list', as he puts it, three times in two months was an ominous signal. Far from getting his act together, which had been the point of returning to Britain, he was heading pell-mell down the slippery slope, and the slalom ride to despair was about to take yet another turn for the worse.

Ron Newman had gone, but still there was no chance of going back to Fort Lauderdale, who had tired of his disruptive behaviour, and on 13 April 1980 George Best made his last, fateful transfer, to San José Earthquakes. He bade a tearless farewell to relegation-bound Hibernian, having scored a modest three goals in sixteen appearances, and headed for California, where Angie was to join him after tidying up their affairs in London. He was met at the airport at San Francisco and driven the forty-odd miles to San José, where he was booked into a hotel. A press conference had been arranged for the Thursday to introduce the new signing to the local media, and his first training session would be the following day.

That was the normal way of things, but by now George was anything but normal. The grip alcohol had on him was growing stronger almost by the day, and on the Thursday morning he skipped his press conference and flew to Los Angeles for a three-day bender. It was a bad start, and it got no better. Within six weeks of signing, he failed to turn up for a match, away to California Surf. He had travelled to LA ahead of the team, but instead of driving to Anaheim with Bobby McAlinden, as arranged, he disappeared to the beach with a six-pack and started yet another drinkathon. As usual, the shortcomings of his team-mates provided a handy excuse. In time, he came to recognize this blaming of others as a character fault of his own, and said: 'Looking back as far as the Manchester United days, I was using situations as self-justification for my drinking. When I couldn't change these situations to my own satisfaction, I would resort to drink. It never occurred to me to change myself to meet the conditions. Like so many alcoholics, I was too self-centred.'

To be fair, like Hibernian, these Earthquakes were never going to do much damage. They were a cosmopolitan bunch even by American standards, with three Yugoslavs of modest pedigree, a South African, an obscure German, Peter Lechermann (whose name, at least, George found promising), and a couple of Dutchmen. One was Hans Kraay, later to play for Brighton, the other Guus Hiddink, who found a much greater claim to fame as Holland's national coach. There was also the usual sprinkling of Football League cast-offs, including Godfrey Ingram, from Luton Town via Northampton, and Mike Czuczman, from Grimsby. The George Best of the sixties would have been hard pressed to make a silk purse out of so many sow's ears. The dissolute, debilitated eighties version was too busy making a pig's ear of his own life.

George's real friends, back in Manchester, found this latest transfer from the worst team in the Scottish Premier Division to the worst in America deeply depressing. David Sadler says: 'He had become a freak show. I didn't like to pick up the papers and see that he was turning out for clubs people knew next to nothing about. Of course, he needed money to live on, and I used to think at least he's getting by, cashing in on his name. Someone would give him a couple of grand to play, and instead of 1,000 people they'd get a crowd of 5,000, but it was sad what he had become. He was still George Best, wasn't he, and it didn't seem right.' Denis Law hated it, too: 'I didn't like seeing it happen. You can't run people's lives for them, but it's not nice to see guys who have been at the very top sinking lower and lower and going through the motions. When you have been at Manchester

United, you don't belong at Fulham and Hibernian, let alone San José wotsits.'

What made it even sadder was that George knew exactly what was going on. 'It was a freak show,' he says. 'That's exactly what it was. People were coming to see me fall over, or whatever. The problem was that I had to do it. I needed the money. The two worst periods I've gone through, drinking-wise, were when I finally left Manchester United, and I had nothing but the clubs, Slack Alice and Oscar's, to occupy my time, and in San José. After United it was non-stop – all I did was drink and sleep. But, if anything, San José was worse.' Rodney Marsh, who was playing against him regularly for Tampa Bay Rowdies, says: 'By this stage, George had "gone". He was a stone or more overweight, drinking very heavily and missing training. I'm not one to slag him off, but he'd had it. He still had the ability to go past defenders, but half the time he didn't know what he was doing. He was in never-never land.'

For the first few months he held it together reasonably well, and a return of eight goals from twenty-six games in a team that finished bottom of the NASL's Western Division was considered good enough to warrant a two-year contract, signed in September. For the first time, he was to play in America all year round, in the North American Indoor Soccer League as well as the NASL, and to his considerable relief the Earthquakes proved more adept at the six-a-side game than the outdoor version, and missed the obligatory play-offs by a whisker. Angie was pregnant by now, so they moved out of the rented accommodation that had been the norm and bought a house of their own, in Los Gatos, California.

Antibuse pills, which produce a violent, allergic reaction to alcohol, worked for a time, but it was the calm before the storm. At the age of thirty-four, fatherhood was supposed to bring George Best to his senses. Sadly, like marriage, it did anything but. Calum Milan Best was born at the Good Samaritan Hospital, San José, at seven a.m. on 6 February 1981 – the thirty-third anniversary of the Munich air crash. The proud father cut the umbilical cord and pronounced it 'the greatest moment of my life'. Yet within a fortnight he was spending the night in jail, for drink-driving. He thought he had conquered the problem, but he had merely been going through what is known as the dry-drunk syndrome – the all-too-brief hiatus while the system readies itself for another binge. At last he acknowledged that he needed help. With his son barely three weeks old, George entered the Vesper Hospital, midway between San José and San Francisco, which specialized in drink and drug dependency. After discussions with the Earthquakes' general manager, John Carbray, it was agreed that he would undertake a rehabilitation course, the expense of which would be met by the club's medical insurance.

Dickie Best believes alcoholics have to sink into the gutter to realize the depths of their debasement, and George was on first-name terms with, if not actually going down, the drain. At one stage, he had gone twenty-six days without eating a proper meal, unable to keep anything but alcohol down. On another occasion he stole money from a woman's purse to fund another of his binges. 'We were sitting in a bar on the beach, and when she got up to go to the toilet I leaned over and took all the money she had in her bag. I felt so bad about it the next day that I went back to try to find her to give it back. It was such a small, close-knit community that everyone heard that I'd done it. It shows you how low I'd sunk.'

Angie, still somehow in love with the lush who was making her life a misery, would go out searching for him, but George knew places to go where she would never find him. 'I used to go to some real dives – the sort normal people didn't even know existed. Angie would hide the car keys so that I couldn't drive, so I would hitchhike, or walk, six or seven miles to this low-life bar that was no more than a little shack. I was drinking vodka, a lot of it, and it was becoming harder and harder to train, or to play. The craving for alcohol was taking over. By now, it was more important to me than football. Before, even at my worst with Manchester United, it was always the other way around.'

Angie tried above and beyond the call of duty to control his drinking. She denied him access to money and transport, locked the doors and pleaded with him, put sleeping pills in his coffee to tranquillize him, even tried to knock him out with a lump of wood. Nothing worked. It was a hopeless task. Sometimes he would be happy with just a couple of beers after training, but then, in his words, 'something in my head would snap' and he would be gone for days at a time. 'To say that Angie suffered terribly would be putting it mildly. When she worked for Cher, she had a lifestyle you wouldn't believe. She was better off than me, really. She lived in, just about everything was paid for, and she was getting good money on top. How she put up with me for so long, I'll never know.'

The Vesper Hospital was, they agreed, their last chance.

chapter twenty

Dinner with George and Calum Best at London's 'Football, Football' restaurant, and daddy's far from little boy takes one look at the bust of his father which has pride of place in the foyer and pronounces it 'gross'. He is thinking just the opposite, of course, but it would be 'uncool' to say it. They see each other once or twice a year, during the school holidays, and love every minute of their time together. Forever pinching and punching, or scoring verbal points, they behave more like mates than father and son.

Calum lives with his mum, Angie, in Los Angeles, and prefers it that way. But if his earliest memories of George as a rampaging alcoholic are too awful to share, all has long since been forgiven, if not forgotten, and it is clear that he idolizes his father now. The nonchalant guard slipping for once, he exclaims 'This place is so cool' as he watches clips of you-know-who on video while tucking into decidedly un-American bangers and mash. During the meal, the usual steady stream of autograph hunters comes to the table, Calum pretending not to notice until he is 'knocked out' to be asked for his. He says his ambition is to be a professional footballer 'like my dad', but talk of chips and old blocks, which would have most fathers preening, is definitely not appreciated. Alcoholism having blighted two generations of the family, the ever-present fear is that it is hereditary, and could claim a third.

It is a real worry for Angie, who has suffered more than

enough, and the phone lines are humming between west London and America's West Coast, the visit nearly curtailed, when the *Daily Star* leads its front page with the banner headline 'Bestie Boy, 15, On The Booze'. The story quotes a source (unnamed, naturally) at Chelsea's Rat and Carrot pub, a short walk from George's flat, as saying: 'I've seen Calum rolling drunk, but George doesn't seem to mind.' The next day, a typically caring follow-up piece by the same newspaper says of Calum: 'His thirst for booze is reminiscent of the faded has-been George has become.'

If the lad has such a craving, he hid it well at 'Football, Football', where he drank orange juice and Coke, but it has to be said that dad struggles when it comes to setting a good example. He came to the dinner date with his son after a dozen games of pool, and nearly as many glasses of white wine, in the Rat and Carrot, and after arranging for Calum to meet me for an interview in his local, the Phene Arms. There, free from parental control, the fifteen-year-old eschewed soft drink in favour of a pint of lager. The staff made a fuss of him but, to his credit, he refused a second pint when the barman suggested it. At fifteen, it shouldn't have been on offer.

The stories George told of the boy's visit would be harmless enough given normal antecedents, but in the context of the Best family history, the thought occurs that they may be playing with fire. Calum had been clubbing it late the previous night.

> He got in at three o'clock. I'd been lying awake, waiting and worrying. I didn't say anything, but then, at three a.m., he decided to phone his girlfriend in the States. I was lying there, listening to him telling her how he loved her, and it got to ten past three, then twenty past. At half past, when he was still talking, I got up and told him to get off the phone, because I wanted some sleep. He said: 'Dad, you're becoming a boring old fart.' I told him to put his hand over the

mouthpiece, and said if he didn't get off the phone straight away I'd tell her he'd been seeing someone else. That did it. He hung up at once. Boring old fart, indeed. I said anything he was getting up to, I'd done in spades.

Entirely comfortable with the do-as-I-say-not-as-I-do approach, George had laid down a maximum of 'a couple of beers' a night, but believes it is best to let the boy have his head, within reason, rather than have him rebel completely:

Of course I worry about him. His mum does a great job with him, and he's a good kid, but he is getting to the age where they go out with their pals, and they'll all have a beer or two. You can't stop that. All you can do is make them aware of the dangers, and keep your fingers crossed. One of the newspapers said we were out drinking pints together, but anyone who knows me will have laughed at that. I haven't drunk a pint for thirty years. If I take him out, he can have a glass of wine with his meal. When he's with his pals, I tell him to stick to a couple of beers. His mum has never said to me that he's come home drunk, and it is not going to happen when he's here because I won't allow it. I tell him if he does that, he won't be welcome the next time he wants to come.

It is a perverse sort of logic, but George believes his own dysfunctional behaviour with drink may have benefited his son: 'Seeing how I was may have helped him, because he knew me at my very worst, when I would do anything to get to the booze, and with a bit of luck that will have taught him that it's a situation to be avoided.' Calum remembers the cursed days all too well, but is understandably loath to talk about them. He says: 'Dad is an alcoholic. I love him more than anything, but because of the fact that he is an alcoholic, I didn't really want to live with him. Just mum was fine.' He has no complaints about his parents living on opposite sides of the Atlantic, and does not feel disadvantaged in any way by the split. On the contrary, he enjoys the contrast between the two cultures. 'I live in Malibu, where there's the beach and not much else. That's nice and relaxed, but you need a bit of excitement sometimes, and when I want the city life – the noise and the craziness – I come to London.' There are other differences. 'In the States,' he says, 'not many people know who my dad is, so I'm not known as George Best's son, which is good. Being compared all the time would be a real pain. But I like the fame thing too, and when I come to visit my dad we have a lot of fun. He's a fun guy with a great sense of humour, and I love to hang out with him. He'll take me to Old Trafford, to all the nice restaurants, and we'll go to see his dad in Ireland sometimes. We have some great times.'

In their days together as a family, he knew only the bad times. The first memories of George he cares to discuss are as a toddler, when he lived with his maternal grandmother in Southend for a year. 'Dad would come down from London to see me at weekends, and every once in a while he'd get a ball out and we'd have a kick about in the garden. He didn't make a big thing of it, though. He's never given me any coaching, or anything like that. He's never given me any encouragement to play football, really. Perhaps he thought it wouldn't be right to pressure me into playing, just because he did.'

In that period, shortly after his return from America, George's alcoholism gave rise to dramatic mood swings and unpredictability, but it is something Calum prefers not to rake over. 'They seemed like good times to me then. Perhaps I wasn't old enough to know any better, but it was fun to me.' Press the point and, just like his father, the responses turn spiky. 'I get asked the same daft questions about my dad every time, so I'm used to it, and know how to answer without saying much.' So what would he like to be asked? 'About him as a footballer. I hate it when people talk to me about his drinking and all that shit. It's none of their business. What does it matter what I think, and whether I'd have been happier if he hadn't been an alcoholic? It wasn't up to me. He does what he wants to do. Let's leave it at that.' How would he describe his feelings for his father? 'I admire the man, I really do, for two reasons. Because he was great at football, and because he's a good guy.' He is too young to have seen George play, 'but I've got a whole bunch of videos of him. I bought them in England and had to have them adapted to play on American VCRs, which was a pain, but it was worth it. One of them is biographical, and tells his whole life story, and the rest are of the big games he played and the great goals he scored. Stuff with him and Denis Law and Bobby Charlton – fantastic players.'

Calum is obsessed with football. He has no interest in any other sports ('I don't like basketball, and American football is boring'), and has no desire to fulfil his mum's ambitions for him by becoming a doctor or a lawyer. He is the star striker with Palisades United, who are rated eleventh out of nearly 2,000 youth teams in California, and trains with them four days a week, as well as playing matches at weekends. Angie, who works as a physical fitness guru to the Beautiful People of Malibu, has turned their garage into a gym where they can both work out. As a footballer, Calum describes himself as a 'cherry picker', an American term which translates as goal-hanger. 'When the other players get the ball,' he says, 'the coach tells them to get it to me.' Like father, like son.

His dream is to follow in those most dexterous of footsteps and join Manchester United but, despite the genes, he is unlikely to be good enough to play professionally in England. George had Alex Ferguson run the most expert of eyes over him, the apologetic reaction merely confirming what dad already knew. 'If he'd grown up here, it might have been different,' George says, wistfully. 'The coaching over there is crap, and there's no money in the game for him to make a career at it in the States.' As yet,

Calum won't accept it: 'I hope to get a soccer scholarship to one of the good colleges, and maybe get into the Major League. Then, ideally, I'd like to come and play for a team in England.' Academically, he was 'not so hot'. His best subject at school? 'Lunch.' If he is not to make a living out of the sport he loves, he would like to be an actor. 'But,' he says, 'in California that is pretty much everybody's dream, so the competition is pretty stiff there, too.'

Judging by the interest the English girls were showing in him, he has a head start.

chapter twenty-one

> We alcoholics are men and women who have lost the ability to control our drinking. We know that no real alcoholic ever recovers control. All of us felt at times that we were regaining control, but such intervals – usually brief – were inevitably followed by still less control, which led in time to pitiful and incomprehensible demoralization. Alcoholics are in the grip of a progressive illness. Over any considerable period we get worse, never better.
>
> – Alcoholics Anonymous literature

For George Best, checking in to the Vesper Hospital for rehabilitation on 2 March 1981 was a waste of time. He was out again on 20 March having 'conned' his counsellors into giving him a clean bill of health. He had identified his problem, that was the easy part. But he did not have the willpower to tackle it. For eighteen days he had gone through the motions, telling everyone what he knew they wanted to hear, but the day he left he knew he had accomplished nothing. He would be going back. He walked out saying to himself: 'Right. I don't want to be stuck in here again. I'm not going to drink for twelve months.' What he was really saying was: 'I'll have a year off, then let's see if I can handle it.' This is classic behaviour. AA says: 'The idea that somehow, some day, he will control and enjoy his drinking is the great obsession of every abnormal drinker. The persistence of this illusion is astonishing. Many pursue it to the gates of insanity, or death.'

Being dry at least improved his home life – and his football. The bar crawls were replaced by an edgy domesticity. George and Angie would go shopping, go to the cinema, go to restaurants together. The proud father redecorated Calum's nursery, complete with a Disney mural. At last Angie could safely invite her friends round, to sunbathe by the pool, or for a meal, without worrying about a raging drunk bursting through the door. But the new leaf was a sham. Every waking minute, George was gasping for strong drink, going through the dry-drunk syndrome. Time hung heavy on his hands, just as it had in the Manchester United days. He built a gym in the garage to occupy himself in the afternoons, after training.

Sobriety allowed him to do justice to his skills on the field, and at thirty-five he enjoyed an Indian summer, to the extent that he scored the goal he rates his finest ever and was invited to return to the old First Division, with Middlesbrough. The Earthquakes were a poor side, destined to finish bottom of the League again despite the efforts of Phil Parkes, the goalkeeper they had signed from Wolves, and Tony Powell, a new defensive recruit from Norwich City. George, however, had a productive resurgence, scoring thirteen times in thirty appearances – his best return since 1977 – and it did not go unnoticed. At the end of 1981, Northern Ireland had qualified for the World Cup in Spain the following year, and George's ultimate ambition took him into transfer talks with Middlesbrough. Their manager, Bobby Murdoch, had checked out his form when San José played a friendly match against Hibernian in October, liked what he saw and made his move. He was not the only one. It was at this game at Easter Road that George met Bill McMurdo, the Glaswegian who was to become his agent. It was a meeting he would regret for the rest of his life.

On 11 December, Murdoch was sufficiently confident to announce that a deal had been done, but three days later the club admitted that they had jumped the gun. George Best would not be joining them after all. Kevin Hamer, one of the directors, said: 'I interviewed Best, with Bobby Murdoch, in London last week, and we met every one of his conditions. I have never felt so let down in my life. He made a verbal contract to join us.' Murdoch said: 'I'm shattered. Best wanted a First Division platform for the World Cup, but that has gone now that he has gone back to America.'

George had got cold feet. Playing in America was one thing, the English First Division quite another, and then, as always, there was the drinking. He was going through one of his dry spells at home with Angie, but living in a hotel in Middlesbrough would be Hibernian all over again, which was the last thing he needed. It was back to the NASL, where his favourite goal of all came against his old team, Fort Lauderdale Strikers, in a 3–2 win in 1981. The bewildering dexterity of his footwork rolled the clock back to the 'El Beatle' days as he received the ball twenty-five yards out and bemused the first defender on the edge of the D, then shimmied past three more near the penalty spot, using opponents like training cones. The goalmouth resembled Whipsnade at feeding time, but he was the coolest man in a stadium baking under a near-ninety-degree sun, swaying left, then right, then left again before confronting a quivering goalkeeper. George put him out of his misery with a killer shot, from whites-of-the-eyes range.

It was a truly breathtaking goal, reminiscent of the supreme footballer at his very best, and it is difficult for the layman to imagine how a raddled alcoholic could reach so far back to dredge up such a gem.

> I can answer that in one word. Pride. Once I got out on the pitch, I put everything else to the back of my mind. I wanted to show these people, who had never seen me at Manchester United, what I was capable of. We were the worst team in the League, really struggling, but I was still enjoying playing

because it was my only release. Everything else was a shambles. I was behaving like a lunatic, my marriage had gone wrong and my personal circumstances were a nightmare, but my football was one thing I knew I could still do well. For me, the games were good because the people were so enthusiastic. San José was a close community and I had a nice little crowd I hung around with. We'd have a game of darts most nights, and go to the local fish and chip shop – it was like a home from home. Until the drink took over again.

When it did, he managed to play on.

The routine I had built into my system served me well over the years. All those stories people tell about the nights before matches when they got drunk with me are rubbish. I didn't drink the night before a game, and I never went out and got stinking drunk for two days beforehand. Over a period of twenty years, that might have happened twice. I've never gone out to play still drunk. Nobody could do that, it's impossible. You'd be throwing up all over the place. I've gone out feeling not too good from a couple of nights earlier, but in the heat we were playing in over there, you had to be careful, and I was.

As his partner in 'Bestie's', their bar on Hermosa Beach, Bobby McAlinden has seen George at his alcoholic worst. He also played with and against him for Los Angeles Aztecs, and confirms that he knew when he had to leave the bottle alone: 'George had long spells when he didn't drink and was really into being fit. And I mean really fit. As any player will tell you, alcohol will not have that great an effect as long as you're working it out every day. During the periods when he played, drinking didn't affect him too much. The real effect came in the off season, when he wasn't playing and had a lot of time on his hands.'

George didn't complete his twelve months off the booze. By early 1982 he had fallen back into the old routine of drinking binges and infidelity, and exactly a year after leaving the Vesper Hospital, he checked in again. This time they tried another tack. They frightened him. On his first visit, his counsellor had told him to look at the patients to either side of him. 'In five years' time,' he had said, 'one of the three of you is going to be dead, one has got a slight chance of making it, and one will be back here within a year.' Now George was back. What, he enquired, had happened to the other two? The man who had sat on his right was dead.

Ouch. George took the programme seriously this time, completing the full thirty days, at the end of which he was nominated the 'Best in Class' and presented with an Alcoholics Anonymous medallion. He was told that he would have to attend AA meetings regularly to have any chance of coping with his addiction, and he did go to a couple, but, as usual, it didn't last. The excuse this time was that, far from anonymous, he was tired of being approached at the end of AA sessions by people who wanted him to open fêtes or coach junior football teams.

Without the support of the AA group, it was inevitable that he would lapse again, and when he did so even the marshmallow-hearted Angie cried 'Enough.' Her husband was a 'drunken bum', she said, and she wanted a divorce. As usual, they arrived at a compromise. George would return to England and go 'cold turkey' with the in-laws, at the house he had helped them to buy in Southend. If he behaved himself, Angie might – just might – be persuaded to sell up and follow. George says:

> I decided to come back because the drinking was getting worse and worse. Everything else was taking a back seat, especially Angela and Calum. When Calum arrived, I hoped it would make such a difference, but it didn't. It didn't stop

> me drinking. That was the worst time of my life – the realization that I couldn't stop, not even for my son. Having him there should have made a hell of a difference, but it didn't. I loved him to death, but the demon was still there. I knew then that it would just go on getting worse unless I did something about it, and God knows what might have happened. I'd gone on the missing list a few times, had a couple of run-ins with the police, and was slowly going mad, so we sat down and decided that one way to try to handle it was for me to come back to England and have a go at sorting myself out here. I'd had two spells in hospital already, and the only alternative was to go back there again, which I didn't want to do.

Again, confusing movement with action is classic alcoholic behaviour. Like so many before him, George convinced himself that he was doing something about his problem, when he was merely moving it from one place to another. He acknowledges the futility of the exercise now. 'Everyone thinks a change of environment might help, but you always know in the back of your mind that it's not going to make any difference. There was no way I was going to go to Southend and sit around all day without wanting, and having, a drink.'

His good intentions lasted about as long as the duty free. On arrival at Heathrow he was still flying, and contacted a friend of Angie's, who met him for lunch at London's Cavendish Hotel. Some friend. It was the start of another affair. George did eventually make it to the in-laws, and did try to behave, but he was merely marking time. He would go for a drink with his father-in-law, Joe. 'Just for a couple.' Again and again he was falling into the trap of believing that he could control his addiction and drink in moderation. For alcoholics, this is impossible. Total denial is the only answer.

> I stayed with Angie's mum and dad for a month or so, but it was murder. All the time I was dying for a drink. I painted the house to try to take my mind off it, but it was no good. It was obvious that things weren't going to work out. Angie's mum, Marion, was a tyrant. The music hall mother-in-law, telling me what I should and shouldn't do all the time. Her stepdad, Joe, was great though. He used to say: 'Don't take any notice of her,' and we'd go down to the Conservative Club for a drink and a game of snooker. Needless to say, the odd drink at the Con Club wasn't enough. I'd sneak off during the day and hit the vodka.

George was not divorced until 1986, but his first marriage was effectively over by the summer of 1982 when he took up with Mary Stavin, the 1977 Miss World who, at the age of twenty-four, was trying to establish herself as an actress. They met at the airport in Belfast, where George had been playing in an exhibition match and Mary had been in the play *Who Killed William Hickey?* The initial introduction was made by George Sewell, the actor, who was also in the play. Best and Stavin were first pictured together on a dinner date in June 1982, and the following month they went public about their 'strong feelings' for each other. George was still married, of course, and Mary was living with another footballer, Don Shanks, formerly of Queen's Park Rangers but then with Brighton. George said at the time: 'I was concerned that I did not come between Mary and Don, and she was equally worried about breaking any last hopes of a reconciliation between Angie and me. But both our relationships were all but finished.' Mary said: 'When the stories first started about me seeing George, so many people advised me to stop and have nothing to do with him. I don't know why. I have found him so trustworthy and considerate. And I don't want anyone to think that I was the cause of the break-up of his marriage. If it had not already been over, I would not have got involved.'

Angie, having remarried, can laugh at George's duplicity now, but she was not amused at the time. Describing the moment when she finally decided that they had no future together, she said:

> Calum was a year old, I hadn't seen George for a week, and I was taking Calum to the doctor for a check-up. I'm driving down the street in San José, it's raining – a really dreary, miserable day – and in the middle of the street, between the two yellow lines, there's this creature walking towards me, soaking wet, miserable, huddled over like a homeless person, and I realized it was my husband. I looked at my son and thought: I can't do this any more. I can't look after two babies. The big one has to go. And he did. I said to him: 'You have to go.' I sent him home to England and I stayed in America, but God bless George, he comes home to England, he meets Miss World and they fall madly in love. And I'm sitting in California thinking: Only he could do this. Only George.

With hindsight, Angie believes the marriage was doomed from the start: 'I think alcohol was a problem from the beginning, but I was young, and knew nothing about alcohol or alcoholics. I thought he was just one of the boys who needed to settle down and be mothered. I could look after him, I could take care of him, I could change him. I tried all that. I had the Florence Nightingale syndrome, but it was a mistake.'

George and Mary stayed with friends in Windsor for a time, then moved into a flat of their own in London's Barbican complex. Not selected for the 1982 World Cup, George did the next best thing and went to Spain as part of the ITV commentary team. He needed the work to occupy time that would otherwise have been spent drinking, and he certainly needed the money. On returning from America he was hit by a claim for £17,996 from the Inland Revenue, who said the money was owed in back tax from his two seasons at Fulham. Unable to pay in full, he offered £10,000 and the rest within six months, but the Revenue insisted on the full amount, and a saga started which was to result in Best being made bankrupt on 5 November 1982.

The taxman clearly did not believe that George Best was unable to lay his hands on £18,000 but, due to a series of misfortunes, it was true. His savings of £27,000 were lost overnight in the collapse of the Irish Trust Bank in 1976, and the £10,000 which was the minimum he expected from the sale of his flat in Putney mysteriously evaporated in intermediaries' 'incidental expenses'. He had asked Angie to sell their house and cars in California and forward his share of the proceeds, but this had not happened. He had, nevertheless, made provision for their son by helping his in-laws to buy their house in Southend (it will eventually be Calum's), and in so doing he had overstretched himself. He is, by his own admission, 'hopeless with money'. Frank Butler, a former sports editor of the *News of the World*, once offered him £10,000 to put his name to some ghost-written columns for the World Cup. 'I'll even write them for you, George,' he said. 'I'd love to, Frank,' came the reply, 'but there's this bird I'm taking to Majorca . . .' The clubs in Manchester, Slack Alice and Oscar's, had been run down while he was in America, and he sold his stake for a pittance. 'I just about gave my shares away.' In short, in 1982 George Best was living hand-to-mouth – even if it was on oysters and champagne.

The Inland Revenue were unsympathetic. Perhaps they had heard George's favourite story of the period, the one in which he won £15,000 in one night out with Mary at a casino. On returning to their hotel, celebrations were in order, and George rang room service for a bottle of Dom Perignon. A wizened little porter from Belfast appeared with the magnum just as Mary came out of the bathroom in a negligée which left little to the imagination. Paddy (it had to be) looked at the 1977 Miss World, panned to the £15,000 George had thrown on the bed, shook his head sadly and said: 'Tell me, Mr Best, where did it all go wrong!'

Technically he may have been broke, but football was still providing enough money to live on, and after a run of lucrative guest appearances (strictly 'readies' only) which took him to Hong Kong, Australia and Malaysia, George was able to move out of the Barbican, which he detested as a soulless 'concrete jungle', and into a flat in Chelsea, just off the King's Road. Ron Atkinson, who always loved a gamble, offered him one final fling with Manchester United:

> Ron was serious about it. He said: 'Come back and do your own thing. Just stroll around and pass it.' I thought about it seriously, because I never wanted to leave in the first place, and the chance to go back had real appeal. Some of the managers they'd had before weren't my cup of tea, but Big Ron was. He tries to play the game the way it was meant to be played, and I was very tempted. In the end, the only reason I didn't do it was the thought that no one could recreate the magic we had there before. There was no Denis Law, no Bobby Charlton, no Paddy Crerand. It was best for the supporters to remember me, and that 1968 team, the way it was. When we won everything.

Instead – and the contrast could scarcely have been greater – George Best's last move as a professional footballer, in March 1983, took him into the old Third Division, with Bournemouth. 'I played five times,' he says. 'It was the usual thing – they wanted me just for the home games, to put a few on the gate.' Brian Tiler, Bournemouth's managing director at the time, had to work hard to get his man. George smiled at the memory of the run-around he gave him:

> I did him twice in one day. He came into a wine bar in London to see me and I wasn't in the mood to talk business, so I had a glass of champagne with him and said: 'I'm going

> to the gents, get another couple of glasses in,' and while he was doing it, I did a runner. I sneaked off to the Inn on the Park hotel, which was my hideaway, where I always went if I didn't want someone to find me. Anyway, I'm sitting there, talking to the Irish barman, and in the mirror behind the bar I can see Brian walking up the slope towards me. Don't ask me how, but he had found me. I pretended not to notice, and he came across and tapped me on the shoulder, and said 'You bugger!' I held my hands up, told him to get the drinks in, and did the same thing to him again. Straight out the back door.

The escapologist's routine was fairly commonplace. Terry Venables tells a story about an occasion during his playing days when George invited him and Bobby Moore for a night out in Manchester. 'We went up to see him, and we'd had one drink when he went to the gents and did a runner out of the window. We couldn't believe it. Bobby said: "Are we that bleedin' boring, or what?" We just looked at each other and laughed.'

Brian Tiler, who died in a car crash near Rome during the 1990 World Cup, did manage to pin his prey down eventually, but probably wondered why he bothered. I saw George at Dean Court when Bournemouth played Newport County, and he cut a sorry, almost pathetic figure, going through the motions in journeyman company. Afterwards, scruffily unkempt, he sat alone in the players' bar drinking vodka out of a half-pint glass, topped up with orange juice to give the impression that he was off the hard stuff. He was still very much on it, still having terrible trouble coping with his craving, and as a last resort he decided to undergo the extreme remedy Angie had first suggested a couple of years earlier. He went to Scandinavia, where they have one of the highest incidences of alcoholism in the world, for a treatment which was outlawed in Britain. Antibuse pellets were sewn into the walls of his stomach, and he was warned that if he carried on drinking while they remained effective, it would kill him.

George had been taking the same pills orally in America, but he would either conceal them behind his teeth before spitting them out, or wait for them to lose effectiveness and go out and get drunk again. This way, there could be no cheating.

> It worked to a degree. I decided to test the things once by having a drink, and it frightened me to death. After one drink your face comes up as if you've got measles and your nose is blocked so that you can't breathe properly. After a couple, you have palpitations. Your heart starts pounding at 100 miles an hour. If you go on drinking after that, you die. It is dangerous – that's why it's banned in most countries.
>
> While the pills were in there, it worked. Desperate as I was when it came to drinking, even I wasn't going to slit open my stomach to get the things out. The trouble was, they only lasted for a certain period, and I was sitting around waiting for them to wear out. It did help, but it certainly wasn't a solution.

George had three treatments, at eighty pounds each, but when a so-called specialist botched the job the third time, he decided quack medicine was not for him. After the last operation the wound would not heal and became infected, necessitating plastic surgery. The illness, as he calls it, has left physical as well as mental scars.

The relationship with Mary Stavin was, he says, 'one of those you think is never going to end'. In fact it was over in just under a year. On 11 May 1983 she moved out of their Barbican flat, saying: 'I've had enough. I love him dearly, but he has a lot of problems. He will have to sort them out by himself. I've walked out of the relationship.' Four days later she left to pursue her acting career in America, having gained a part in the James Bond film *Octopussy*. 'She decided she wanted to be a serious actress,' George says. 'She wanted to go to Hollywood and be a superstar. I told her LA was the worst place to go. I said: "You may have been Miss World, but they've got girls who look that good on every street out there." After a while I went after her to see how she was getting on, and she had to admit: "It's just not happening." It never did from the acting point of view, but she met a guy and had a baby, and she seems to be OK.'

George, too, soon found a new soulmate, another stereotypical blonde bombshell by the name of Angie Lynn. In June 1984 the twenty-six-year-old photographic model who worked under the name of 'La Fox' walked out on Chris Quinten, the actor who played Brian Tilsley in *Coronation Street*, and went with George on a trip to Norway. As he started seeing more of her, so did everybody else. In July she 'bared all', as they say, in the top-shelf magazine *Mayfair*. The two of them could be found most nights at Blondes, a private members' dining club in London's West End. It was widely believed at the time that George owned the place – a misapprehension the real owners did nothing to correct. In fact he had no stake in the club, they were paying him to drink there for the publicity he guaranteed. *Paid* to *drink*. George thought he had 'died and gone to heaven', and was not about to come back down to earth for something as mundane as a benefit bash. On 20 October 1984 he was in Blondes with Angie while 200 guests kicked their heels in Manchester at a dinner in his honour. And if that was not exactly the sort of publicity Blondes was looking for, they'd seen nothing yet.

chapter twenty-two

On Christmas Day 1984 George Best didn't look for the presents, he looked for the pail, to slop out. He was in Pentonville prison. Drink having brought him to a new low, he was jailed for three months in December for drunken driving, assaulting a policeman and failing to answer bail.

On 2 November, a Friday, he had decided, as was his wont once in a while, 'I'm going to get drunk' and, unwisely, he drove to the chosen venue, a wine bar called Blushes in Chelsea's King's Road. He parked the car on a meter, accomplished his objective, walked to a nearby club to make sure, then thought he'd have a nightcap or seven in Tramp, the most fashionable and exclusive disco in London. He should have taken a cab to Jermyn Street. He took the car.

George had weaved as far as The Mall when, just before two a.m., the police pulled him over and proferred the breathalyser, knowing they were on a winner. The test showed 112 milligrams of alcohol in 100 millilitres of breath, seventy-seven over the limit, and he was taken to Cannon Row police station, charged and bailed to appear at Bow Street court later the same morning. He had not arrived when the case was called at 11.45, whereupon the magistrate, Mr William Robins, raised his eyebrows and said: 'No answer? My goodness, you'd better try to bring him in.'

What followed was like a scene from *The Untouchables*. George takes up the story: 'They let me out of the police station at six o'clock in the morning and said I had to be in court at nine.

I thought they meant Monday morning, I didn't know courts sat at weekends, so I staggered home and fell asleep.' He slept through attempts by police to wake him by banging on the front door at eight o'clock, got up and showered in the afternoon, then returned to Blushes for a 'livener' in the early evening when regulars said they had heard on the radio that there was a warrant out for his arrest. Instead of doing the logical thing and contacting the police to check, George stayed out drinking all day and into the night and arrived home at breakfast time on Sunday to find his flat surrounded by reporters, who told him that the police had been round looking for him. In the middle of a binge, and needing another drink, he locked himself in his flat, ignoring all calls on the intercom system. 'The next thing I knew,' he says, 'there were police everywhere, trying to arrest me for not answering my bail. There were dozens of them outside the flat. My first thought was to do a runner, so I telephoned a girl I knew who lived just across the road and said: "Open the door for me, I'll be over in a second."'

Unable to gain either a response from their quarry or entry to Best's Oakley Street flat, the local police summoned two Special Patrol Group units to help. An eyewitness, Nick Prettejohn, a twenty-five-year-old management consultant who lived in the same building, said: 'I was woken by the police hammering at the front door. I heard one of George's windows open and saw him climb out into the garden. Then the police realized what was happening and rushed around the back. I was standing on the doorstep in my dressing gown when George sauntered by, saying with a cheeky grin: "How are you today?"' After taking refuge, briefly, with the girl across the road, – an ex-date by the name of Diana Janney – George was discovered and dragged away. But not without a fight. Prettejohn said: 'He was waving his arms and carrying on when they forced him into the van.'

'Carrying on' was an understatement. George says: 'There was no back way out of Diana's flat, so eventually I had to give myself up. I can remember shouting: "Tell everyone it took twenty-five of the bastards to get me." The SPG bundled me into the van and then one of them started mouthing off. It was "You little Irish wanker" and "You Irish scum", all that rubbish, so I stuck the nut on him. Butted him. They beat the shit out of me in the wagon. There were eight of them, and they all had a go, everywhere but my face, so that there would be no bruises visible when I went to court.' Back at Cannon Row police station, George collapsed as the charges were read to him and was taken to Westminster Hospital, where bruising to the chest was noted by the doctor who examined him in the casualty department.

When he finally appeared at Bow Street, on 5 November, the stipendiary magistrate, Ronald Partel, granted him a one-month adjournment, on unconditional bail of £500. On the charge sheet he was described as unemployed. On 3 December, back at Bow Street, George pleaded guilty to all three charges. Miss Amanda Pugh, prosecuting, told the court that he had punched (not butted) one of the arresting officers in the face, and pointed out that he had been convicted of drink-driving, and disqualified for a year, in 1975. It sounded bad, George feared the worst. Up to this point, he had clung to the unlikely hope that he might get away with a fine or a suspended sentence. To gasps from Angie Lynn and others in the public gallery, he was given three months' imprisonment and banned from driving for five years by the stipendiary magistrate, Mr William Robins, who told him: 'I regard an assault on the police as an extremely grave matter. Those who commit it do so at their peril. I see no reason to distinguish your case from others because you happen to have a well-known name.'

Within hours the defence had successfully applied to a High Court judge, Mr Justice Skinner, for bail, pending an appeal. George was released on a surety of £500 from his agent, Bill McMurdo. For the appeal, at Southwark Crown Court on 17 December, two distinguished journalists, Hugh McIlvanney of the *Sunday Times* and the *Daily Mail*'s Jeff Powell, acted as character witnesses. McIlvanney says: 'In the court canteen, I told George that having us on his side might make him the first man to be hanged for a driving offence. But such feeble efforts at cheering him up were soon stifled by the realization that he was probably going to jail, and before long everybody was staring into the bottom of the coffee cup, with nothing to say. Then he glanced across at me with a smile. "Well, I suppose that's the knighthood fucked," he said.' The gallows humour, and the smile, gave way to a feeling of 'sheer terror' when Judge Gerald Butler QC dismissed the appeal, telling Best the sentence was 'neither excessive nor unduly severe'. George, visibly shaken, clutched the rail of the dock before being taken down. His counsel, Philip Havers, said his client was 'terrified at the prospect of going to prison'.

For his first eight days, including Christmas Day, George was in London's Pentonville, which was 'disgusting', he says. The rest of his sentence was served in Ford open prison in Sussex, which was 'much more civilized'. The first regime was 'pretty sobering'. On Christmas Day a cooked breakfast, complete with bread and margarine, was served at 7.30 and eaten in the cells. After breakfast, everyone was 'banged up' until 11.30 when prisoners started queuing to collect their lunch – the traditional turkey and Christmas pudding. By way of a treat, there was a spoonful of sprouts – unheard-of luxury at other times. Again the meal was taken in the cells. After lunch there was a video in the association hall, until tea at 4.30 when there was a choice between fish fingers and chips and cottage pie. The rest of the afternoon was 'association time', which meant chatting with fellow inmates, playing snooker or table tennis, and by 7.30 George was locked up for the night with a sticky bun and a hot drink for supper. He is not ashamed to admit that he 'had a little cry'. He was 'appalled' by the 'sheer degradation' of his circumstances. The 'stomach-churning stench' of slopping out seemed to symbolize it all.

Ford, near Arundel, was much better. The doors were not locked, the windows were all open. On arrival George was told that he could leave at any time, but that if he did he would be taken back to Pentonville. He stayed put. There were no cells, prisoners slept in Nissan hut dormitories, twelve men in each. There were parades and roll calls, but a lot of free time which George put to good use, working on his fitness in the gym. 'While I was at Ford,' he says, 'the governor got a letter with a Belfast postmark, saying "the boys" were coming to get me out. He called me in to his office and said: "We might have to take this seriously, and if we do we'll have to send you back to Pentonville. What do you think?" I said: "Well, if these boys come, they'd better be able to fight, because I'm not going anywhere." Nothing happened. It was just another crank.' One inmate did leave, under cover of the commotion caused when it was reported that George was going to play for the prison football team:

> It was funny. They had this game away from home, and no end of press men came, thinking I was going to play. I didn't, but while this great scrum was going on outside, one of the lads did a runner out the back. The head warder at Ford was a nice man. He had a disabled kid who I sent some pictures and autographs, and we became quite friendly. He told me that the guy telephoned him and said: 'I'm in France, can I come back?' The warder told him: 'Well, if you do, you'll be sent to a closed prison,' and he said: 'Fuck it then, I ain't coming back' – and he never did.

George refused to play for the prison football team, or become involved with it in any way. He was not inclined to give the press their 'pound of flesh' by being pictured, and ridiculed, in such a humiliating setting. He contented himself with training in the gym for five or six hours every day. He also stayed off the booze, which is not as silly as it sounds. 'You could get absolutely anything in there, and I mean *everything*,' he says. 'It was not just drink, there were drugs of every sort – soft and hard – coming in. I never touched any of it, but there were offers all the time. Everyone wanted to be mates with George Best, and all the Jack the Lads were sidling up to me and saying: "I can get you this or that." They used to get parcels delivered every night, over the fence.'

George kept himself to himself, avoiding all attempts to befriend him. 'When I first went in there,' he says, 'the governor told me: "Just keep your nose clean. Don't get involved with any of the inmates, and don't have any contact with them when you get out. I don't want to see you back, and if you do get involved with any of them, you'll end up in here again." I've bumped into one or two since, and I know it was good advice. They had some dodgy ideas, but there's no way I'd risk going inside again.' By 'keeping his nose clean' he earned full remission and was freed after two months, on 8 February 1985. The police, however, were not finished with him. Within hours of his release no fewer than eighteen plain-clothes officers raided Blondes, shortly before midnight when 'Flanagan', the well known model, was among the diners questioned. No one was arrested, but a list of club members was confiscated. George was not present, and heard no more of the affair. His agent, Bill McMurdo, had sold the story of 'My Prison Hell' to the *Sun* newspaper, who took George and Angie Lynn to Mauritius for a fortnight as part of the deal.

It was an idyllic spot, but a less than happy occasion. George had emerged from Ford fighting fit after all the gym work – 'I was like Superman' – and after two months on the wagon he really thought he had his demon under control at last. It was the classic triumph of hope over experience. In the plush surroundings of the Le Touessrok hotel, he lasted just four days without a drink. When his willpower crumbled yet again, it sent him into deep despair, and the familiar vicious circle was rounded when he sought to blot out his depression by going on a protracted bender:

> I'd been dry 'inside', so I was in good shape when I got to Mauritius, and I was running a couple of miles or more every day to stay that way. February is the rainy season out there, and it was pouring down every day, but I love running in the rain, so that was no problem. Unfortunately, though, because of the weather there was not much else to do. There was no chance of any sunbathing, or the usual holiday stuff, and Angie got pretty bored. Anyway, after four days I've come back after my run, and you had to pass the bar to get to our room. Something snapped and I thought: Oh fuck this, and had a couple of large vodkas. When I got to the room, Angie took one look at me and said: 'You've had a drink, haven't you?' and that was that. I was off the wagon and back on a binge.

Angie, like so many before her, had really thought he had cracked it. Prison had taught him a lesson and dried him out. They could have a normal life, at last. She had stood by him when he was in jail, now she felt badly let down. On their return to London she moved out of the Oakley Street flat and in with a friend, Page Three girl Nikki Clarke, in Fulham. George was, he says, 'infatuated' and, distraught, he disintegrated and fell into an alcoholic stupor. In mid-March 1985 he was barred from Tramp after a drunken brawl when he found Angie in the company of Tim Jeffries, the ex-husband of Koo Stark. A witness told the *News of the World*: 'George arrived alone, and had been drinking. He said he and Angie had quarrelled. About an hour later Angie turned up, and George was furious. She was with a group of her friends when he stormed across. After the argument [with Jeffries] George was led away.' As George tells it, he had gone to Tramp, drunk, with another girl, had left after a verbal exchange, but had gone back and ended up fighting with Jeffries, who had just started taking Angie out.

They made up briefly, and holidayed together in Ibiza, but by the end of June it was all off again, and a 'heartbroken' George told the *Sunday Mirror*: 'We'd been talking about a wedding, the children we wanted to have and where we wanted to live. I gave her £300 to go shopping, and we said we'd go out to dinner that evening. Then I went to put a bet on, and when I got back Angie had gone and lots of our stuff was missing, including all her things. I've done nothing but search for her. I am screwing everything up for the chance of bumping into her – not turning up for things I should.' He had lost £8,000 by missing exhibition matches.

George and Angie Lynn were undoubtedly a love match, but theirs was an overwrought and mutually damaging relationship, iniquitous influences who dragged one another into bad places and dangerous situations. When George couldn't find her, the last port of call was always a seedy club off Regent Street habituated by prostitutes and drug addicts (of which she was neither). George hated her going there, and they would end up fighting. It happened so often that he was barred – from a dive inhabited by 'the scum of the earth'. Unable to live with or without each other, they split and reunited on countless occasions. 'In the end,' he says, 'we had to call it a day. We used to fight like cat and dog, and we'd have ended up killing each other.'

Before they did, Angie fell pregnant, in September 1986, and they spoke of marriage. But in December she lost the baby and the wedding plans were cancelled. The last act of an always dramatic liaison came soon afterwards, in February 1987. By this time they no longer lived together, and the police questioned George after he put his fist through a window at Angie's Kensington flat. She had reported him, alleging criminal damage, and the inevitable newshounds noticed a boot mark on the front door. She told them: 'The window was smashed and the door kicked in. Of course I called the police. Wouldn't you?'

Today, George still has a soft spot for the girl he was close to marrying on more than one occasion. Alone among his exes, she has never sold the newspapers a single damaging story about him. 'Of the lot of them,' he says, 'the two Angies definitely had it the worst – I treated both of them so badly. With Angie Lynn, to say it was fraught between us would be the understatement of the century. It couldn't have been more heavy, but she has been as good as gold. Never a word to the papers and, of all of them, she could have sold most stories and she could have done with the money the most. She was a great girl, but totally nuts, so the two of us made an explosive combination. She lives in Ibiza now, which was always her favourite place. Good luck to her.'

By 1987 George was heading for skid row. Constantly threatened with bankruptcy by the Inland Revenue, he had given up trying to beat his alcoholism and was missing as many bookings as he fulfilled – be it personal appearances or exhibition matches, for both of which he was still much in demand. Angie Lynn had brought out the worst in him. Fortunately, the next woman to share his life could scarcely have been more different. Dark and sultry, of Egyptian extraction, Mary Shatila was a break from the seemingly endless production line of aerobic blondes. She turned him around in the nick of time.

When Mary first saw George, in Blondes, and asked who he was, her half-sister, Fiona, said: 'He's a womanizer and a drunk. Don't go within a hundred feet of him,' but fate decreed that they met two days later, in Blushes, where George memorized her phone number and rang to ask her out. It was one of his better pick-ups. Over the next eight years she was everything to him – lover, nurse, secretary and agent all rolled into one. He thanked her by bedding her sister, and anyone else who took his fancy, but she bears him no malice, saying 'That's George' with a wanly whimsical smile.

In 1987, her first job was to improve his cashflow with a view to settling with the Inland Revenue and gaining a discharge from bankruptcy. At the age of forty-one, he was playing fewer exhibition matches now, and the personal appearances, opening bars and shops, and occasional television work were never going to be enough to pay off debts spiralling (the Inland Revenue were charging him ruinous interest) towards the six-figure mark. The George Best legend was there to be exploited, but how?

With the help of Mary, and some of his friends, he overcame his innate shyness with strangers and launched a new career on the lucrative public-speaking circuit. He was much too self-conscious to start on his own, but he didn't have to:

> Bobby Moore and Kenny Lynch, the comedian, got me going. They were both good pals, and Bobby had done a deal with a string of local councils who put us on in town halls all across the country. We showed a video of the World Cup and told a few stories, and Kenny kept it moving along nicely as compère. That was the start of it. I was new to it, and hated it, but I was getting well paid. Then, as more and more people saw us, I started getting invitations to speak after dinners and lunches, and the thing just snowballed.
>
> I was nervous as hell at first, which was a new experience really. I'd had no nerves at all when I was playing. But I found the reaction – the feedback – gave me a buzz, and gradually, as I got used to it, I began to enjoy it. I teamed up with Denis Law as a double act and then later [from 1993] with Rodney Marsh for a tour that sold out everywhere. Doing the London Palladium was the highlight. What a night that was. People don't realize what hard work it is. The actual show is the easy part. It's what goes with it. The hours of travelling between

venues, the endless handshaking, the chatting, the photographs. That seems to go on all night. There may be 800 people there, and at the end of the show you might have to sit there for another two hours to satisfy them. It's part of the job.

Mary's job was to negotiate the fees, take the bookings, make the travel arrangements and ensure that George not only turned up, but arrived sober enough to work. It was not an easy task, and she did not always succeed, but she did well enough to improve his reputation, and therefore his income, significantly. It would be years before the stigma of bankruptcy was removed, but the means to do it came in 1988, courtesy of the people of Northern Ireland.

Manchester United may have refused George Best a testimonial, but Belfast rallied round its favourite son in his hour of need, and on 8 August 1988 a crowd of 25,000 – the largest at Windsor Park for twenty years – braved persistent rain to watch two all-star XIs run through their party pieces in a 7–6 romp. Two months earlier, George had played with Eusebio, Kevin Keegan and Paolo Rossi in a charity match in Tokyo to raise money for Aids research. Bloated by booze, he puffed his way through the game, then struck a bet with the Dutchman Johnny Rep that he would shed twenty pounds before his testimonial. With the help of the Henlow Grange health farm in Bedfordshire he won his money and, back to his best weight, delighted his home-town public by scoring with a delicious chip. Liam Brady, Ossie Ardiles, Paul Breitner and Frank McAvennie were also among the scorers on a night which produced net receipts of around £110,000. Interviewed after the game, George said, with ironic prescience: 'I find it difficult to watch football these days. No one in Britain, and very few in Europe, really excites me. I think Paul Gascoigne has got a chance of becoming a great player [he had just turned twenty-one at the time] if they leave him alone. They're doing to him what they do to all great sportsmen – running him down when he's barely started. They'll only be happy when he falls off the pedestal. He's accused of being overweight, arrogant, unable to cope with the press and a boozer. Sounds like he's got a great chance to me!' On a more serious note, he said, with heartfelt emotion: 'The people of Belfast have saved me. They have given me the means to sort out my finances, and my life.' It is a debt he continues to acknowledge today. Unable to bank the money because of his bankruptcy, George put it in a trust fund for his son, Calum. It was a decision he would have cause to regret.

With more and more work coming in, and regular spots on television and commercial radio, George's finances should have been improving dramatically, but his twin addictions, alcoholism and gambling, were like an anchor, constantly dragging him back. In yet another ill-conceived attempt to drink and make money at the same time, Mary opened a second 'Bestie's' in London's Marylebone using £125,000 put up by her wealthy Egyptian father and her half-sister, Fiona. It was not a good idea. Fronting a wine bar is hardly the way to curb your liquid intake, and Malcolm Wagner was deeply upset by the state his old friend lapsed into on one visit at this time:

> In Manchester, I never really had George down as an alcoholic because whenever I saw him he always seemed to be in control. It was only later, when I went down to London a couple of times, that I saw him really drunk and out of it. Yeah, I'd seen him pissed and good fun – one of the chaps – in Manchester, but now he was out of his head and I really didn't like it. There was a bar next door to Bestie's, in Crawford Street, that sold vodka. Only vodka. We'd had a couple of drinks in Bestie's – nice social drinking – and then George said: 'Come on, I'll take you to this vodka place.' So we went next door and there were thirty bottles on a shelf, all different vodkas. I think George tried to have one of each –

neat. I had a couple and said: 'Look, I can't,' I was practically throwing up. But he kept on, and I watched him go glassy-eyed. It was very sad. I got most upset. He won't remember it, but I said: 'George, turn it in, son. At this rate I'm going to be standing over a wooden box, putting you away.' I filled up. I was terribly upset at the way he was going. I said: 'For God's sake, pal, get a grip.'

He couldn't, of course, and drinking was not the only problem. The gambling that first took hold in the Slack Alice days had never gone away, and it was not only in London that Malcolm Wagner found himself wondering where it was all going to end:

> He was blowing money as fast as he could earn it. He really had the gambling bug. He came up to Manchester to do a personal appearance, for which he was paid £600. He gave the money to Mary, and we all went out for dinner. George insisted on going to a casino which, as far as I'm concerned, is the worst place to go for a meal. I've never gambled, and it has no interest for me. Anyway, we'd had a nice dinner and we were sitting chatting, and George said: 'Come on, let's go and have a game' – not to me, to Mary. You should have seen the change come over him. Every time he lost it was, 'Give me some more money.' She said 'George, you've done it all,' but he wouldn't have it. It was: 'I know you've got money in your bag, give me some more money,' and it started to get really nasty.
>
> It's like his drinking, there's no stopping. There's no saying: 'Let's do £100 or £200 and call it a day.' Everything he's got has got to go. It happened at a testimonial dinner in London. His friends set it up for him – Michael Parkinson was the speaker and Jimmy Tarbuck and Billy Connolly were there. After the auction of mementos, George got about

> £20,000 at the end of the night. He sold all his medals, the shirt Pele gave him, everything. To me, it was like selling your soul. He auctioned off all the things you would have thought he wanted to treasure for ever, then went round the corner to the Playboy Club and blew the lot.

It was not all bad news. George did try to break the cycle, but his willpower always crumbled – usually at the first sign of adversity. Before and after his testimonial, in the summer of 1988, he managed to stay off the drink for two months, giving everyone around him fresh hope. Mary recalled how his skin 'glowed' and his eyes 'sparkled' but said he would go whole days at a time without speaking to her because he had to concentrate so hard on staying sober. Malcolm Wagner said: 'When I saw him around that time he looked like a million dollars. He was down to about eleven stones and he looked absolutely terrific. His hair was shining, his eyes were bright. The old George was back.' His dad, Dickie, was optimistic, in a fingers-crossed way:

> George rang me to tell me that he was down in Kildare, opening a bar for a friend, and said if I caught the train to Dublin, he'd pick me up there by car. So I got the train to Dublin and there was this big Daimler waiting. George didn't meet me on the platform because he didn't want any fuss. He was clean shaven, which was always a good sign, and he hadn't had a drink for three weeks. He was bright-eyed, bushy-tailed and as trim as could be. He looked about twelve years younger. I was with him for four days, and he didn't have one drink. It was a vast improvement.

Mary told him: 'You're through with it,' but George knew better. 'No way,' he said. 'Not a moment goes by when I don't have to stop myself having a drink.'

It was another false dawn. By 1989 the monkey was perched

on his back again, and Mary winced when a report of a 'punch up' with a journalist in Adelaide, Australia, ended with the words: 'Best – at the casino with two leggy blondes – denied the attack.'

It was in 1989 that I met Mary Shatila, at a match between Crystal Palace and Manchester United. Girlfriends, or wives, are not normally allowed to sit with reporters in football press boxes, but an exception was always made for the exceptional, and Mary sat between George (who was working for a London radio station) and me at Selhurst Park. I was struck by the way she doted on him. Nothing was too much trouble for her. When he wanted a cup of coffee, she fetched it. When he wanted something stronger after the game, she supplied it. When it was time for the taxi to collect them, she went to see if it was there. She was also a charming woman. Everyone knew how much she loved her George, and everyone admired her devotion to what seemed like a thankless task.

Mary suffered with the rest of us when George appeared on the *Wogan* television show in 1990 as a lolling, slurring drunk. He had gone on the programme to promote an autobiography, *The Good, the Bad and the Bubbly*, ghost-written by a showbiz journalist, Ross Benson from the *Daily Express*, but the book was forgotten as the host led his interviewee down the path to ridicule. George had already called Tommy Docherty a 'bullshitter' and his press critics 'arseholes' when, having been asked persistently about his predilection for young women, he said: 'Terry, I like screwing, all right?', to which Wogan's follow-up question was: 'So what do you do with your time these days?' George, clearly the worse for wear, replied with one word, 'Screw', and the host, smiling at a job well done, wrapped up the interview with: 'Ladies and gentlemen, George Best.'

The reaction made the front pages of the more sensationalist newspapers, which may well have been the intention all along. The viewing figures for *Wogan* were well down at the time and, with its tired format, it certainly needed all the publicity it could get. For his part, George has often told me that public interest in him is fuelled more than anything by his hell-raising image. Among those well placed to know, however, there was a strong impression that he was used. No one had thought to control the drinks he had during the two hours he spent in the 'Green Room' hospitality suite before the programme, and the *Sun* quoted a BBC source as saying: 'The *Wogan* show has been flagging for some time. This has got people talking about it again.' A spokeswoman for Simon and Schuster, publishers of *The Good, the Bad and the Bubbly*, said: 'Terry Wogan and his researcher chatted with George at length before the show. They were aware of his condition, and made the decision to let him on.' George professed to be unrepentant at the time, and told Sky TV: 'I don't give a shit what people say about me,' but his true feelings are betrayed by the fact that he has never been able to watch the video he was given of *Wogan*, and prefers not to talk about it. Mary took it on the chin, as stoical as ever. She told the press that she had lived in Lebanon for eight years. 'I witnessed bombings, shootings and death. When you've been through that, George is pretty easy to cope with.'

She was much more interested in finding a way of resolving his ongoing disputes with the taxman and his former agent, Bill McMurdo, with whom he was involved in another costly wrangle. Here, at least, salvation was at hand. By 1991, it was estimated that George owed up to £100,000 in back tax, interest, legal fees and to a variety of other creditors. 'I was working, and earning well, but everything I was getting was going to the lawyers. They were telling me they'd sort it out in a couple of months, but the months became a year, then a couple of years, and so on.' His 'saviour', as he calls him, was Bryan Fugler, a solicitor then working for Tottenham Hotspur. 'I went to see him in September 1991, with Mary, on a recommendation, and he looked at all the papers and said: "You know what they are doing, don't you? They are keeping it going because they are all earning money out of the case. You're being screwed. Leave it to me, I'll sort it out in no time."'

In October 1991 Fugler wrote to Stoy Hayward, the insolvency practitioners appointed by the bankruptcy court, as follows: 'It would seem to me to be a grave miscarriage of natural justice for a person to go bankrupt for approximately £22,000 and to find himself being required to pay over £60,000 to discharge that bankruptcy.' To settle the bankruptcy, and pay his accumulated legal costs, George needed some of the money from his testimonial, but getting access to it proved maddeningly difficult. It was tied up in a trust fund for Calum, the legality of which was dubious at best, and was being contested by Stoy Hayward. A protracted battle ensued. 'Trying to get the money was a nightmare,' George says. 'The whole idea of the testimonial was to help me, and I ended up having to fight like hell to get what I needed to get me out of trouble.' Bryan Fugler says:

> It was a superhuman task. George was bankrupt and the trustee in bankruptcy [George Auger, from Stoy Hayward] was about to grab his testimonial money. He challenged the trust fund set up for Calum and, because it had not been set up correctly, there is no doubt that had it gone to court he would have lost all of it. And he would still have been bankrupt. The more I got involved, the more amazed I was by what I discovered. In November 1982, George went bankrupt for £22,918, of which about £16,000 was a Revenue debt. In December 1991, when the 1986 Insolvency Act came into effect, all those who had been bankrupt for three years were discharged automatically. But this trustee applied to the court for George Best's automatic discharge to be suspended *sine die* on the basis that he had not cooperated with them.
>
> The real reason they did that was that they were on a meal ticket. All the money was going in fees. If they'd carried on as they were, George would have ended up with nothing.

> I had no grounds to stop them, so I went to them and said: 'This is a bloody disgrace. You're taking the piss out of a national hero. My client is threatening you. If you don't do a deal with me, he's going to go to the press and expose you.' That did it. In the end I had to pay them some more money, and we ended up with George getting about £50,000 out of his testimonial, which was a travesty, but it was the best I could do. The main thing it achieved was to get him out of his bankruptcy.
>
> George had been really badly advised. Presumably on the advice of a solicitor, he had sworn an affidavit saying he had no money and no liabilities, so any time he earned any money, the trustee [Auger] claimed it, saying he had no overheads. He should have been advised to say that he needed £500 a week to meet his commitments. For example, he had a son he was supporting. What he was doing was telling them nothing, for fear that if he earned a few bob they would take it all. While he was bankrupt, the trustee would grab everything because George had sworn an affidavit saying he didn't need it. He desperately needed to get out of this situation, and that's what I did for him.

Eventually, his testimonial money freed, George paid his creditors £32,500 and finally, after nearly ten years, his bankruptcy was discharged on 5 May 1992. Relieved, and grateful, he celebrated by asking Mary to marry him. It was not the first proposal – by her reckoning it was the second of four. 'I said "Yes" the first two times, but we never got round to it.' By the fourth, she didn't bother answering.

By 1993, the 'road shows' with Rodney Marsh were in full swing and Best's earnings were underpinned by weekly appearances on Sky TV, who have always paid him more than their other panellists. It is unclear whether this is because they prize his name and his contributions so highly, or in the belief that the premium serves as an extra incentive to turn up. His unreliability is such that they always have a reserve (it was Clive Allen for a long time) on stand-by. Marsh, too, has been let down:

> He went missing for a show at Oxford, so I went on and did it on my own. I told all of Bestie's stories, only coherently, which made a change! That's the only one he's actually missed, but quite a few have been a struggle, because he's had a good drink. When that happens, I have to keep prompting him, and it's hard work. He has another side to him, though. At about the time you're talking about we were doing a show in Bournemouth, and a headmaster had written to George asking if he'd do an afternoon's coaching. So on the way to Bournemouth we stopped at this school in Petersfield and put on a bit of a clinic. There must have been a couple of hundred kids there, and George wouldn't leave until every one had done a bit with him. We were there three hours, his knee came up like a balloon, but he wouldn't go until he'd signed every autograph. That didn't get in the papers, of course. They're only interested in the boozing.

George Best always kept the popular prints topped up there, and in January 1994 his intake reached a new personal best when he was plunged into desperate melancholia by the death of his old mentor, Matt Busby. George, in Los Angeles at the time, disappeared during dinner and went on a pub crawl that lasted twenty hours. Mary understood, just as she put up with everything else, and after seven years together (easily a record for George) it seemed that they were made for each other, and that this time it really was for real. For keeps. George's two great, enduring friends, Malcolm Wagner and Mike Summerbee, thought so. Wagner says: 'Mary was terrific. She worked very hard for George and loved him to bits. I think he thought a lot of her, too, but he was always open to temptation, always open to a phone number being slipped to him.' Summerbee agreed that Mary was 'a lovely person', adding: 'She organized his life brilliantly, and helped him tremendously. It was Mary who got him into the way of life he's got now – the dinners and promotional work. Before she came along, he was struggling. She was a big influence, and a positive one. Unfortunately for her, she got sucked into the worst side of his character – the drinking and what have you.'

Perhaps she was too forgiving, too much of a doormat. Perhaps he will always be vulnerable to a leggy blonde. Whatever the reason, by the middle of 1994 the relationship was moribund, and in July George met Alex Pursey, the twenty-two-year-old Virgin flight attendant who was to become the second Mrs Best. Was Mary bitter about the break-up, which became final in January 1995? She says no, George begs to differ. An interesting insight into life with an alcoholic was provided by an open letter, published in the *Daily Mirror*, in which Mary wrote:

> When you needed a brandy in the morning, I brought it to your bedside. If you needed a glass of wine so that your hand was steady enough to sign an autograph, I poured it for you. My relationship with you was like sailing on a ship with a hole in the side. I stood on the deck, bailing out water with a bucket instead of mending the leak. At first, we lived hand to mouth. I'd have to search around the house for £5 to get a paper and your favourite baked beans. But George being George, you could always get someone to buy you a drink.
>
> During our eight years together, I used every trick in the book to slow down your drinking. I would put ice in the glass to make you think you were knocking back more than you were. My maternal instincts came into play, and I let you become the centre of my life. When you were drinking, I made sure there was plenty of food and fruit juices and your favourite drinking food – trifle – in the fridge. Three times a night I would get up and cook your favourite meals – mussels

in white wine, or chicken – because you'd wake up hungry from the alcohol. Every need was catered for. I would bathe you, shave you, cut your toenails and trim your beard. You tried to give up drinking at least ten times. Sometimes it lasted two days, sometimes two months, but you usually gave in when the first thing went wrong. I'd wake up afraid you'd be dead beside me. I'd check for swelling and read every book on treating alcoholism. But nothing helped me deal with you. If you were flat out, drunk, or had embarrassed yourself, I never criticized. Instead I provided love, food, warmth and nourishment. I knew it would not save the day, but it would save the situation.

Underneath, you are a good little boy, who really wants to do the right thing by giving up drinking, but at the same time you're indifferent. You live life the way you want. You are a happy drunk who loves life. You have always got away with your drinking. People still love you, whatever. In time, you have come to accept your alcoholism. You say you can control it, but it is so severe I don't believe you'll ever beat it completely.

As everyone knows, you love women. After a night out alone, you'd come home with six or seven different females' phone numbers. Picking up girls was a reflex when you got drunk. I'd say: 'How could you do this to me?' You would say: 'It's only a game.' You said you'd wake up with a girl next to you and think: 'What have I done?' One night was different. You came to me drunk and told me you had slept with my half-sister, Fiona. You said you had made love once, and now you could not get rid of her. But I never blamed you. It was a one-off situation, and she led you on.

When a journalist rang out of the blue that week to say you were getting married to Alex, I was so numb I didn't care. In the end, you married her in the love-heart tie given to you by the girlfriend after me. That was typical. If there was a perfect person for you, I'd say it is your mother, which is frightening. You told me I reminded you of her. You need a woman who is a partner, friend, companion, lover and parent in one.

The memories are not all fond ones. Far from it. Mary says George hit her twice – 'and hard' – but admits to provoking him on both occasions. The first time, he refused to get out of bed to fulfil a booking in Edinburgh. 'I started on him,' she said. 'I pushed him, emotionally and verbally, for the better part of an hour.' The argument ended with a blow to Mary's face. The second time, George had £1,000 on him after a gig and went out and blew the lot, gambling. Another fight resulted, and again Mary came off worst. For all that, there is more than a suspicion that she still loves him, but George is not interested, and changed his phone number to stop her ringing. He says:

When she left, she took just about everything – documentation and diaries I needed for tax purposes and personal stuff that was no good to her. She took a bracelet Mary Stavin had given me and a keepsake from some handicapped children in Australia. Her father had given her the money to start Bestie's, which was too small to make any money, and closed. I gave her some of that back and told her to take what she needed from the flat. The worst thing was that she took all the paperwork. She'd handled all the business side of things, and everything went with her. The personal stuff was of sentimental value only. I spoke to her about it, and she sent one or two little things back, but not the lot.

I won't speak to her now. She put her name to a couple of newspaper stories which my solicitor wanted to do something about. It was a pity it had to end like that, because she had been good for me, but I had met someone else – Alex – and it was hard for her to take. We were splitting up anyway. I'd dated a couple of girls just before I met Alex. Then when I met her, that was it. Mary kept calling once in a while, and I had to tell her to stop. It was over. It's a shame when any relationship ends, but I had met someone I fell in love with and wanted to marry.

chapter twenty-three

July 1997, and George and Alex Best wind down after a trip to Mauritius in celebration of their second wedding anniversary with a week at Henlow Grange health farm in deepest Bedfordshire. Surrounded by portly Arab princes, pampered housewives and anorexic models, they are 'bored out of their brains', but suffer in the cause of detoxification. Alex has learned that the only way to slow George's drinking from, a torrent to a stream, is to get him out of his daily routine at the pub. She reins him in at Henlow four or five times a year, at up to £1,000 a visit.

An invitation to 'come up and see us' conjures visions of carrot juice, lettuce leaves and perspiration, but fears of a day of monastic denial prove groundless. 'Fancy a bit of lunch at the pub round the corner?' George says. 'They do a great lasagne.'

'Why not? A nice brisk walk?'

Horrified looks all round. 'Nah. We'll take the car' (their BMW 318i, complete with personalized registration, was a present from Alex's well-to-do father, Adrian). At the pub, George has one Perrier, then it is back to his staple diet, white wine. Henlow can forget him for the afternoon.

Neither of the Bests bothers with the exercise equipment or the swimming pool (Alex makes Kate Moss look like Roseanne, and George can't swim). There is no serious attempt at weight reduction or conditioning, the break is merely intended to minimize alcohol intake. So how do they while away their time among the towelling robes and leotards in what is a cross between an upmarket gym and a rambling country house hotel? People watching. 'See that big guy over there? He's a Kuwaiti prince. His dad has told him he has to stay here until he loses five stones. He's been here six months, and hasn't lost a pound. Keeps sending out for six Big Macs at a time. He loves being surrounded by all the birds, and doesn't want to go home.' They also do a fair bit of reading. Alex, who admits she is 'seriously bored', is on Jilly Cooper's *Riders*. George, heavily into biographies, is lapping up Oscar Wilde's. 'It's a great story. He died of syphilis. At the end, shit was coming out of every hole in his body. They say he stayed for a time in Oakley Street – it might even have been where our flat is now.' The suggestion that they change the toilet seat has everyone falling about.

As well as a good read, George loves newspaper crosswords, quizwords and general knowledge tests of every type. In his local, a somewhat dowdy West London 'drinker' called the Phene Arms (all scampi and Mitchell brothers lookalikes leching over Kelly Holmes on the 'affeletics') he is the ultimate arbiter in such things. Waiting for him one lunchtime, I joined the regulars perusing the *Daily Mirror* crossword, and we were all stumped on the last clue. 'Got him!' cackled the pub know-all. 'George will never get this one.' On arrival, he was quickly put to the test. 'Twenty-five across. Play by Eugene Ionesco. Starts with R and there's an E in the middle.' Within seconds George had jaws sagging all round with 'Rhinoceros'. Philistines all, we had to wait until the solution was printed the following day to check if he was right. He was. Television's *Countdown* conundrum is another speciality and, with a vast fund of accumulated information, he would be a banker bet on *Mastermind*. Specialist subject: Bedrooms, 1965–95.

Today, he is testing Alex with a Mensa sampler. 'A man goes into a pub and pays eleven pounds for lunch and a drink. He pays ten pounds more for his food than his drink [it can't have been George]. What did each cost?' To her husband's glee, Alex ventures ten pounds and one pound. The correct answer is ten pounds fifty and fifty pence. After much good-natured teasing, with the word bimbo prominent, she heads for their room to catch up on the soaps while George leads me in search of a quiet corner to fill in some gaps in a love life that makes Warren Beatty look like a wallflower. 'The smoking room is favourite,' he says. 'There's never anyone in there.' Duly ensconced, with the windows thrown open (he is a zero tolerance man when it comes to the deadly weed), we are just getting into Mary Stavin's unusual proclivities when a pair of conspiratorial matrons come in for a quick gasper, and spoil the tale. With the sort of deft manoeuvre that characterized his work on the field, the subject is changed. *Top Gear* had been to interview him the previous day for a feature on E-type Jaguars, of which he had six. 'But not all at the same time!' He had welcomed the diversion, but thought his fee was stingy. 'They paid me £150 and kept me fannying about for ages. They couldn't make up their minds whether to film the thing inside or out, and the basic question threw me a bit. They wanted to know what driving an E-type meant to me. I think they expected a deep, meaningful answer. I just said it was a bloody nice car.'

A couple of weeks earlier, the Bests (still very lovey-dovey, they call each other 'Bestie', as a pet name) had been in Mauritius, at a hotel within a mile of where George stayed with Angie Lynn on his release from prison in 1984. Then, the trip had been paid for by the *Sun*, this time the *Daily Star* picked up the bill in return for a series of 'exclusive' interviews. On 31 September 1996 they had called George a 'faded has-been', an 'unshaven wildman' and 'exposed his boozy pub sessions with his 15-year-old son'. Now, little more than nine months later, he was 'the ultimate legend', 'the Belfast hero' and 'still brilliant in bed, even when he's been on the booze'. Small wonder he has nothing but contempt for the tackier tabloids, taking their money but ignoring 'all the crap they write'.

The hook on which the *Star* hung their eight-page spread was the Bests' second wedding anniversary. They had met in July 1994, when George was still living with Mary Shatila, and married a year later, when Alex was twenty-three. Her mother, Cheryl, is the same age as George, her father Adrian, the managing director of an industrial belting company based in Wimbledon, is just one year older. Alex had been to public school near the family home in Cheam, Surrey before going on to college to do a two-year course in business studies. She worked in sales for a reprographics company before becoming a flight attendant with Virgin. She had been flying their transatlantic routes for nearly three years, and was just coming out of a long-term relationship with John Scales, whom she met in his Wimbledon days, when a mutual friend introduced her to George on what was her first visit to Tramp. 'I'd gone with a girlfriend, who was a member,' she says. 'When I met George it wasn't a case of "Ooh, its George Best!" I've never been much of a football fan, and while I'd heard his name, I didn't know very much about him. I knew nothing at all about his colourful past. I just knew that he'd played football.'

After a couple of dates – 'lunch, dinner, drinks, the usual things' – they were pictured together in the newspapers, and she was shaken by the publicity that followed. Mary Shatila, who thought this was 'just another fling' and that she and George were still a couple, put her name to a searing piece in one of the papers which had the desired effect. Alex backed off:

> Reading all that stuff about George's past put me off, and I stopped seeing him. I was still busy flying anyway, so there wouldn't have been that much opportunity. I hadn't seen him from August to January, and then we bumped into each other, by accident, in the Dover Street wine bar. It was my birthday and I was out with a few friends for dinner, and he was there as well, on his own. The two guys who run the place are good friends of his, and he was stood talking to

them. I was sitting, having a meal and didn't see him, but someone said: 'George is over there.' He came over and bought me champagne, for my birthday, and we started seeing each other again.

Friends warned her what she was getting herself into, that there was a lot of dirty washing in the baggage George brought to the relationship, but she thought he was 'really nice', and decided to take him at face value. The age difference meant nothing to her. 'George doesn't look, or behave, like an old man, so I never notice it.' She was disconcerted, at first, by his appetite for alcohol, but she, too, likes a drink (although on nothing like the same scale), and it did not put her off. 'He got drunk a lot, and I thought it was a bit odd, but I got used to it after a while, and he never behaved badly in front of me, otherwise that would have been that.'

Alex knew nothing of George's mad, bad ways, but she was to get a crash course. After the archetypal 'whirlwind romance', they were to marry on 18 July 1995, but the bride-to-be returned from a flight to America to find the groom out on a bender, in female company. To no one's great surprise, he failed to turn up for the wedding. Like so many suffering women before her, she forgave him, and they were married, at Chelsea register office, the following week. Denis Law, who was one of the guests, said: 'The reception was at a pub at Heathrow, which was right on the end of a runway. You could hardly hear yourself speak for planes taking off. We called it "Four terminals and a wedding". I remember Alex's mum and dad stood in the corner, looking shell-shocked.'

The second Mrs Best has been portrayed, variously, as a gold-digger, a groupie and an airhead, but the pigeon holes are all too convenient. She is none of these things. There is more 'gold' to be struck at her parents' home than she is ever likely to find in George's mortgaged-to-the-eyeballs flat, she has had only one other serious boyfriend, so is hardly the voracious manhunter, and she brings to the marriage secretarial and bookkeeping skills which should prevent another ruinous run-in with the taxman. 'I do all George's paperwork, all his accounts and take care of all the bills,' she says. 'He's hopeless when it comes to managing money.' Running the household can be hard work, given George's extravagances, and there are regular rows which, since they often end up with one or both partners nursing a black eye, tend to get into the newspapers. Alex says: 'I get very annoyed and very hotheaded and so does George. When we get on, we get on very well, but when we have a row we both get physical, running around hitting each other and pulling hair. Things get smashed in the flat. When we're fighting, it's no holds barred.'

The marriage endured a particularly torrid time in September 1996. George, on a protracted bender, missed successive gigs in Merthyr and Plymouth, then left the flat on Saturday the 14th, saying he was going to get the morning papers, failed to turn up for his weekly spot on Sky TV, and was not seen again until eight p.m., by which time there was no reasoning with him. The cost, in forfeited fees, of his three days on what he calls 'the missing list' was £4,000. In his absence the phone rang twice, on successive days, and when Alex answered it the caller hung up. Suspicious, she convinced herself that it was a girl ringing George.

On 20 September, her husband still out of control, Alex moved out of the flat, taking all her personal possessions with her. It was enough to bring the wild rover to his senses. Tearful, fearful, and full of remorse, George went AWOL on Sky for the second Saturday in succession to track down his missing wife. The search was conducted from his usual HQ, the Phene Arms, and when a couple of phone calls to her mum persuaded Alex to ring the pub, her first question was: 'Are you going to behave?' George said: 'I'll behave if you come back,' and the crisis was over. Was she embarrassed by some of his behaviour? 'Sometimes, when he's really drunk, but then I try to stay out of the picture and let him get on with it. Knowing what he's really like, and how good he can be, it infuriates me to see him like that. I'd rather not be there. I speak to his ex-wife, Angie, quite a lot, and she says: "You're lucky. With me, he used to go missing for days." I've never experienced that. I don't think I could put up with it.'

After the September contretemps, all was forgiven, if not entirely forgotten, during a lucrative two-week series of speaking engagements and coaching clinics in Malaysia and New Zealand, on the second leg of which they were continually disturbed by a guest playing the piano in the next room. George thought of complaining to the hotel management, but was glad he didn't when a note poked under the door said Dudley Moore apologized for the noise, and that he would like to meet one of his heroes, if it was possible. After 'a few drinks', they got on like the proverbial house on fire. It was not the only starry diversion. On a day off, George and Alex were given complimentary tickets for a Michael Jackson concert, after which they were asked if they wanted to go backstage to meet the great Wacko. 'I told them no thanks,' George says. 'He had all these kids on stage with him. Weird.'

Alex accompanies George everywhere, as his 'personal assistant'. She enjoys the first-class travel, VIP treatment and exclusive hotels, and can handle the downside of being married to a high-profile alcoholic – indeed she seems to thrive on the row-and-make-up cycle. In January 1997 their private business was public property again, the *Sun* leading its front page with the headline 'Raging Best Beat Up Wife'. 'Yeah, it happened,' Alex says, 'but our domestic tiffs are always blown out of proportion. I've given him a black eye once or twice, and he's done it to me. As far as we're concerned, it's no big deal, so why should anyone else make a big thing of it? When we fight, he hits back. That's all there is to it.'

Much more damaging than the occasional bout of fisticuffs would be proof that George had been with another woman, but she has had no hint of that. 'It has probably happened, but I don't know. I'd rather not know, to be honest. He comes home every night which, in view of his past record, must be a good sign.' It is not womanizing or his drinking, *per se*, that makes her lose her temper, although the behaviour – particularly jealousy – alcohol exacerbates is a contributory factor. 'I just ignore his drinking now. I'll never be able to do anything about that, it will always be part of him. I just let him get on with it, because if I don't, it's just going to infuriate him. It's normally something he says to me that starts me off. He can be very finicky about things. Everything has to be just so in the flat, exactly how he likes it. If it's not, he goads me, and tries to provoke a row. That does make me angry and it's not all my fault, which is what he says.'

Two incidents the author witnessed point to an obsessive, unreasoning jealousy on George's part. The first was the occasion in the Phene Arms when Alex and Tom Graveney's son, Tim, chatted briefly at the bar. When she came to join us George snapped: 'Don't embarrass me in here again.' On another occasion, when we were driving to Belfast airport, George told a story about a gig in Athlone when, in the middle of the night, two men walked into their hotel room. 'Imagine if I'd been in the bar, and Alex had been in bed on her own,' he said, to which Alex, joking, responded: 'I might have had a good time.' George didn't like it and, shooting her a meaningful glance, said: 'I'll have a word with you about that later.' She looked genuinely apprehensive.

Alex says: 'He is very jealous. He imagines things that I'm doing when I'm not. He's a chauvinist in that he hates me talking to other guys, completely innocently, but it's all right for him to chat up any girl who walks into the pub. That really annoys me. And I don't like the way he always pretends that I'm the one who starts the fights and hits him in the head. I never get to tell my side of the story in the papers because I keep it all to myself. That's the way I am.' Would she say he was hard to live with? 'Yes, he can be a pain in the neck. There's one rule for him and another for me. He objects to me going out to see my girlfriends in Wimbledon, for example, but it's all right for him to spend all day with his mates in the pub. And if I have a drink he'll say: "God, you're not drinking at lunchtime, are you?" Yet he can start at breakfast.' While she recognizes the futility of trying to stop him, she is worried by the amount George puts away:

> He goes to the Phene every day, and when he's not actually drinking he's thinking about it all the time, so I do find myself thinking: How much longer can your body cope with that? It does frighten me. That's why I like to go to Henlow Grange. He won't stop drinking while he's in the pub, but at the health farm he can read and watch telly, try to relax, and if there's not a drink in front of him he has to slow down. Mind you, it worries me just as much when he gives up completely for a couple of days, just like that. Your body can't be dependent on something like alcohol and then do without it totally just once in a while. I say: 'Why not have just a couple of drinks in the evening?', but no. That's George. It has to be all or nothing.

To curb his legendary profligacy, she collects his fees and doles out pocket money. 'He's quite good now,' she says. 'We don't go to the casino that often, but when we do he'll only spend £200 or £300, and he can handle that. If he had a lot of cash on him it would be different, but I get my hands on as much as I can and bank it at once.' When George does win at the tables, it tends to be a lot, fuelling the habit. In April 1997, after one of their rows, he stormed off to the Palm Beach casino in London's West End: 'I had about £300 on me and at first it wasn't going well.' Playing roulette, he was soon down to his last twenty-five pounds.

> Then I started to roll. I was playing two tables at the same time, and when I started to win they were giving me bigger and bigger chips, up from £25 to £100 and finally to £1,000. They said: 'Let us cash a few of these for you,' but I wouldn't let them. It's bad luck.
>
> By the time I'd finished, I'd won £11,000 and I wanted a drink, so I went to the Dover Street wine bar – with £11,000-worth of chips still on me. When I finally got home, at about 3.30, Alex said: 'Where the hell have you been?' I said 'Out,' and we went through the usual nonsense. Eventually, I told her I'd been to the casino, and she said: 'How much did you take with you?' I said 'A couple of hundred – maybe three hundred quid.' She shook her head. 'I suppose you lost the lot.' I said. 'Actually, I did quite well,' and I started to pile the chips on the table. They were coming out of every pocket, and she was stacking them up. The £25 chips were in piles of £100, then she counted the £100 chips, and she came to the pink ones. 'How much are these worth?' I said £1,000, and there were four of them. When she'd finished counting she was gobsmacked. We went back to the Palm Beach the next night, with all the chips, but this time it just wasn't happening. We got a few zeros and I said: 'Let's call it a day.' We cashed in £10,000. It was enough to decorate and carpet the flat.

Alex has to remind him that he doesn't always win. She also has to remind him to eat: like a lot of alcoholics, when it comes to solids he has the appetite of a sparrow. 'I try to make him have one proper meal every day,' she says, 'especially when he's drinking a lot. I'll cook a shepherd's pie or a lasagne, for when he comes home from the pub in the afternoon. Even if I'm not cooking, I'll put something in front of him and make him eat.' She was living, she said, with a very complex and difficult man. 'It takes a long time to learn what he is really like, but I think I know him now, and know exactly what he is going to do next.'

If that sounds dangerously like a case of famous last words, George did seem, after two years, to be doing a very good impression of a happily married man. He knows now that he will never beat the demon alcohol, but in his fifties he has just about run out of wild oats to sow, and his gambling is under control. It is hard to believe, but George Best is ready to settle for his version of domesticity:

> When I think about it, I'm a lucky man to be enjoying the life I have today. In 1981, when I came back from America, I was in a desperate position. I was a bankrupt alcoholic with no work, and nothing but one suitcase full of clothes to my name. That was my lowest ebb – when my first marriage broke up. My mum got to the stage where she was so low she wanted to die, and I thought about that. I thought: What the hell is the use? I couldn't see any light at the end of the tunnel. But when I was deep in despair, and there was a temptation to leave all the shit behind with a few pills, I used to think back to the good times and say to myself: No, I wouldn't want to miss out if they came round again. I got as depressed and as low as you can get, but I couldn't ever bring myself to end it all. Thank God I didn't, because the good times are back. I still go out and get pissed and can't remember things in the morning, but nowadays when I've had enough I go home, to bed. That's the difference. In the old days, I could never get enough. If I was in the pub with my pals and it shut at eleven, a couple would go home, and I'd go on with the others to a wine bar until two. Then the others would go home and I had to go on to somewhere that

stayed open until four. Now, if I'm in the pub at eleven and I've had enough, I go home. Because there's someone worth going home to.

Alex and I get on great. We have our set-tos and knock lumps out of each other, but she's given me more slaps than I've given her. I've had to cry off from Sky TV three times because she's given me a black eye. She may be a skinny little so and so, but she's a feisty one all right. She can look after herself.

With the help of a devoted inner circle of friends, he feels he has turned his life around. Mary Shatila, sadly, doesn't get a mention, but she started the process by getting him on the public-speaking circuit and giving him the will to sort out his bankruptcy. Her good work was carried on, and the task all but completed, by his solicitor, Bryan Fugler, by Alex, and also to a significant extent by a London-based Welsh entrepreneur and Manchester United nut by the name of Phil Hughes, who performs the role of agent on a non-commission basis, happy to be of service to a hero-turned-friend. 'The three of them have pulled me through,' George says, his gratitude plainly sincere. 'Together, they just made my life better and better. I still have my bad days, but 90 per cent of the work I'm booked for, I do.' How does he account for the other 10 per cent?

The problem is, if I don't think I can perform to the standard I set for myself, I won't do the job. I don't want to go on Sky and look bad, so I take the easy way out. It's the same if I'm speaking at a dinner in front of 500 people. If I'm not in a fit state to do it, I won't. I know it's wrong, and that I'm letting people down, and I do feel guilty. The trouble is, that only makes me worse. My solution is to go out and get drunk and forget it, so it becomes a vicious circle. But I am getting better. It doesn't happen so often now.

> The nice thing is that the phone still rings, I'm still wanted. I read people saying they feel sorry for me. Why? I'm having a whale of a time, and I've got plenty of work. I did an interview for the Chris Evans programme and he paid me £5,000, and I got the same for going on 'Richard and Judy' – £5,000 for seven minutes of my time. If that's being a has-been, I'll settle for that. On the rare occasions when I get up early, I go out and see people queuing for buses or stuck in traffic and think to myself: You lucky bastard. At fifty I'd gone through stuff that should have killed me by thirty and now look at me. In the past twelve months, Alex and I have been to Malaysia, New Zealand, Mauritius and Portugal working. It's a marvellous life.

A cloud which had darkened the horizon for years was blown away in May 1998, when a long-running dispute with Bill McMurdo, George's erstwhile agent, was finally resolved. Their business relationship had ended in 1989, but McMurdo, a Scot who also represented Charlie Nicholas and Frank McAvennie, had facilitated the purchase of the Chelsea flat that had been the Best bolthole since July 1984.

The property had been bought in the name of George Best Management Limited, a company in which McMurdo had acquired 85 of the 90 shares, and he claimed at the Central London County Court that it was 'for the benefit of the company shareholders', and that George had been allowed to occupy it 'on a non-exclusive basis.' George contended, through Jonathan Crystal QC, that all the money generated by the company was earned by him, and that there was a 'gentlemen's agreement' that the shares were to pass to him when he was discharged from bankruptcy.

George had not paid the mortgage to the Clydesdale Bank, for three years because of the dispute and, claiming £72,000 in arrears, the bank sought repossession. After a three-day hearing, an out of court settlement was reached. George agreed to leave the flat and McMurdo to help finance the purchase of alternative accomodation. The loss of a home that had been his refuge for nearly fourteen years was a body blow but, as ever, George bounced back and moved into a more desirable property just around the corner, in fashionable Cheyne Walk.

chapter twenty-four

On 22 May 1996, George Best's fiftieth birthday, BBC2 cleared their regular schedule and devoted a whole evening – six programmes – to a celebration of his career under the umbrella 'Best Night'. It is hard to envisage the Beeb paying such effusive homage to any other living sportsman, the implausibility of a Gazza or a Giggs Night pointing up the futility of contemporary comparisons.

George was not simply the best British footballer of modern times (can there ever have been a more apt surname?), he was also, by a long way, the most glamorous. His enduring fascination for people of both sexes, and all ages, is impressive testimony to looks and personality as charismatic as his talent. He left Manchester United before David Beckham was born, but when he went back to Old Trafford in March 1997 for a speaking engagement, the queue for his autograph had more twists than an alpine coach tour, and put the new 'Babes' in their proper context.

His allure transcends all barriers. Fortunate enough to have seen him in his pomp, I have been asked how good he was by the landlady at my local, by a police sergeant who found me a full quire to the wind on leaving the Phene Arms, and by Teddy Sheringham, the England striker who, when we met for interview, was more interested in discussing this biography than his own transfer to Manchester United.

The second question, much more difficult to answer, is

always: 'What's he really like?' He is an alcoholic, and like all addicts his chosen poison has a profound effect on his personality, causing huge mood and behavioural changes. He can be riveting company, or taciturn to the point of embarrassment, engagingly witty at two o'clock, boorish drunk at half past. He is a tender, giving lover according to those in a position to know, but he has physically abused most, if not all, his women. An incorrigible flirt, he is fiercely jealous if his partner so much as looks at another man. He is careful with his money these days (casinos notwithstanding) but can also be incredibly generous, producing £2,000 in cash to pay off the bailiffs when they called at his favourite pub. The greatest conflict of all is that the bane of his life is also his greatest enjoyment. Drink. Therein lies the solution, if only he could find it.

First things first. George Best remains the most gifted and exciting performer I have seen in forty years of watching football, nearly thirty of them as a professional observer. It was a goal he scored at White Hart Lane in February 1968 that convinced this rugby-playing Spurs supporter that the Beautiful Game was the true path. When he received the ball on the edge of the penalty area, there were six defenders between George and Pat Jennings, but he shimmied one way and then the other to wrong-foot them all before planting an unstoppable shot past his great friend and Northern Ireland room-mate. Goodnight Barry John.

George was the best in an era fondly remembered as the best. Mackay and Moore, Baxter and Giles, Greaves, Law and Charlton – they all deserve their place in the pantheon, but George was the one who had the seated jumping, the standing craning and the hairs dancing an Irish jig on the nape of the neck. When the force was with him, as it usually was in the sixties, this Nureyev of the masses seemed to epitomize those heady, devil-may-care days when all you needed was love. And five bob to get in.

That black Beatle mop was like a matador's cape – you could almost hear 'Chopper' Harris muttering 'I'll have the long-haired git' as the Bestie boy jinked inside him, outside him or, the ultimate humiliation, poked the ball through his legs before leaving him for dead. Harris always tried to 'do' him, as did Tommy Smith, Peter Storey and all the legendary hackers in the days when defenders had *carte blanche*. They ended up on their backsides. George was tough enough to withstand the most brutal of challenges, and he could dish it out with the best/worst of them. Matt Busby used to say he was as good a tackler as anyone in that European Cup-winning team.

His other attributes are documented elsewhere in this book. To recap, as a winger, rather than a through-the-middle striker, he was Manchester United's leading scorer for five successive seasons, from 1967–8 to 1971–2, at a time when Bobby Charlton and Denis Law were among his rivals. His accomplishments received international recognition in 1968 when, at the unusually early age of twenty-two, he was the European Footballer of the Year, and he was picked for a World XI, to play in Eusebio's testimonial in 1973.

The acid test for any player's reputation is how he is rated by his peers, and George's contemporaries will entertain no quibbling. There was no one better. Denis Law says: 'From 1964 to 1969, he was the best player in the country. It's sad as hell, but I don't think we saw the best of him. I think he went on the blink at a time when he could have got even better. You hit your peak as a player at around twenty-eight, and he was gone by then. Even so, I'd put him on a par with the top six I ever saw. I wouldn't like to choose between George, Di Stefano, Cruyff, Maradona, Pele and big John Charles. Bestie definitely belongs among that elite.' Rodney Marsh believes that for two years, George was the best player in the world. 'Overall, Pele was the greatest I have ever seen, but for that window between 1968 and 1970, George was unstoppable, and I would say that he was the top man. The most important thing a great player has is balance. Zola is a good example today, Bobby Charlton always had it. Pele would get whacked, and it would enable him to keep his footing. George had it like nobody I've ever seen. He was like a Subbuteo man, he just wouldn't go over.'

There is no love lost between Best and Tommy Docherty, but 'The Doc' says: 'For me, George is one of the best three in the world – ever. In my book, he's right up there with Pele and Tom Finney. I think Finney was the best I've seen. He and George are probably on a level as regards ability, but I give Tom the benefit because he was the better pro.' Bobby Charlton, too, fell out with George during their playing days, but says now: 'He was on a par, at least, with anyone you can name, and from the conversations I've had with him over the years, I know Pele would tell you the same thing. From a talent and style point of view, I would say Cruyff was probably the nearest thing to him. George was braver, but Cruyff had great organizing ability. George looked after number one really when he was on the pitch. He wouldn't dictate tactics or have a chat about what we were going to do. Cruyff had that.' Johnny Giles says: 'George was the most naturally gifted player I have ever seen. He had the lot: balance, pace, two good feet, he was brave, strong and a good header of the ball. Pele wasn't as gifted as George Best. He couldn't beat players as many ways as George could. And I would definitely put George above Cruyff, because he had more heart. Maradona would be close, because he was more of a team man.'

The most remarkable tribute of all is paid by David Sadler:

> He was definitely the greatest player I've ever seen. I'm talking from experience, on the basis of what I saw every day, in matches and in training, and I would say you could have put George in just about any position in our 1968 team and he would have been better than the person who was playing there. Sounds stupid, doesn't it, but at that time Tony Dunne was probably the best left-back in Europe, and George could have done the job better than him. In Nobby Stiles's position,

he would have been quite capable of winning the ball, because he was a tremendous tackler, and when he got it, he'd have used it better than Nobby. He could head the ball better than me, and probably as well as Bill Foulkes, and he could do everything Bobby Charlton did, and more. People say Pele didn't tackle because he didn't have to. George didn't have to, but he did. You couldn't beat him on a football pitch. There was nothing a player could do to defeat him, mentally. You couldn't kick him out of the game because he'd bounce straight back and tackle you twice as hard.

Alex Ferguson ridicules comparisons with Ryan Giggs: 'He'll never be a Best. Nobody will. George was unique, the greatest talent our football ever produced, easily. Look at the scoring record – 137 goals in 361 League games and a total of 179 goals for United in 466 matches played. That's phenomenal for a man who did not get the share of gift goals that come to specialist strikers. George nearly always had to beat men to score.'

Mention of Giggs serves only one useful purpose, calling to mind the different treatment the two prodigies received from the same club in their formative years. George, as the first footballer to cross over into pop stardom, was left to fend for himself. Manchester United had no idea what to do about the creeping corruption of their innocent young genius, so they did nothing. Busby fiddled while Best's fuse burned. Alex Ferguson, who admits he learned from those mistakes, threw up a protective wall around Giggs when he first came to prominence, keeping him on a tight rein off the field and denying the media access to him until he had attained maturity, and was judged ready to cope with interviews, photo shoots, all the head-turning paraphernalia of celebrity. George says he could have done with more guidance, *in loco parentis*. Instead, he was left to his own devices after training every day, and the devil soon found work for his idle hands. 'Boredom was my problem.' Unlike today's cosseted millionaires, he was not advised on how to invest his money, or warned about the perils of strong liquor and bad company. In short, while he may have been predisposed to the playboy lifestyle, he was shoddily served by a management too ready to turn a blind eye to his indiscipline off the field for as long as he 'did the business' on it.

The experts from Alcoholics Anonymous say that alcoholism, which curtailed his career and still blights his life, can be nipped in the bud if the signs are spotted early enough. 'The difficulty is that few alcoholics have enough desire to stop while there is yet time.' The critical time for George was 1968 when, at the watershed age of twenty-two, he lost the wise counsel of Mike Summerbee and David Sadler, the two footballing pals who told him when it was time to go home, and how to behave when he got there. Summerbee and Sadler were both married that year, and it was the removal of their stabilizing influence, more than the feeling that Manchester United could only go downhill after winning the European Cup (George's preferred excuse), that accelerated the lurch towards dissolution.

The void in his inner circle was filled by nightclub owners, bookmakers, rag trade wide boys and beauty queens who, despite his loyal protestations to the contrary, were hardly the sort of company to keep a young footballer on the straight and narrow. His mother's sad descent into, and premature death from, alcoholism is also of major significance, with medical opinion increasingly suggesting a hereditary aspect to the illness. This theory, that susceptibility may be passed on in the genes, is more persuasive than Dickie Best's notion that the family were found wanting when his wife's incapacity prevented them from moving to Manchester to chaperon their wayward son. By the time that despairing proposal was made, in Frank O'Farrell's day, the die was well and truly cast.

Thirty years on, some notable players – Paul Gascoigne, Tony Adams and Paul Merson among them – have drawn back from the same precipice with the aid of counselling, but Matt Busby sent George Best to a psychiatrist once, and he sat laughing at the questions. He says: 'You can have counselling and come out thinking: That was a load of crap, give me a drink. It depends on the individual. I don't think it would have worked for me because I didn't want to change. I liked drinking. But at least they have the chance now. I didn't have that.' George's scepticism about the efficacy of counselling is shared by an eminent authority, Dr Thomas Stuttaford, who, writing in *The Times*, says:

> Suggestions of treatment are sometimes accepted by patients with a personality disorder if they are made by those in whom they are in awe. Usually, however, the would-be patients accept counselling only if they feel that it might help them to have a more profitable or enjoyable life. The truth is that most patients with a personality disorder don't give a damn what others think about them.
>
> In most cases when counselling is used, the result is disappointing. Many of the patients have little desire to change their personalities, and are not troubled by an uneasy conscience. Treatment is made even more difficult because they not only usually fail to make deep, long-lasting sexual relationships, they also lack trust in those who are trying to help them.

Our man in one.

Dickie Best is not alone in suffering we-could-have-done-more pangs of guilt. Some of George's old team-mates feel they played priests and Levites, passing by on the other side of the road when a good Samaritan or two might have saved the day. David Sadler, who shared digs with George up to 1968 and roomed with him on away trips afterwards, says: 'I did try to talk him round, but did I try hard enough? There were one or two of us who were closer to him than the rest, and we certainly had his ear. He would have listened to us and we could have done more. I think Bobby [Charlton] could have helped George more, at the time when George had enormous respect for him. But all this is with the benefit of twenty-odd years of hindsight. At the time, we were all busy looking after our own careers – I know I was.' Charlton says: 'If we'd known then what we know now, it might have been different. We [Manchester United] have learned from our experience with Eric Cantona. We had to treat him a bit differently, make allowances. If, instead of being hostile to George, which I was, we had leaned a bit his way and tried to help him, who knows? I think we might all have tried to do a little bit more, but I doubt if it would have worked. George hasn't changed over the years, and he won't change. He's just that sort of individual.' Denis Law takes another view: too many allowances were made by *laissez-faire* management. 'If I'd known then what I know now, I'd have given him a right smack. It would have been: "Now don't mess about Bestie, or else." If it happened today, I'd have no trouble sorting it out, but at the time we all had enough on our own plates without trying to solve his problems.'

Today, instead of basking in the reverential esteem enjoyed by Charlton, Law and less gifted contemporaries, the football fantasist's dream (and a few women's) finds himself used as a depressing example, with all sorts of micro-celebs going into rehab saying things like: 'I don't want to end up like George Best.' How *will* the best footballer of his generation end up? Sadly, the prognosis is not good. He continues to drink in quantities that would kill most of us, with the result that, like Jeffrey Bernard, he is often unwell. There is also a real danger that he will lose the one rock he has clung to since the dark days of 1984. His Chelsea flat. He says he is a happy man, but alcoholism and lasting happiness are incompatible, and those tormented eyes tell a different story.

Those close to him worry constantly. His father Dickie, after losing his wife to the ravages of alcohol, cannot bring himself to think about it happening again. 'Despite everything, I still keep hoping that for George, one day the problem will disappear. Or that he can handle it so that it doesn't handle him. I still look for light at the end of the tunnel. But in reality, there comes a time when you have to accept that it's not going to go away.' George's wife, Alex, says: 'It does frighten me. How much longer can his body cope?' His oldest friends share her concerns. Malcolm Wagner says: 'It's absolutely heartbreaking how he has ended up. After earning so much money, he should have had such an easy life. I still love him, he's still my best pal, but I fear for what is going to happen.' Mike Summerbee says: 'Deep down, I don't think he's a happy man. Don't ask me what's at the root of it, because I don't know. The way his mother died, perhaps. You look at the amount he drinks and wonder how long he can go on? My fear is that one day I'll wake up and it will be on the news that he's been found dead somewhere. Mind you, we've all been saying that for twenty years!'

Those of us of a certain age will wish him another twenty years, at least, for in the words of another genius: 'There'll never be another.' Thanks for the memory.

index

AC Milan 182–3
Adam, Ken 286
Anderson, Willie 46, 62, 64, 101
Armstrong, Joe 27, 33, 34, 45
Aston, John 39
Aston Junior, John 46, 111
Atkinson, Ron 323
Aztecs *see* Los Angeles Aztecs

Ball, Alan 177, 195, 214
Barr, Billy 127–8
BBC2 'Best Night' 363
Beal, Phil 278, 284
Belfast Telegraph 63
Bell, Colin 142
Benfica
  European Cup match against United (1966) 93–9, 143
  European Cup final against United (1968) 145–52
Best, Alex (second wife) 4, 5, 6, 129, 354–5
  background 353
  relationship with Best 282–3, 346, 353–4, 355–6, 356–8
Best, Angie (first wife) 312
  ending of marriage with Best 320, 321
  relationship with Best 273, 275, 277, 280–1, 283–4, 299–300, 306, 307, 318, 356
Best, Ann (mother)
  and alcoholism 105, 204, 264, 289–91, 292, 294–5
  death 204, 286–7, 292
  early years 9, 11, 12–13, 289
  relationship with son 64, 105
Best, Barbara (sister) 13, 264
Best, Calum (son) 305–6, 308–13, 319
Best, Carol (sister) 10, 15
Best, Dickie (father) 6, 7, 9, 16, 288–97
  amateur footballer 10, 11
  attitude to son playing football 17, 21–2, 25, 29–30

misses son's debut matches 62–3
parental philosophy 17, 22
relationship with son 292–3, 295–7
relationship with wife 289–91
on son's Chelsea performance 72, 289
on son's drinking 264, 371–2
and son's early years 10, 13, 14–15, 19
and son's football career at United 33–4, 44–5, 64, 79–80
on son's international career 160–1
and wife's alcoholism 204, 289–91, 292

BEST, GEORGE [References to this entry are grouped under the following headings: Early Years; Football Career (America; Clubs; General; International; Manchester United); Business/off-the-field career; Drinking; Personal; Relationships]

EARLY YEARS
birth 9
childhood scrapes 13–14
and death of grandfather 16–17
first football matches watched 11–12
and grandparents 10
living in Northern Ireland 15–16
not considered for schoolboy cap 23
obsession with football 20
physique 22, 24
plays at Cregagh Boys Club 22–3
plays rugby 18
practises football in street 10–11, 12, 13
and printing trade 31
relationship with parents 14–15
and religion 15
schooling 16, 17–19
supports Wolverhampton Wanderers 20–1
upbringing 9–10, 13, 14–15

FOOTBALL CAREER
– AMERICA
asked to play for New York Cosmos 237
at Detroit Express 286
plays for Fort Lauderdale Strikers 285–6, 298–9, 303
plays for Los Angeles Aztecs 269–70, 270–1, 272, 278–9, 284–5
plays for San José

Earthquakes 173, 303–4, 305, 315, 316–17
– CLUBS
approach from Chelsea to play 269
at Fulham *see* Fulham
invited to play for Middlesbrough 315–16
plays at Dunstable Town 268
plays at Bournemouth 323–4
plays at Cork Celtic 271
plays at Hibernian 300, 301–3
plays for the Jewish Guild in South Africa 265
plays at Stockport County 268–9
– GENERAL
abilities 41, 61, 70, 108, 109–10, 114–15, 115–16, 159, 190, 364
accomplishments 365
announces retirement 219, 227
appoints an agent 82–3
best goal scored 316–17
cartilage injury 101
change of heart over retirement 227
charity match in Tokyo 337
determination to become two-footed 40–1, 73, 107, 108
European Footballer of the Year 134, 154, 185, 266
global ban imposed by FIFA 286, 298
love of crowds 58, 59
named *Daily Telegraph* Sportsman of the Year 217
pace 41–2
popularity and fame 100, 114, 202, 252
press reviews 64, 70, 95, 99, 152, 166
and tackling 41, 365
talent for goal scoring 115–16
testimonial in Belfast 337–8
tributes to 367–8
voted Player of the Year 154
voted supporters' Player of the Year 277
– INTERNATIONAL
arrival in squad 159–60
attitude towards playing for Northern Ireland 68, 157, 162, 169
comeback 172–3
debut against Wales 67–8, 157–8
disappointment at not

playing in a World Cup 157, 174–5
enjoyment off the field 168–9, 170
goals scored 161–2
match against Scotland 157, 163–6
matches against England 161, 167–8
misses matches 163, 166, 170–1
second game against Uruguay 160
suspensions 230
– Manchester United
accomplishments at 365
arrival 26–8
asks to be captain 211
attitude towards training 40–1, 107, 108
blossoming in 1964–5 season 69
bookings and sendings off 178, 205, 214
Busby's relationship and handling of 61, 88–9, 106, 205, 229, 251, 252–4, 254–5, 255–8
disciplined and dropped 88–9, 216
early dedication 43
early social life 43, 48–50, 84–6
early view of talent 36–7
earnings 35, 44, 83–4, 154, 155, 214
final departure 242–8
first goal scored 63
first taste of adulation 99–100
first team debut 50, 57–60
'go-it-alone' attitude on the field 98, 116–18, 221
goals scored 14, 67, 94, 96, 114, 115–16, 137, 139, 141, 145, 189, 192, 198, 208, 209, 213, 214, 367
invited back by Atkinson 323
lack of advice and supervision given to 252, 256, 367–8
misses training 107, 205–6, 216, 218, 228
offered professional contract 44–5
performance in European Cup Final 148, 152
performance in match against Chelsea (1964) 69–72, 289
plays as winger 64–5
plays for youth team 46–7
relationship with Charlton 118–19, 221–6
requirement to play as

amateur due to protectionist rule 34–5
re-signing of by Docherty 240–2
returns home after first day due to homesickness 28–32
routine before matches 57–8
second match played 62–4
severance of all legal ties 268
sexual misconduct before match 191–2, 252
speed of elevation at 38
suspensions and fines 190, 205, 206–7, 230
talent spotted by Bishop 24–5
testimonial refused 300–1
transfer-listed 230–4, 253
treatment of at beginning 26, 367
BUSINESS/OFF-THE-FIELD CAREER
and advertising 154
clothing contracts 231
guest appearance at opening of O'Neill's Irish pub 129–30
and Inland Revenue 321–2, 336, 342
modelling contract 154
opening of 'Bestie's' 278, 338
opening of boutiques 100, 195
opening of Slack Alice 156, 249–50, 259–60, 261
owning of Oscar's 156, 267–8
personal appearances 3, 6–7
public-speaking circuit 246, 282–3, 336–7, 344
sells boutiques 237
sells stakes in nightclubs 322
share in a racehorse 195
Sky TV appearances 4, 344–5
This is Your Life appearance 217
trust fund for Calum 338, 343–4
Wogan show appearance 289, 341–2
DRINKING
4, 107, 185, 200–5, 218, 219, 358, 370
AA sessions 318
antibuse pellet treatment 324–5
attempt at controlling 272–3, 318–19, 340
and Brown Bull pub 121, 127–8, 202–3
checks into Vesper Hospital

for rehabilitation 306, 314, 318
effect on football 194, 205, 228, 299, 305
introduction to 47–8
liking of vodka 121, 200, 201, 338–9
losing control 195, 205, 216, 228
and mother's alcoholism 295, 369
out of control 280, 288, 299, 303, 305, 306–7, 333
reasons for 200–1, 203
returns to England to rehabilitate 318–20
routine 267
starting of heavy 153
PERSONAL
appeal and popularity 4, 363
arrest and imprisonment 327–32
arrested for stealing from Marjorie Wallace 263–4
assault on waitress 130, 236–7
bankruptcy 322, 337, 343–4
and birth of son 305–6
car crash 277
characteristics 200, 364
Cusack incident 206–7
daily routine 267
death threats received 171, 215–16
driving convictions 103, 136, 185
eating habits 5, 8, 359–60
effect of Busby's death on 345
ending of first marriage 320
engagement to Eva Haraldsted 194
enjoyment of life in Los Angeles 279
fiftieth birthday 363
financial problems 322
first house 208–9
friends outside football 124–7
gambling 265–7, 339–40, 358–9
girlfriends and women 42–3, 89, 106–7, 121–2, 216
girls adulation of 201, 202
guilt over mother's death 204, 287, 293–4, 294–5
at Henlow Grange 350–1, 358
holidays in Majorca 155–6
interest in pool 130
involvement in fight at Rat and Parrot pub 130–1
jealousy 130, 282, 357–8, 364

and newspaper crosswords 351
nightclub scene 91–2, 103–4, 106, 121
physique 34, 114
purchases first car 45
spending of money 83, 155
and sports cars 68, 155
thrombosis of the leg 238–9
RELATIONSHIPS
Alex (second wife) 282–3, 346, 353–4, 355–6, 356–8, 360–1
Angie (first wife) 273, 275, 277, 280–1, 283–4, 299–300, 306, 307, 318, 320, 321
Angie Lynn 326, 333–5
David Sadler 38, 39, 48, 104, 368, 369–70
Denis Law 74, 117, 221, 222–3
father 292–3, 295–7
Jackie Glass 119–20, 153
Marjorie Wallace 262–4
Mary Shatila 335–6, 337, 340, 341, 342, 345–6, 346–9, 361
Mary Stavin 320, 321, 325–6
Mike Summerbee 89–92, 100, 119, 120–2, 201, 203–4, 368
parents 64
Rodney Marsh 274–5, 277
son (Calum) 308, 309–10, 319
Best, Ian Busby (brother) 104, 288
Best, James 'Scottie' (grandfather)11
Best, Julia (sister) 17
'Bestie's' 278, 338
Bingham, Billy 173
Bishop, Bob 20, 23–5
Blanchflower, Danny 162, 172
Blondes 326
Bournemouth 323–4
Boyce, Carl 237
Boyland Youth Club 23, 24
Brennan, Liz 133
Brennan, Shay 131–3, 138, 142, 189, 195
Broadbent, Peter 21
Brown Bull pub 121, 127–8, 202–3
Buchan, Martin 217–18, 228
Burne, Colin 259, 266
Burns, Francis 136
Bursk, Danny 103, 124, 125, 126–7
Busby, Matt 36, 39, 143–4
achievements 51–2
on Best's abilities 61, 70, 116
death 345
and European Cup (1966) 95–6, 102, 135–6, 176

and European Cup (1968) 144, 147, 151
as general manager 188, 193
handling of and relationship with Best 61, 88–9, 106, 205, 229, 251, 252–4, 255–8
and Johnny Giles 54–5
and McGuinness 184, 186, 188–9, 193, 196–7
managerial style 86, 187–8
and Munich air disaster 135, 176, 181
neglect in rejuvenating team in (1968–9) 176–7
offering of professional contract to Best 44
reappointment as manager 196–7, 199, 210–11
receives knighthood 153
signings 52
stands downs after second term 211
steps down from being manager 180–2
tactics and strategy 187
Butler, Frank 322

Callaghan, Ian 285
Campbell, Bobby 7, 276
Cantona, Eric 370
Cantwell, Noel 41, 52, 65
Cargill, Sandra 123
Catterick, Harry 176
Cavan, Harry 170–1
Chaffetz, John 270, 279, 284
Charlton, Bobby 370
on Best's abilities 37–8, 98–9, 107, 115–16, 366
on Best's 'go-it-alone' attitude on field 98, 117–18
on Best's international career 174
on Busby's relationship with Best 254–5
character 225–6
and European Cup (1968) 146, 147, 148
European Footballer of the Year 103
on McGuinness 186
relationship with Best 118–19, 221–6
retirement 240
two-footed 73, 107–8
at United 42, 56, 66, 112, 138, 141
Chelsea 44
declares interest in Best 269
match against United (1964) 69–72, 289
Cher 281, 307
Chisnall, Phil 56–7, 65
Cohen, George 103
Collins, Bobby 77
Connelly, John 72–3, 74, 75, 110–11
Connor, David 47

Cooke, Charlie 272
Cork Celtic 271
Corriere dello Sport 94–5
Crane, Fraser 208
Cregagh Boys Club 22–3
Crerand, Noreen 227
Crerand, Pat 102, 166, 194–5, 224
  on Benfica game 97–8
  Best on attributes of 97, 151
  on Best's abilities 38, 60, 64, 70–1
  on Best's final departure 247–8
  on Busby leaving 181
  and European Cup (1968) 146, 150
  on McGuinness 186
  at Manchester United 52, 64, 65, 86, 112, 113, 141
  on O'Farrell 234
  on refereeing decisions in European Cup (1969) 183
  relationship with Best 97, 246–7
  and Stein 211–12
Crompton, Jack 38, 41
Cryuff 367
Cusack, Sinead 206, 207–8
Czuczman, Mike 304

Daily Mirror 70
Daily Star 352
Daily Telegraph 217
Dalglish, Kenny 24
David, Steve 278, 279
Davies, Ron 272
Davies, Wyn 228
Delaunay, Henri 134
Demmy, Selwyn 124–5, 126
Detroit Express 286
Docherty, Tommy 156
  on Best 366
  and Best's final departure from United 242–6
  as manager of United 232, 239–40
  post-United career 244
  re-signing of Best 240–1
  transfer-listing of Best 332–3
Dougan, Derek 8, 169
  How Not to Run Football 175
Doyle, Mike 47
Dunne, Pat 73–4, 110
Dunne, Tony 65, 111, 240, 366
Dunphy, Eamonn 38
Dunstable Town 268

Earthquakes *see* San José Earthquakes
Edelson, Michael 126
Edwardia 100
Edwards, Duncan 254
Edwards, Louis 102, 181, 231
Elder, Alex 64, 67
England
  matches against Northern Ireland 161, 167–8

England, Mike 177
Estudiantes 178
European Championship 171–2
European Cup
  inauguration (1955) 134
  (1966) 88, 101–2
    Busby's disappointment at elimination 102, 135–6, 176
    match against Benfica 93–9, 143
  (1968) 134, 137, 177
    final against Benfica 145–52
    last chance theory 138, 146
    quarter-final against Gornik Zabrze 139–40
    second round match against Sarajevo 138–9
    semi-final against Real Madrid 140–1, 142–5
  (1969) 179, 182–3
European Cup Winners Cup 66, 145–6
Eusebio 149, 365
Evans, Chris 362
Evans, Ian 280

FA Cup
  (1948) 51
  (1963) 44, 52–3, 54
  (1964) 65, 66
  (1965) 77–8
  (1966) 92, 101, 103
  (1967) 113
  (1968) 140
  (1969) 182
  (1970) 190–1
FA Youth Cup 43–4, 46–7
Ferguson, Alex 26, 51–2, 61, 367
Finney, Tom 367
Fitzpatrick, John 32, 34, 42, 46, 84–5
Forsyth, Alex 240
Fort Lauderdale Strikers 285–6, 298–9, 303
Foulkes, Bill 65, 138, 142, 144–5, 178, 188–9, 195
Fry, Barry 38, 39, 268
Fugler, Bryan 342–4, 361
Fulham 172, 273–8, 279–80
  Best charged with bringing the game into disrepute 276–7
  Best's reluctance to fulfil second year of contract 279
  dispute with Aztecs over transfer of Best 279, 286
  growing disillusionment with 275
  (1976–7) season 273–5, 276
  (1977–8) season 279–80
  offering of contract 273
Fullaway, Mrs Mary 28, 32, 33, 48

Gallacher, Hughie 255
Gascoigne, Paul 337–8

Gaskell, Dave 65, 73, 110
Gento, Francisco 40
'George Best Rogue' (boutique) 195
Giggs, Ryan 61, 115, 163, 367
Giles, Johnny
on Best 36, 191–2, 256–7, 366
dropped from United 53–5
at Leeds 55, 76, 77–9
on United's decline 179–80
view of Busby 255–7
Glass, Jackie 119–20, 153
Glentoran club 11–12, 20
Gornik Zabrze 139–40
Graham, George 240
Graveney, Tim 282, 357
Great Universal Stores 154
Greaves, Jimmy 201
Green, Geoffrey 95, 113, 147, 148–9
Gregg, Harry 7, 27, 65, 110, 158, 159
Grosvenor High School 16, 17
Guardian 207–8
Guttman, Bela 93

Hansen, Alan 65
Haraldsted, Eva 194
Hardman, Harold 135
Hart, Tom 301, 302
Haynes, Johnny 21
Herd, David 45, 52, 53, 65, 75, 112, 136
Hibernian 300, 301–3
Hickton, John 285
Hiddink, Guus 304
Higgins, Alex 200
Holton, Jim 240
Hopcraft, Arthur 235–6
Hortop, Graham 274
Hudson, Ray 285
Hughes, Phil 361

Ingram, Godfrey 304
Inland Revenue 321–2, 336, 342
Inter-Cities Fairs Cup 81
IRA 215
Irving, David 285
Izquierdo-Moreno, Felix 156, 260–1, 266–7, 267–8

Jackson, Michael 356
Jagger, Mick 261
Janes, Angela *see* Best, Angie
Janes, Marion 283
Jeffries, Tim 333
Jennings, Pat 67, 157, 168–9, 209
Jewish Guild (South Africa) 265
Jones, Ken 70

Keegan, Kevin 24, 231
Kendall, Howard 67
Kidd, Brian 108, 136, 143–4, 146, 151, 183, 248
Kinsey, Albert 47
Kraay, Hans 304

Law, Denis 83, 336, 370
on Benfica match 99
on Best's abilities 60, 365
on Best's deterioration 249, 304–5
on Busby 181, 255
knee injury 101, 137, 142, 145
on McGuinness 186
on O'Farrell 234
popularity with fans 56, 74–5, 114
relationship with Best 74, 117, 221, 222–3
transfer-listed 195
transferred 240
at United 52, 53, 56, 65, 72, 74, 75, 116
League Cup 110, 190
Leeds 55, 80
bad blood between United and 76–7
matches against United 75–6, 77, 111
organization 77–8, 179–80
physical side 78–9
Leicester City 53
Lloyd, Cliff 83
Los Angeles Aztecs 269–70, 270–1, 272, 278–9, 284–5
Lynch, Kenny 119, 336
Lynn, Angie 326, 333–5

McAlinden, Bobby 47, 270–1, 272, 278, 317
Macari, Lou 240
McBride, Peter 32, 46
McCreadie, Eddie 269
McDonald, Colin 82
MacDougall, Ted 228
McFarlane, Bud 20, 22, 23
McGuinness, Wilf 235–6
attempts to drop Best for sexual misconduct 191, 252
on Best 109–10, 160, 193–4, 198–9
and Busby 176, 184, 186, 187–9, 193, 196–7
part of coaching staff 37, 102, 109
players' view of 186
post United career 198
sacked as manager 196–8, 254
succeeds Busby 184–5, 185–6
team changes 195–6
McIlroy, Jimmy 82
McIlvanney, Hugh 115, 128, 329–30
Mackay, Dave 66
McLaughlin, Jimmy 158
McMillan, Sammy 27
McMordie, Eric 25, 26–7, 29, 166–7, 169
McMurdo, Bill 315, 332, 342
Manchester City 47, 142
Manchester Evening News 205, 228

Manchester United
bad blood between Leeds and 76–7
Busby steps down as manager 180–2
coaching philosophy 39–40
crowd attendances 114
decline in (1968–9) season 176–7
and European Cup *see* European Cup
and FA Cup *see* FA Cup
and FA Youth Cup 43–4, 46–7
finding replacement for Busby after second term 211–13
league form
(1950s) 51–2
(1962–3) 52–3
(1963–4) 56, 62, 65–6, 66–7
(1964–5) 73–4, 75–6, 79, 80–1
(1965–6) 88, 89, 92, 93, 101, 103
(1966–7) 110, 111–12, 113
(1967–8) 136–7, 138, 139, 140, 141–2
(1968–9) 176, 178–9, 179–80, 182, 185
(1969–70) 189–90, 192–3
(1970–1) 196, 208, 209, 210
(1971–2) 213–14, 215, 217–18
(1972–3) 227–8, 232, 239, 240
(1973–4) 242, 250
McGuinness succeeds Busby 184–5, 185–6
O'Farrell appointed manager 213
pre-season training 42
relegation (1974) 250
sacking of McGuinness 196–8, 254
youth development system 26
see also Best, George: football career (Manchester United); Busby, Matt
Manchester United Luncheon Club 129, 185
Mancini, Terry 270, 284
Marsh, Rodney
on Best's abilities 365–6
on Best's deterioration 305
at Fulham 273, 274–5, 279
public-speaking circuit 336, 344, 345
relationship with Best 274–5, 277
Martin, Mick 240
Martin, Ricci 281, 283
Meek, David 205, 228, 234
Middlesbrough 315–16
Miller, Sir Eric 275–6
Moir, Ian 56, 57
Mooney, Malcolm 100, 124, 206

Moore, Bobby 273, 336
Moore, Carolyn 216
Moore, Dudley 356
Moore, Graham 65
Moorhead, Dr 295
Morgan, Willie 178, 214–15
Munich air disaster 52, 90, 135, 137–8, 146, 176, 181
Murdoch, Bobby 315
Murphy, Jimmy 39, 187, 229–30, 254
Murphy, Noel 131
Musgrove, Malcolm 215

Neill, Terry 158–9, 161, 164–6, 169–70, 172
New York Cosmos 237
Newman, Ron 285, 286, 298–9
News of the World 64
Nicholson, Bill 176
Nicholson, Jimmy 27
Nile club 122
Noble, Bobby 46, 111, 112
Norman (brother-in-law) 6–7
North American Soccer League 269–70 *see also* Best, George: football career (America)
Northampton Town 190
Northern Ireland (team) 158, 168–9, 170, 171–2 *see also* Best, George: football career (International)

O'Farrell, Frank
  departure 232, 234–5, 236
  handling of Best 217, 219
  as manager 213, 215, 227, 228
  players' view of 234–5
  transfer-listing of Best 230, 232, 253
Oscar's 156, 267–8, 322

Pardoe, Glyn 47, 280
Parkinson, Michael 253
Partizan 101
Pele 3–4, 366
Phonographe, Le 121–2
'Phyllis's' 20, 122–3, 185, 252
Piper, Norman 285
Platt, Alan 129
Professional Footballers' Association 83

Quixall, Albert 54, 55

Ramsey, Alf 92
Rapid Vienna 182
Real Madrid 93, 135
  European Cup match against United (1968) 140–1, 142–5
Reaney, Paul 76, 78
Reid, Gary 264
Revie, Don 77, 179–80, 213
Revson, Peter 262
'Richard and Judy' 362
Rimmer, Jimmy 46

Rives, Jean-Pierre 302
Rogers, Don 47
Rous, Stanley 135
Ryan, Jimmy 32, 85, 139

Sadler, David 177
on Best's abilities 109, 249
on Best's downward spiral 219–20, 304
on Best's early behaviour 48–50, 84, 104
on Best's international career 174–5
on Busby's handling of Best 257–8
on Charlton 224–6
marriage 203
on O'Farrell 234–5
relationship with Best 38, 39, 104, 368, 369–70
tribute to Best 366–7
at United 38–9, 56, 111
San José Earthquakes 173, 303–4, 305, 315, 316–17
Sarajevo 138–9
Scotland
match against Northern Ireland 157, 163–6
Semprese, Emile 266
Setters, Maurice 52, 65, 74
Sexton, Dave 215
Shanks, Don 320
Shatila, Mary 353
ending of relationship with Best 346, 348–9
relationship with Best 335–6, 337, 340, 341, 342, 345–6, 346–8
Shearer, Alan 115
Shellito, Ken 70–1
Sheringham, Teddy 363
Sibald, Bobby 284
Sky TV 4, 344–5
Slack Alice 156, 249–50, 259–60, 261, 322
Slim Gypsy (racehorse) 195
Sloniecka, Stevie 236
Smethurst, Derek 270
Stanley, Ken 81–2, 83, 100
Stavin, Mary 320, 321, 325–6
Stein, Jock 211–12
Stepney, Alex 110, 149, 242
Stiles, Nobby 52, 65, 74, 77, 142–3, 178
Stockport County 268–9
Storey, Peter 168, 280
Storey-Moore, Ian 217, 218, 228
Stuttaford, Dr Thomas 369
Stylo 231
Summerbee, Mike 103, 124–5, 371
at Manchester City 120, 123
marriage 203, 369
on Mary Shatila 346
relationship with Best 89–92, 119, 120–2, 201, 203–4, 369

Sun, the 88
Swindon Town 47

This is Your Life 217
Tiler, Brian 324
Times, The 70, 95, 113, 147, 166, 206–7
Top Gear 352
Toshack, John 18
Tottenham 115

Ure, Ian 188, 189, 210
Uruguay 160, 161

Venables, Terry 71–2, 324
Vesper Hospital 306, 314, 318
Violett, Dennis 255
Vytacil, Rudolf 182

Wagner, Malcolm 125, 127, 153, 264, 371
  on Best's drinking and gambling 202, 338–40
  business ventures with Best 124, 259, 261, 267
  on Mary Shatila 345–6
  sets up Jewish Guild deal 265
Walker, Ian 195
Wallace, Marjorie 262–4
West Ham 112–13
Whelan, Tony 285
White, John 'Chalky' 156
Williams, Graham 58–9, 60, 67
Wilson, Harold 191
Withers, Granny 9–10
Wogan 289, 341–2
Wolverhampton Wanderers 20–1
World Club Championship 178–9
World Cup 170, 171, 172–4
  Best's disappointment at not playing in 157, 174–5
World Indoor Soccer League 237

Young, John 278
Youth Cup *see* FA Youth Cup